HEARTBEAT

DANIELLE STEEL

HEARTBEAT

Delacorte
Press

Published by
Delacorte Press
Bantam Doubleday Dell Publishing Group, Inc.
666 Fifth Avenue
New York, New York 10103

Library of Congress Cataloging in Publication Data

Steel, Danielle.
   Heartbeat / Danielle Steel.
        p.   cm.
   ISBN 0-385-29908-7
   ISBN 0-385-30321-1 (Limited Ed.)
   I. Title.
   PS3569.T33828H44   1991
   813'.54—dc20   90-3044   CIP

Manufactured in the United States of America
Published simultaneously in Canada

March 1991

10 9 8 7 6 5 4 3 2 1
BVG

To Zara,
sweet heartbeat
of my life,
may your life be ever
full of love and joy . . .

and to your daddy, who has
filled my life to the brim
with love and joy and heartbeats

with all my heart and love,

d.s.

HEARTBEAT

thumping,
pitter pat,
 wondering
 where it's at,
heartfelt,
 heart sweet,
 sweet dreams,
 heartbeat,
precious music
 in my ears,
hand to hold
to still my fears,
 loving footsteps
 in the night,
 treasured hopes,
 forever bright,
 brightest love,
 gift from on high,
 gentlest
 sweetest lullaby,

miracle of tiny
      feet,
    born of one
single,
    precious
        beat,
singing
    sweetest
        little song,
  my heart
        to yours
        will e'er belong,
      this final bond,
    this tie so sure,
from our love
    so strong and pure,
      now whisper softly
  while babe sleeps,
      our love
        will always
              ever keep
  and as the magic
  stardust soars,
      my heart is ever,
        always, yours.

CHAPTER

••1••

THE SOUND OF AN ANCIENT TYPEWRITER SANG OUT STAC-
cato in the silence of the room, as a cloud of blue smoke hung
over the corner where Bill Thigpen was working. Glasses
shoved up high on his head, coffee in styrofoam cups hovering
dangerously near the edge of the desk, ashtrays brimming, his
face intense, blue eyes squinting at what he was writing.
Faster, faster, a glance over his shoulder at the clock ticking
relentlessly behind him. He typed as though demons were
lurking somewhere near him. His graying brown hair looked
as though he had slept and woken several times and never
remembered to comb it. The face was clean-shaven and kind,
the lines strong, and yet something about him very gentle. He
was not a man clearly defined by handsome, yet he seemed
strong, appealing, worth more than a second glance, a man
one would have liked to spend time with. But not now, not as
he groaned, glanced at the clock again, and let his fingers fly at

the typewriter still harder. Then finally, silence, a quick fix with a pen as he leapt to his feet, and grabbed handfuls of what he had been working on for the past seven hours, since five o'clock in the morning. Nearly one now . . . nearly air time . . . as he flew across the room, yanked open the door, and exploded past his secretary's desk like an Olympic runner, heading down the hall as quickly as he could, darting around people, avoiding collisions, ignoring surprised stares and friendly greetings, as he pounded on doors that opened only inches as he shoved a hand inside clutching a sheaf of the freshly written changes. It was a familiar procedure. It happened once, twice, sometimes three or four times a month when Bill decided he didn't like the way the show was going. As the originator of the most successful daytime soap on TV, whenever he was worried about the show, he stopped, wrote a segment or two, turned everything upside down, and then he was happy. His agent called him the most neurotic mother on TV, but he also knew he was the best. Bill Thigpen had an unfailing instinct for what made his show work, and he had never been wrong. Not so far.

A Life Worth Living was still the hottest daytime soap on American TV and it was William Thigpen's baby. He had started it as a way to survive when he'd been starving in New York years before as a young playwright. He had started playing with the concept and then the first script during a time when he was between plays in New York. He had started out writing plays on off-off Broadway, and in those days he had been a purist. The theater above all. But he had also been married, living in SoHo in New York, and starving. His wife, Leslie, had been a dancer in Broadway shows, and at the time she was out of work too, because she was pregnant with their first baby. At first he had kidded around about how "ironic" it would be if he finally made it with a soap, if that turned out to be the big break of his career. But as he wrestled with the script, and a bible for a long-term show, it stopped being a joke, and became an obsession. He *had* to make it . . . for Leslie . . . for their baby. And the truth was, he liked it. He loved it. And so did the network. They went crazy over it. And the baby, Adam, and the show had been born at almost the same time, one a strapping nine-pound baby boy with his father's big blue eyes and a mist of golden curls, the other a tryout on the summer schedule that brought the ratings through the roof and an instant outcry when the show disappeared again in September. Within two months, *A Life Worth Living* was back and Bill Thigpen was on his way as the creator of the most successful daytime television soap ever. The important choices came later.

He started out by writing some of the early episodes himself, and they were good, but he drove the actors and director crazy. And by then his career on off-off Broadway was all but forgotten. Television became his lifeblood in a matter of moments.

Eventually, he was offered a lot of money to sell his concept and just sit back and go home to collect residuals, and go back to writing plays for off-off Broadway. But by then, almost as much as his six-month-old son, *Life,* as he called it, was his baby. He couldn't bring himself to leave the show, much less sell it. He had to stay with it. It was real to him, it was alive, and he cared about what he was saying. He talked about the agonies of life, the disappointments, the angers, the sorrows, the triumphs, the challenges, the excitement, the love, the simple beauty. The show had all his zest for life, his own sorrow over grief, his own delight for living. It gave people hope after despair, sunshine after storms, and the basic core of the story line and the principal characters were decent. There were villains, of course, too, and people ate them up. But there was a basic integrity about the show that made its fans unshakable in their devotion. It was in effect a reflection of the essence of its creator. Alive, excited about life, decent, trusting, kind, naive, intelligent, creative. And he loved the show, almost like a child he was bound and determined to nurture, almost as much as he loved Adam and Leslie.

And in those early days of the show he was constantly torn, endlessly pulled, always wanting to be with his family and yet keep an eye on the show, to make sure it was on the right track and they hadn't brought in the wrong writer or director. He viewed everyone with suspicion, and he maintained complete control. They understood nothing about his show . . . his baby. And he'd pace the set like a nervous mother hen, going crazy inside over what might happen. He continued to write random episodes, to haunt the show much of the time, and kibitz from the sidelines. And at the end of the first year, there was no point pretending that Bill Thigpen was ever going back to Broadway. He was stuck, trapped, madly in love with television and the show of his own making. He even stopped making excuses to his off-off-Broadway friends, and admitted openly that he loved what he was doing. There was no way he was going anywhere, he explained to Leslie late one night, after he'd written for hours, developing new plots, new characters, new philosophies for the coming season.

He couldn't abandon his characters, his actors, and the intricacies of the plot and its avalanche of tragedies, traumas, and problems. He loved it. The show was shot live five times a week, and even when he had no real reason to be on the set, he ate, drank, loved, breathed, and slept it. There were daily writers who kept the show going day by day, but Bill was always watching over their shoulders. And he knew what he was doing. Everyone in the business agreed. He was good. He was better than good. He was terrific. He had an instinctive sense for what worked, what didn't, what people cared about, the characters they would love, the ones they would enjoy hating.

And by the time his second son, Tommy, was born two years later, *A Life Worth Living* had won two critics' awards and an Emmy. It was after the show's first Emmy that the network suggested they move the show to California. It made more sense creatively, production arrangements would be easier out there, and they felt that the show "belonged" in California. To Bill, it was good news, but to Leslie, his wife, it wasn't. She was going back to work, not just as a kid in the chorus on Broadway. After watching Bill obsess about his show for the past two and a half years, she had had it. While he had been writing night and day about incest, teenage pregnancy, and suburban extramarital affairs, she had gone back to classes in her original discipline, and now she wanted to teach ballet at Juilliard.

"You're *what* ?" He stared at her in amazement one Sunday morning over breakfast. Everything had been going so well for them, he was making money hand over fist, the kids were terrific, and as far as he knew, everything was just rolling along perfectly. Until that morning.

"I can't, Bill. I'm not going." She looked up at him quietly, her big brown eyes as gentle and childlike as when he'd met her with her dance bag in her hand outside a theater when she was twenty. She was from upstate New York, and she had always been decent and kind and unpretentious, a gentle soul with expressive eyes and a shy but genuine sense of humor. They used to laugh a lot in the early days, and talk late into the night in the dismal, freezing-cold apartments they rented, until the beautiful and very expensive loft he had just bought for them in SoHo. He had even put an exercise bar in for her, so she could do her ballet warm-ups and exercises without going to a studio. And now suddenly she was telling him it was all over.

"But why? What are you saying, Les? You don't want to leave New York?" He looked mystified as her eyes filled with tears and she shook her head, turning away from him for an instant, and then she looked back into his eyes and what he saw there made his heart ache. It was anger, disappointment, defeat, and suddenly for the first time he saw what he should have seen months before, and he wondered in terror if she still loved him. "What is it? What happened?" How could he have missed it? he asked himself. How could he have been so stupid?

"I don't know . . . you've changed . . ." And then she shook her head again, the long dark hair sailing around her like the dark wings of a fallen angel. "No . . . that's not fair . . . we both have. . . ." She took a deep breath and tried to explain it to him. She owed him that much after five years of marriage and two children. "We've changed places, I think. I used to want to be a big star on Broadway, the dancer who made good and became a star, and all you wanted to do was write plays with 'integrity,' and 'guts,' and 'meaning.' And all of a sudden you started writing. . . ." She hesitated with a small sad smile. "You started writing more commercial stuff, and it became an obsession. All you've thought about for the last three years is the show . . . will Sheila marry Jake? . . . did Larry really try to kill his mother? . . . is Henry gay . . . is Martha? . . . will Martha leave her husband for another woman? . . . whose baby is Hilary in truth? . . . will Mary run away from home? . . . and when she does will she go back to drugs? Is Helen illegitimate? Will she marry John?" Leslie stood up and started to pace the room as she reeled off the familiar names. "The truth is, they're driving me crazy. I don't want to hear about them anymore. I don't want to live with them anymore. I want to go back to something simple and healthy and normal, the discipline of dancing, the excitement of teaching. I want a normal, quiet life, without all that make-believe bullshit." She looked at him unhappily, and he wanted to cry. He had been a fool. While he had been playing with his imaginary friends, he was losing the people he really loved, and he hadn't even known it. And yet, he couldn't promise her he'd give it up, sell his control of the show and go back to the plays he'd had to beg to get put on. How could he do that now? And he loved the show. It made him feel good and happy and accomplished and strong . . . and now Leslie was leaving. It was ironic. The show was a huge success, and so was he, and she was longing for their days of starvation.

"I'm sorry." He tried to force himself to stay calm and reason with her. "I know I've been wrapped up in the show for the last three years, but I felt I needed to control it. If I let it get completely out of my hands, if I let someone else do it, they could have cheapened it, they could have turned it into one of those ridiculous, trite, maudlin soaps that make your skin crawl. I couldn't let them do that. And the show *does* have integrity. Whether you admit it or not, Les, that's what people have responded to. But that doesn't mean I have to sit on top of it forever. I think in California things will be very different . . . more professional . . . more in control. I should be able to get away from it more often." He only wrote occasional segments now. But he still controlled it.

Leslie only shook her head with a look of disbelief. She knew him better. It had been the same when he was writing his early plays. He worked for two months straight without taking a break, barely eating or sleeping or thinking of anything else, but that had been only for two months and in those days she still thought it was charming. It no longer was. She was sick to death of it, sick of the intensity and the obsessiveness, and his mania for perfection. She knew that he loved her and the boys, but not the way she wanted him to. She wanted a husband who went to work at nine o'clock, and came home at six, ready to talk to her, to play with the kids, to help her cook dinner and take her to a movie. Not someone who worked straight through the night and then rushed out of the house exhausted and wild eyed at ten a.m. with an armload of memos and edicts and script changes to deliver by rehearsal at ten-thirty. It was too much, too exhausting, too draining, and after three years she'd had it. She was burnt-out, and if she ever heard the words *A Life Worth Living* again, or the names of the characters he was constantly adding and subtracting, she knew she would have hysterics.

"Leslie, give it a chance, baby, please . . . give *me* a chance. It'll be great in L.A. Just think of it, no more snow, no more cold weather. It'll be great for the boys. We can take them to the beach . . . we could have a pool right in our backyard . . . we can go to Disneyland. . . ." But she was still shaking her head. She knew him better.

"No, *I* can take them to Disneyland and the beach. *You'll* be working all the time, you'll either be up all night writing someone out of the show, or running in for rehearsal or to watch them air, or frantically rewriting something else. When was the last time you took the boys to the Bronx Zoo, or anywhere for that matter?"

"All right . . . all right . . . so I work too hard . . . so I'm a terrible father . . . or a bastard or a rotten husband or all of the above, but for chrissake, Les, for years we were starving to death. And now look, you can have anything you want, and so can they. We can send them to decent schools one day, we can give them everything we wanted to, we can send them to college. Is that so terrible? So okay, we've had a few hard years and now it's going to get better. And now you're going to walk out before it does? What timing." He stared at her, tears brimming in his own eyes as he held out a hand to her. "Baby, I love you . . . please don't do this . . ." But she didn't move toward him, and she lowered her eyes so she couldn't see the pain in his. She knew he loved her, and she knew better than anyone how much he loved the boys. But it didn't matter. She knew that, for her own sake, she had to do what she was doing.

"Do you want to stay here? I'll tell them we won't move the show. If that's what this is all about, to hell with California . . . we'll stay here." But a note of panic had crept into his voice as he watched her, sensing that California was not the issue.

"It won't make any difference." Her voice was low and soft, and she was very sorry. "It's too late for us. I can't explain it. I just know I have to do something different."

"Like what? Move to India? Change religions? Become a nun? How different is teaching at Juilliard? What are you saying to me, dammit? That you want out? What the hell does that have to do with Juilliard or California?" He was hurting and confused and suddenly, finally, he was angry. Why was she doing this to him? What had he done to deserve it? He had worked hard, done well, his parents would have been proud of him if they'd been alive, but both had died when he was in his early twenties, of cancer, within a year of each other, and he had no siblings. All he had was her and the boys, and now she was telling him that they were leaving, and he was going to be alone again. All alone, without the three people he loved, because he had done something wrong, he had worked too hard and been too successful. And the unfairness of what she was doing to him made him suddenly burn with fury.

"You just don't understand," she insisted limply.

"No, I don't. You're telling me you won't come to California. So I'm telling you that if it makes a difference, we'll stay here, and to hell with what the network says. They'll have to live with it. So what now? Where do we go from here? We go back to the way things were, or what? What's happening, Les?" He was torn between anger and despair and he wasn't sure what to say to her to change it. But what he hadn't understood yet was that she had made up her mind, and there was no way now to dissuade her.

"I don't know how to say this to you. . . ." Her eyes filled with tears as she looked at him, and for an instant he had the insane feeling that he had walked into one of his own shows and couldn't get out now . . . would Leslie leave Bill? . . . can Bill really change? . . . does Leslie really understand how much Bill loves her? . . . He wanted to laugh suddenly, or cry, but he did neither. "It's over. I guess that's the only way to say it. California doesn't have anything to do with it. I just haven't wanted to admit it to myself until now, and now I have. I can't do this anymore. I want my own life, with the boys. I want to do my own thing, Bill . . . without living with the show day and night . . ." And without him. But she couldn't bring herself to say it. The look of pain in his eyes was so overwhelming, she thought she might faint just looking at him. "I'm sorry. . . ."

He looked as though lightning had just struck him. He was deathly white, and his eyes were big and blue and filled with anguish. "You're taking the boys?" What had he ever done to deserve that? They both knew that, no matter how busy he had been for the past three years, he adored them.

"You can't take care of them by yourself in California." It was a simple statement as he stared at her in horror.

"No, but you could come with me to help." It was a weak joke, but neither of them felt like joking.

"Bill, don't . . ."

"Will you let them come out to see me?" She nodded, and he prayed that she meant it. For a moment, he thought of abandoning the show, staying in New York, and begging her not to leave him. But he also sensed that no matter what he did now, it was too late for her. In heart and soul and mind, she had already left him. And what he reproached himself for now was not having noticed sooner. Maybe if he had, he could have changed things. But now, he knew her well enough to know he couldn't. It was all over, without a whimper or a wail. He had lost the war long since and never known it. His life was over.

The next two months were an agony that still made him cry when he thought of it. Telling the boys. Helping them move to an apartment on the West Side before he left. His first night alone in the loft without them. Again and again, he thought of giving up the show, and begging her to take him back, but it was clear that the door was closed now, never to be reopened. And he discovered, before he left, that there was another teacher at Juilliard whom she was "very fond of." She hadn't carried on an affair, and Bill knew her well enough to believe that she had been faithful to him, but she was falling in love with the guy and that was part of her reason for leaving. She wanted to be free to pursue her relationship with him without guilt, or Bill Thigpen. She and her teacher friend had everything in common, she insisted, and she and Bill no longer did, except their children. Adam had been heartbroken to see him go, but at two and a half he had readjusted pretty quickly. And Tommy was only eight months old and seemed not to know the difference. Only Bill really felt it as tears filled his eyes and ran slowly down his cheeks as the plane soared slowly over New York and headed for California.

And once there, Bill threw himself into the show with a vengeance. He worked day and night, and sometimes even slept on the couch in his office, as the ratings continued to soar, and the show won innumerable Daytime Emmys. And in the seven years he'd been in California, Bill Thigpen had become only slightly less manic. *A Life Worth Living* had become his pride and joy, his daily companion, his best friend, his baby. He had no reason to fight it anymore. He let his work become his daily passion.

The boys came out to visit him on alternate holidays and for a month in the summer, and he loved them more than ever. But being three thousand miles away from them when he really wanted to see them every day remained extremely painful. And there had been a parade of women in his life, but the only constant companion he had was the show, and the actors in it. And he lived for his vacations with Adam and Tommy. Leslie had long since married the Juilliard teacher and had two more kids, and she had finally given up teaching. With four kids at home under the age of ten, she had her hands full, but she seemed to love it. She and Bill talked on the phone now and then, particularly when the boys were coming out, or if one of them was sick, or if there was a problem, but they didn't have much to say to each other anymore, except about Adam and Tommy. It was hard even to remember what it had been like when they were married. The pain of losing her was gone, and the memories of the good times were dim. Except for the boys, it was all gone now. And they were the real loves in his life. In the summer, when they spent the month with him, his passion for them was even greater than anything he'd felt for the show, his attention to them more intense. He took a month's vacation every year and they usually went somewhere for part of it, and spent the rest of the time in L.A., going to Disneyland, seeing friends, just hanging out while he cooked for them and took care of them, and ached all over again when they went back to New York and left him. Adam, the older one, was almost ten now, responsible, funny, serious, and a lot like his mother. Tommy was the baby, disorganized, still a baby some of the time, even at seven, and whimsical, vague, and sometimes very, very funny. Leslie frequently told Bill that Tommy was the image of him in every way, but somehow he couldn't see it. He adored them both, and on long, lonely nights alone in L.A., his heart still ached wishing that they all lived together. It was the one thing in his life that he regretted, the one thing he couldn't change, the one thing that really depressed him at times although he tried not to let it. But the idea that he had two kids he loved and hardly ever saw seemed a high price to pay for a mistaken marriage. Why did she get to keep them and not he? Why did she get the reward for the lost years, and he get the punishment? What was fair about that? Nothing. And it only made him sure of one thing. He was never going to let it happen again. He was never going to fall madly in love, get married, have kids, and lose them. Period. No way. And over the years, he had found the perfect solution to the problem. Actresses. Hordes of them. When he had time, which wasn't often.

When he had first come to California, aching from the pain of leaving Leslie and the kids, he had fallen gratefully into the arms of a serious lady director, and had had an affair that lasted six months and almost led to disaster. She had moved in with him and taken over his life, inviting friends to stay, furnishing his apartment for him, running his life, until he felt as if he had been strangled. She had previously gone to UCLA, done graduate work at Yale, talked constantly about a Ph.D., and was into "serious film," and she kept insisting that *A Life* was beneath him. She talked about it like a disease from which he might soon be healed, if he would only let her help him. She also hated kids, and kept putting away the photographs of his children. Remarkably, it took him a full six months to catch his breath and let her have it. It took six months because she was great in bed, treated him like a six-year-old at a time when he desperately needed nurturing and liked it, and she seemed to know everything about the television industry in L.A. But when she told him he ought to stop talking about his kids, and forget about them, he rented a bungalow at the Beverly Hills Hotel for a month, gave her the key, told her to have a great time, and not to bother to call him when she found an apartment. He moved her things to the bungalow the same afternoon, and didn't run into her for the next four years until they saw each other at an awards ceremony, where she pretended not to know him.

And what had come after that had been intentionally lighthearted and easy. Actresses, starlets, walk-ons, models, girls who wanted a good time when he was free, and enjoyed going to an occasional party with him when he wasn't in a period of high stress due to some change on the show, and they wanted nothing more from him. They fitted him in among the other men in their lives, and seemed not to care when he didn't call them. Some of them cooked dinner for him occasionally, or he for them since he loved to cook, and the ones who were good with kids were sometimes called on to go to Disneyland with him when the boys were in town, but more often than not he enjoyed keeping the boys to himself during their visits to California.

More recently, Bill had gotten involved with one of the actresses on the show. Sylvia was a pretty girl from New York, and she had an important part on the show. And it was the first time in a long time that he had allowed himself the indulgence of getting involved with someone who actually worked for him. But she was a sensational-looking girl, and she had been hard to resist. She had come to the show via years as a child actress and model, the cover of *Vogue*, a year in Paris working for Lacroix, and six months in L.A. doing bit parts in an assortment of unsuccessful movies. She was a fairly decent actress, surprisingly enough, and a sweet girl, which came through on the air, and Bill was surprised himself by how much he liked her. Liked. Not loved. Love was something he reserved for Adam and Tommy, who were, respectively, nine and a half and seven. Sylvia was twenty-three, and sometimes he thought she behaved like a child herself. Along with her sweetness there was a kind of simplicity and naiveté that both touched him and amused him. Despite her worldly experiences, acting and modeling for the past nine years, she seemed to have remained relatively unsophisticated through all of it, which was at times both refreshing and annoying. She was singularly unaware of the inevitable politics that went on behind the scenes on the show, and some of her performances were superb, but she was also easy prey for the more jaded women with whom she acted. And Bill found himself constantly warning her to be more alert to the games they played and the trouble they surreptitiously tried to cause her. But childlike, she floated through all of it, and seemed to keep herself amused when Bill was too busy to entertain her, as he had been for weeks, working on the addition of two new characters, and the surprise removal of yet another. He was always careful to keep the show fresh, and keep the audiences fascinated with the never-ending plot turns.

At thirty-nine, he had become the king of daytime soaps, as his row of Emmys lined up on a shelf on his office wall clearly attested. But he was, as always, totally unaware of them, as he returned to his office and began to pace, wondering how the actors in today's show would react to the unexpected last-minute changes. Two of the women usually handled it well, but one of his male actors frequently blew his lines when surprised at the last minute, and if the alterations made him too nervous. He had been on the show for two years, and Bill had thought more than once about replacing him, and yet he liked the human quality he brought to the show, and the power of his performances when he believed in what he was saying.

It was a show which seemed to mean a lot to untold millions across the United States, and the volume of mail Bill and the actors and the producers got was nothing short of amazing. The cast and crew had become a kind of family over the years, and the show meant a great deal to all of them. It had become a home and a way of life for a lot of very talented people.

That afternoon, his own ladylove, Sylvia, was going to be playing her part as Vaughn Williams, the beautiful younger sister of the show's principal heroine, Helen. "Vaughn" had been lured into an affair with her brother-in-law, and introduced to drugs by him as well, unbeknownst to anyone in her family, particularly her own sister. Trapped in a web from which she seemed unable to free herself, Vaughn's brother-in-law, John, was luring her deeper and deeper into his clutches and leading her toward her own destruction. In an unexpected turn of events on that day's show, Vaughn was going to be witness to a murder committed by John, and the police would begin seeking Vaughn for the murder of the drug dealer who had been supplying her drugs since John introduced her to him. It had been a difficult series of events to orchestrate and Bill had been closely supervising the writers, with an eye to stepping in himself if he had to. But it was exactly the kind of plot turn that had kept the show going for close to ten years, and Bill was clearly pleased with the morning's work sketching out the next developments as he sat down in a chair in his office, lit a cigarette, and took a sip from the steaming mug of coffee his secretary had just put there. He was wondering what Sylvia would think of the script changes he had just handed her through her dressing room door. He hadn't seen her since the night before, when he left her place at three a.m. and came to the office to start working on the idea that had been gnawing at him all evening. She had been asleep when he left, and he had gone home to shower and change before going to his office at four-thirty. And by twelve-thirty, the atmosphere in his office was still electrically charged as he got to his feet, stubbed the cigarette out, and hurried to the studio, where he watched the director carefully going over the last-minute changes.

The director was a man Bill had known for years, a Hollywood veteran who had come to the show after directing reams of successful television movies. He had been an unusually serious choice for a soap opera on daytime TV, but Bill had obviously known what he was doing. Allan McLoughlin kept everyone on their toes, and he was speaking seriously to Sylvia and the actor who played John, as Bill walked into the studio and stood discreetly in a remote corner of the room where he could observe but not disturb them.

"Coffee, Bill?" A pretty young script girl inquired. She had had an eye on him for a year. She liked him. He was what some people would have described as a "teddy bear," tall, powerful, warm, smart, nice-looking but not gorgeous, with easy laughter and a gentle style that somehow softened the intensity with which he worked. But Bill only smiled and shook his head. She was a nice kid, but he had never thought of her as anything but the script girl. He was too busy working while he was there to concentrate on anything but what was happening in front of the cameras, or in his head, as he plotted the show's future turns and detours.

"No, thanks, I'm fine." He smiled at the girl and turned his attention back to the director. He noticed that Sylvia was studying her lines, and the actors who played Helen and John were conferring quietly in a corner. There were two men dressed as policemen, and the "victim," the drug dealer "John" was going to kill on today's show, was already wearing a blood-drenched shirt that looked disturbingly realistic. He was laughing and exchanging jokes with one of the grips. It was his last day on the show, and he had no lines to learn. He was going to be dead when the camera first saw him.

"Two minutes," a voice said, loud enough for everyone to hear, and Bill felt a faint flutter in the pit of his stomach. He always did. He had felt that twinge since his very early days as an actor when he was in college. And in New York, he had actually felt sick for an hour every night before the curtain went up on one of his plays. And now, ten years after *A Life* had been born, he still felt a twinge every time they were about to go on the air. What if it bombed? . . . if the ratings fell? . . . if no one watched? . . . if all the actors walked off? . . . if everyone fluffed their lines? . . . if . . . the possibilities and potential for horror were endless.

"One minute!" The noose at the top of his stomach tightened further. Bill's eyes scanned the room. Sylvia with her eyes closed, memorizing the lines one last time, and maintaining her composure. Helen and John at their marks on the set, ready for the colossal argument that was to open the day's show. The drug dealer eating a huge pastrami sandwich in his blood-drenched shirt offscreen, and no one uttering a sound as the assistant director held up a hand, fingers extended, indicating five seconds before they went on the air . . . four . . . three . . . two . . . one finger . . . a leap in the pit of Bill's stomach, and the hand is down, and Helen and John are fighting furiously on the set, the language abusive but just inside what the censors will allow them, the situation tense to the point of explosion. The words are familiar to Bill, and yet here and there, as they always do, they wing it. Helen more so than John, but for her it works, and Bill doesn't mind it as long as she doesn't go too far afield, or throw off the other actors. It's working so far . . . the door slams after four minutes of intense drama, and they break away for a commercial. Helen comes off the set looking deathly pale. The work they do is brief and intense, the dialogue and the situations so real that somehow they all believe them. Bill catches her eye and smiles. She did a good job. She always does. She is a very fine actress. She disappears. The hand goes up again. Total silence. Not a sound, not a coin clanking in a pocket, or a key on a key ring, or a footstep. John has gone to the remote country home of the drug dealer, who has anonymously called Helen and told her of her husband's affair with her sister. Shots ring out, and all we see is the prone body of the man in the blood-soaked shirt, lying on the floor, clearly dead. Extreme close-up of John's face, a murderous look in his eye, as Vaughn stands beside him. Fade out. Fade in. Extreme close up of Vaughn, looking incredibly beautiful in a small but luxurious apartment. John has set her up as a good girl gone bad, and we see her saying good-bye to a man. We sense without being told that she is a call girl. Vaughn's eyes meet the camera, troubled, beautiful, and somewhat glazed. Bill watches intensely as the plot unfolds and he begins to relax as they fade out for another commercial. It is a like a new play every day, a fresh drama, a whole new world, and the magic of it never ceases to intrigue him. Sometimes he wonders why it works, why the show is so immensely successful, but he wonders if it's because he himself is still so wrapped up in it. He wonders, but only rarely, what might have happened if he had sold his concept, or left the show years before . . . if he had stayed in New York . . . gone on to something else . . . stayed married to Leslie, and stayed with the boys . . . would they have had more kids? Would he be writing Broadway plays by now? Would he ever have made it? Would they have gotten divorced by now anyway? It was odd to look back and try to second-guess it.

Bill left the studio then, assured that the segment was going well and he didn't need to stay till the end. The director had it in control, and Bill walked slowly back to his office, feeling spent, relieved, and sure of the direction of the next several segments. One of the things that he loved about the show was that he could never get lazy or complacent, he couldn't just coast, or use a formula, or follow the same old plot lines. He had to keep it fresh, moment by moment, hour by hour, or the show would simply die. And he liked the excitement of the daily challenge. The challenge met, he went back to his office, and sprawled his frame across the couch, staring out the window.

"How'd it go?" Betsey asked. She had been his secretary for nearly two years, which in television was half a lifetime. She was a stand-up comedian at night, and she thought Bill walked on water when no one was looking.

"It went okay." He looked relaxed and pleased. The knot in his stomach had turned into a peaceful hum of satisfaction.

"Did we hear anything today from the network?" He had sent over some new concepts for some interesting directions for the show, and he was waiting to hear, although he knew they would pretty much let him do anything he wanted.

"Not yet. But I think Leland Harris is out of town, and so is Nathan Steinberg." The gods who ran his life, omniscient, omnipotent, all-thinking, all-seeing, all-knowing. He and Nathan went fishing together from time to time, and although the guy was said to be a son of a bitch, Bill actually liked him and insisted that he had always been very pleasant to him. "Are you leaving early tonight?" Betsey looked at him hopefully. Once in a while when he'd come in at the crack of dawn, he left before five o'clock, but it was rare, and he shook his head as he walked across the room to his desk where his ancient typewriter sat on a small table just behind it. It was a Royal, and it was one of the few souvenirs he still had left from his father.

"I think I'll hang around. The stuff we put in today worked, which means they've got a lot of changes to make for the next few segments. They have to write out Barnes completely. We just killed him. And Vaughn is going to wind up in jail, not to mention the fact that Helen is getting wise to John. And wait till she finds out that her little sister has been turning tricks to support her drug habit thanks to her own darling husband." He beamed happily as he stretched his legs under the desk and leaned back with his hands behind his head in a pose of total delight and relaxation.

"You have a sick mind." Betsey made a face, and closed the door to his office, and then popped her head back in. "Do you want me to order anything from the commissary for tonight?"

"Christ . . . now I know you're trying to kill me. Just get me a couple of sandwiches and a Thermos of coffee and leave it on your desk. I'll grab it if I get hungry." But more often than not, it was midnight before he even saw the time, and by then he was no longer hungry. It was a wonder he didn't starve to death, Betsey often said, when she saw evidence that he had worked through the night, leaving overflowing ashtrays, fourteen mugs of cold coffee and half a dozen Snickers wrappers behind him.

"You should go home and get some sleep."

"Thanks, Mom." He grinned as she closed the door again. She was a terrific person and he liked her.

He was still smiling to himself, thinking of Betsey, when the door opened again, and he looked up. As always when he saw her, he felt a sharp intake of breath at how she looked. It was Sylvia, still wearing her costume and makeup from the show, and she looked stunning.

She was tall and thin and shapely, with full high silicone breasts that just begged for men to reach out and touch them, and legs that seemed to start at her armpits. She was almost as tall as Bill, and she had cascades of thick black hair that hung to her waist, creamy white skin, and green eyes that were strikingly catlike. She was a girl who would have stopped traffic anywhere, even in L.A., where actresses and models and beautiful girls were commonplace. But Sylvia Stewart wasn't commonplace anywhere, and Bill was the first to say that she did wonderful, healthy things to their ratings.

"Good job, babe. You were great today. But you always are." He stood up as she smiled, and he came around his desk to give her a half-serious kiss as she sat in a chair and crossed her legs, and looking down at her, he felt his heart beat a little faster. "God, you destroy me when you come in here looking like that." She was wearing the sexy little black dress that she had worn in the last scene on the show, and it was clearly a knockout. Their costume department had gotten it on loan from Fred Heyman. "The least you could do is put a sweatshirt and some jeans on." But the jeans weren't much better. She wore them skintight and all he could think of when he saw her in jeans was taking her clothes off.

"Costume said I could have the dress." She managed somehow to look both innocent and sultry.

"That's nice." He smiled at her again and settled back behind his desk. "It looks good on you. Maybe we can go out to dinner next week and you can wear it."

"Next *week*?" She looked like a child who had just been told her favorite doll was in the shop for repairs until next Tuesday. "Why can't we go out *tonight*?" She was pouting at him, and he looked faintly amused by her. These were the scenes that Sylvia was singularly good at. They were the downside of her incredible good looks and irresistibly sexy body.

"You may have noticed on today's show that several new developments occurred, and your character just wound up in jail. There are a ton of new scenes for the writers to write and I want to be around to write some of it myself, or at least check on how they're doing." Anyone who knew him knew he was going to be working eighteen- to twenty-hour days for the next few weeks, kibitzing and coaxing and rewriting it himself, but the material he would get out of it would be worth it.

"Can't we go away this weekend?" The incredible legs uncrossed and recrossed, causing a disturbance in Bill's jeans, but she still appeared not to have understood him.

"No, we can't. If I'm lucky and everything goes okay, maybe by Sunday we can play a little tennis."

The pout deepened. Sylvia did not look pleased. "I wanted to go to Vegas. A whole bunch of the kids from *My House* are going to Vegas for the weekend." *My House* was their stiffest competition.

"I can't help it, Sylvia. I've got to work." And then, knowing that it would be easier if she went without him than if she stayed and complained, he suggested that she go to Vegas with the others. "Why don't you go with them? You're not on the show tomorrow, and it might be fun. And I'm going to be stuck here anyway all weekend." He waved at the four walls of his office, and even though it was only Thursday then, he knew he had at least three or four more days of intense work overseeing the writers, but Sylvia looked cheered by the suggestion that she go without him.

"Will you come to Vegas when you finish?" She looked like a child again, and sometimes her ingenuousness touched him. In truth, her body appealed to him more and it had been an easy relationship for him for the past several months, although not one he was overly proud of. She was a decent person and he liked her, but she was less than challenging for him, and he knew he didn't always meet her needs either. She wanted someone who was free to run around and play with her, to go to openings and parties and ten o'clock dinners at Spago, and more often than not he was tied up with the show, or writing new scenes, or too tired to go anywhere, and Hollywood parties had never been his forte.

"I don't think I'll be finished in time to go anywhere. I'll see you Sunday night when you get home." The timing was going to be perfect for him and it would keep her off his back, although he felt mean thinking of it that way. But it was easier knowing that she was happy somewhere else rather than calling him at the office every two hours to ask him when he'd be finished working.

"Okay." She stood up, looking pleased. "You don't mind?" She felt a little guilty leaving him, but he only smiled and escorted her to the door of his office.

"No, I don't mind. Just don't let the 'kids' from *My House* try to sell you a new contract." She laughed, and this time he kissed her hard on the mouth. "I'm going to miss you."

"Me too." But there was something wistful in her eyes as she looked at him and for the flash of an instant he wondered if something was wrong. It was something he had seen in other eyes before . . . starting with Leslie's. It was something that women said at times, without actually saying the words. It had to do with feeling alone and being lonely. And he knew it well, but there was nothing he was going to change now. He never had before, and at thirty-nine, he figured it was too late to do much changing.

Sylvia left his office, and Bill went back to work. He had a mountain of notes he wanted to make about the new scripts, and all the upcoming changes, and by the time he looked up from his typewriter again, it was dark outside, and he was startled to realize it was ten o'clock when he looked at his watch, and he suddenly realized he was desperately thirsty. He got up from his desk, turned on some more lights, and helped himself to a soda water from the office. He knew Betsey would have left a bunch of sandwiches for him on her desk, but he wasn't even hungry. The work seemed to feed his spirit when it was going well, and he was pleased as he glanced over what he'd done, and leaned back in his desk chair, sipping the soda. There was just one more scene he wanted to change before giving it up for the night, and for the next two hours, he banged away on the old Royal, totally forgetting everything except what he was writing. And this time when he stopped, it was midnight. He had been at it for almost twenty hours and he was hardly even tired, he felt exhilarated by the changes he'd made and the way the work had been flowing. He took the sheaf of pages he'd been working on since that afternoon, locked them in a desk drawer, helped himself to another soda water on his way out, and left his cigarettes on the desk. He seldom smoked except when he was working.

He walked past his secretary's desk, with the sandwiches still sitting in a cardboard box, and walked out into the fluorescent-lit hall, past half a dozen studios that were closed down now. There was a late-night talk show in one, and a bunch of odd-looking kids in punk clothes had just arrived to make an appearance. He smiled at them, but they didn't smile back. They were all much too nervous, and he walked past the studio where they did the eleven o'clock news, but that was dark now, too, having already been readied for the morning broadcast.

The guard at the front desk handed Bill the sign-out sheet and he scrawled his name and made a comment about the most recent baseball game. He and the old guard shared a passion for the Dodgers. And then he walked out into the fresh air, and took a deep breath of the warm spring night. The smog didn't seem so bad at that hour, and it felt good just to be alive. He loved what he did, and it made it seem somehow worthwhile to work those ridiculous hours, making up stories about imaginary people. Somehow when he was doing it, it all made sense to him, and when he was finished, he was always glad he had done it. Now and then it was an agony, when a scene didn't go right or a character slipped out of control and became someone he had never intended, but most of the time doing it was something he loved, and there were times when he missed doing it full-time, and he envied the writers.

He sighed happily as he started his car. It was a '49 Chevrolet woody station wagon, and he had bought it from a surfer seven years before for five hundred dollars and he loved it. It was maroon and it was in less than perfect condition, but it had soul, and lots of room, and the boys loved riding around in it when they came to visit.

As he drove home on the Santa Monica Freeway toward Fairfax Avenue, he realized suddenly that he was hungry. He was more than hungry. He was starving. And he knew that there was nothing in his apartment. He hadn't eaten there in days. He had been too busy working and before that he'd eaten out, and he had spent the weekend before at Sylvia's place in Malibu. She rented it from an aging movie star who had been in a retirement home for years but still kept the house in Malibu she had once lived in.

Bill stopped at Safeway on his way home, and it was after midnight as he pulled his woody into the parking lot and slid into a space right in front of the main entrance. He parked it next to a battered old red MG with the top down, walked into the brightly lit all-night store and helped himself to a cart as he tried to decide what he wanted to eat. There were chickens barbecuing in a nearby aisle, and he noticed that they smelled terrific. He helped himself to one of them, a six-pack of beer, some potato salad from the deli area, some salami, some pickles, and then he headed to the produce section for lettuce and tomatoes and vegetables to make himself a salad. The more he thought about it, the hungrier he got, and he could hardly wait to get home and have dinner. He could no longer remember if he'd eaten lunch, or if he had, what it had been. It seemed like years suddenly since he had eaten. He remembered then that he needed paper towels, too, and toilet paper for both bathrooms, he knew he needed shaving cream, and he had a feeling that he was running out of toothpaste. It seemed like he never had time to shop for himself, and as he roamed through the store feeling wide-awake, it seemed like the middle of the afternoon as he helped himself to cleaning products, olive oil, coffee beans, pancake mix, sausages, syrup—for the next time he had breakfast at home on a weekend—and then bran muffins, some new cereals, a pineapple and some fresh papaya. He felt like a kid going wild as he kept putting things in his basket. For once, he wasn't in a hurry, he didn't have to get to work, there was no one waiting for him anywhere, and he could explore the store at his leisure. He was just trying to decide if he wanted some French bread and Brie with his dinner, as he rounded a corner, looking for the bread, and collided with a girl who seemed to rise up out of the floor with an armful of paper towels. She seemed to come up out of nowhere, and before he could do anything about it, he had almost run her down with his cart, and she jumped back, startled, dropping everything around her as he watched her. There was something striking about her, and beautiful, in a clean, wholesome way, and he couldn't help staring at her as she turned away, and gathered up her paper towels.

"I'm sorry . . . I . . . here, let me help . . ." He abandoned his cart, and stopped to give her a hand, but she was quick to stand up, and smile, blushing faintly.

"No problem." Her smile was powerful, strong, her eyes were huge and blue, and she looked like someone who had a lot to say, and he felt like a kid as he stared at her, and she drove her cart away, smiling at him again over her shoulder. It felt almost like a movie scene, or something he might have written for a show. Boy Meets Girl. He wanted to run after her . . . hey, wait . . . stop! But she was gone, with her shining dark hair that just brushed her shoulders as it swung freely, her wide ivory smile, and blue eyes that seemed enormous. There was something so straightforward about the look she gave him, yet something quizzical about her smile, as though she had been going to ask him a question, and something friendly as though she had been going to laugh at herself. She was all he could think about as he tried to finish his shopping. Mayonnaise . . . anchovies . . . shaving cream . . . eggs? Did he need eggs? Sour cream? He couldn't concentrate anymore. It was ridiculous. She was pretty but she wasn't that great-looking after all. She had the kind of preppy good looks of a girl fresh out of an eastern college. She'd been wearing jeans, a red turtleneck, and sneakers, and his heart skipped a beat when he saw her unloading her cart at the checkout a few minutes later. He stopped pushing his own cart for a moment, and looked at her. She wasn't *that* fantastic after all, he told himself. Nice-looking, yes . . . very nice-looking, in fact, but for his taste, his current California taste in any case, she was by far too normal. She looked like someone you could talk to late at night, someone who could tell a joke, someone who could make dessert from scratch, or tell a good story. What did he need with a girl like that when he had girls like Sylvia to keep his bed warm? But as he watched her put her empty cart away, he couldn't have explained why, but he felt a kind of empty longing for her. She was someone he would have liked to know, and he wondered what her name was, as he rolled slowly toward her. Hi . . . I'm Bill Thigpen . . . he rehearsed in his head as he pulled his cart into the checkout lane where she was paying. She seemed not to notice him this time. She was writing a check, and he glanced over but he couldn't read her name. All he could see was her left hand holding the checkbook. The left hand with the gold ring. Her wedding band. Whoever she was, it didn't matter anymore. She was married. He felt his heart plummet, like a disappointed child, and he almost laughed at himself as she glanced over at him and smiled again, recognizing him from when he'd collided with her a few minutes before with the paper towels. Hi . . . I'm Bill Thigpen . . . and you're married . . . what a damn shame, if you get a divorce, give me a call. . . . Married women was one kind he didn't mess around with. He wanted to ask her why she was doing her shopping so late at night, but there was no point. It no longer mattered.

"Good night," she said, in a soft husky voice, as she picked up her two grocery bags, and he unpacked his cart.

" 'Night," he answered as he watched her go, and a few minutes later, he heard a car roar off, and when he went back to his own car in the parking lot, the little MG next to his car was gone, and he wondered if that was what she had been driving. He grinned to himself then. He was obviously working too hard if he was starting to fall in love with total strangers. "Okay, Thigpen," he muttered as he started his car with a roar of exhaust fumes, "take it easy, boy." He chuckled as he drove out of the parking lot, and as he drove home, he wondered what Sylvia was up to in Las Vegas.

CHAPTER

••2••

As Adrian Townsend drove away from the supermarket, her thoughts were full of Steven waiting for her at home. She hadn't seen him in four days. He had been stuck in meetings at a client presentation in St. Louis. Steven Townsend was the bright shining star of the ad agency where he worked, and she knew that one day, if he wanted to, he would run the L.A. office. At thirty-four, he had come a long, long way from humble beginnings in the Midwest, and she knew just how much his success meant to him. It meant everything to him. He had hated everything about poverty, his childhood, and the Midwest, and in his opinion he had been saved sixteen years ago by a scholarship to UC Berkeley. He had majored in communications, as Adrian had three years later at Stanford. Her passion had been TV, but Steven had fallen in love with advertising from the beginning. He had gone to work for an ad agency in San Francisco right out of school, and then he'd gone to business school at night and earned his MBA once he got to southern California. There was no doubt in anyone's mind that Steven Townsend was going to succeed, no matter what it took, or cost him. He was one of those people who were determined to get where he wanted to go, who planned things out in great detail. There were no accidents in Steven Townsend's life, no mistakes, no failures. He would talk to Adrian for hours sometimes about clients he was going to get, or a promotion he had set his sights on. She marveled at him sometimes, his determination, his drive, his courage. It hadn't been easy for him. His father had been an autoworker on the assembly line in Detroit, with five kids, three daughters and two sons, of which Steven had been the youngest. His older brother had died in Vietnam, and the three girls had stayed close to home, perfectly content not to go to college. Two of them had been married while still in their teens, both pregnant, of course, and his oldest sister had married at twenty-one, and had had four children before her twenty-fifth birthday. She had married an autoworker like her dad, and when there was a strike they all went on welfare. It was a life Steven still had nightmares about, and he seldom talked to anyone about his childhood. Only Adrian knew how much he had hated it, and how much he had come to hate them. He had never gone back to Detroit once he left, and Adrian also knew that it had been more than five years since he had communicated with his parents. He just couldn't talk to them anymore, he had explained it to her once when he'd had a little too much to drink and they'd come home after an office party. He had hated them so much, hated their poverty and despair, hated the look of constant sorrow in his mother's eyes over all that she could not do for, or give, her children. But she must have loved you all, Adrian had tried to explain, sensing the woman's love for them, and her sense of helplessness in the face of what they needed and she couldn't give them, in particular, her youngest child, anxious, ambitious Steven.

"I don't think she loved anyone," Steven had said bitterly, "she had nothing left in her . . . except for him . . . you know, she even got pregnant the year I left, and by then she must have been almost fifty . . . thank God she lost it." Adrian felt a twinge of distant pain for her, but she had long since stopped pleading their cause to Steven. He obviously had nothing in common with them anymore, and even talking about them was far too painful. She wondered from time to time what they would have thought of him, if they could see him now. He was handsome, athletic, outspoken, well educated, intelligent, bold, and sometimes even a little too brassy. She had always admired his fire, his ambition, his drive, his energy, and yet from time to time she wished that it were only a little tempered. Perhaps that would come in time, with age, with love, with kindness from those who loved him. Sometimes she teased him, she said he was like a cactus plant. He wouldn't let anyone come too close, or touch his heart, except when he decided to allow it.

They had been married for almost three years, and the marriage had done them both good. Steven had continued to rise in the agency meteorically in the past two and a half years, after moving to Los Angeles twelve years before when he finished college. He had worked in three different ad agencies over the years, and he was known in the industry as being smart, good at what he did, and more than occasionally ruthless. He had taken over clients from friends, and wooed them from other agencies in circumstances that occasionally bordered on the improper. But the agency where he worked never lost out from his maneuvers, nor did Steven. They were growing day by day, and so was Steven's importance.

She and Steven were very different, Adrian knew, and yet she respected him. Most of all, she respected what he had come from. She knew, just from the little she had heard, that surviving his early beginnings must have been brutal. Her own were at the opposite extreme, from an upper-middle-class family in Connecticut, she had always gone to private schools, and she had one older sister. She and Adrian didn't see eye to eye, and in recent years, Adrian had drifted away from her parents, too, although every few years they came out to California to see her. But it was too different from their comfortable life in Connecticut, and the last time they had come, her parents hadn't gotten along with Steven. And Adrian had to admit he'd been difficult with them. He'd been openly critical of her father, and his genteel pursuits. Her father had never had a great interest in pursuing a major career. He was an attorney, and he had retired early on, and for years he had taught at a nearby law school. She'd been embarrassed by Steven's almost grilling him, and she'd tried to explain to them that that was just Steven's way and he meant no harm by it, but after they went back, her sister, Connie, had called Adrian and given her hell about the way Steven had treated her parents. She'd asked how Adrian could "let him do that to them." Do *what?* she'd asked. "Make Dad feel so insignificant. Mom said Steven humiliated him. She said Dad says he'll never go back to California."

"Connie . . . for heaven's sake . . ." Adrian was upset to realize how hurt her father had been, and she had to admit Steven had been a little . . . well . . . *exuberant* when he pressed him, but that was just his style. And she tried in vain to express that to her sister. But they had never been close. They were five years apart, and Connie had always somehow disapproved of her, as though she didn't quite measure up. Which was why, in the end, after college, Adrian had stayed in California. That, and the fact that she had wanted a job in TV production.

Adrian had gone to Los Angeles to take graduate courses in

film at UCLA, and she had done very well. She had had several extremely interesting jobs, and then Steven had come along, and he had seen different career opportunities for her, and in some ways, that had changed things. He thought the milieu of film or even films for TV was far too arty, and he kept insisting she should be doing something more hard-edged, more concrete. They'd been living together for two years when she got the offer to work in TV news, and it was certainly more money than she'd earned before, but it was also very different from anything she'd ever dreamed of. She'd agonized over whether or not to take the job, she just felt it wasn't "her," but finally Steven talked her into it, and he'd been right. In the past three years she'd come to love it. And six months after she'd taken the job, she and Steven went to Reno for a weekend and got married. He hated big weddings, and "family ordeals," and she had agreed with him so as not to upset him. But that had been upsetting for her parents too. They had wanted to do a beautiful wedding at home for their youngest daughter. Instead, she and Steven flew east, and her parents had been anything but pleased to learn that they were already married. Her mother had cried, her father had scolded them both, and they had both felt like errant children. Steven had been really irritated with them, and as usual, Adrian had gotten in a big fight with her sister, Connie. Connie had been pregnant with her third and last child by then, and as usual, she made Adrian feel inadequate somehow, and as though she had done something really awful.

"Look, we didn't want a big wedding. Is that a crime? Big ceremonies make Steven nervous. What's such a big deal about that? I'm twenty-nine years old, I should be able to get married any damn way I want to."

"Why do you have to hurt Mom and Dad? Can't you make an effort *for once* in your life? You live three thousand miles away, you do whatever you please. You're never here to help them, or to do anything for them. . . ." Her voice had trailed off accusingly as Adrian stared at her, wondering at just how much bitterness was building up between them, and how much worse it was going to get. In recent years, their relationship had begun to seriously depress her.

"They're sixty-two and sixty-five years old, how much help do they need?" Adrian asked, and Connie looked livid.

"A lot. Charlie comes over and shovels Dad's car out every time it snows. Did you ever think of that?" There were tears in Connie's eyes, and Adrian had had an overwhelming urge to slap her.

"Maybe they should move to Florida, and make things easier for both of us," Adrian had said quietly, as Connie burst into tears.

"That's all you know about, isn't it? Running away. Hiding on the other side of the country."

"Connie, I'm not hiding. I have a life out there."

"Doing what? Working as a gofer on production crews? That's crap and you know it. Grow up, Adrian. Be like the rest of us, be a wife, have kids, if you're going to work, then at least do something worthwhile. But at least stand up and be normal."

"Like who? Like you? Are you 'normal' because you were a nurse before you had kids, and I'm not okay because I have a job you don't understand? Well, maybe you'll like my newsroom job better. It's called 'production assistant,' maybe you can understand that a little better." But she hated the venom that had crept into their relationship over the years, the bitterness, the jealousy. They had never been close, but at least early on they had been friends, or pretended to be. Now the veneer appeared to have worn off, and there was nothing left but Connie's anger that Adrian was gone, and free, and doing what she wanted in California. And Adrian didn't tell them that she and Steven had agreed not to have children. It was something that meant a lot to him, after the horrors of his childhood. Adrian didn't agree with him, but she knew he blamed his parents' misery on the fact that they had children, or certainly too many of them. But he had told her long since that children were not on his agenda, and he wanted to be sure that Adrian was in full agreement. He had talked more than once about having a vasectomy, but they were both afraid that if he did, there might be physical repercussions. He had urged her to have her tubes tied instead, but she had hedged about it because it seemed so radical, and finally they had settled on alternate methods of assuring that they wouldn't have children. It made Adrian sad sometimes to think of never having children of her own, and yet it was a sacrifice she was willing to make for him. She knew how important it was to him. He wanted to pursue his career without encumbrances, and he wanted her to be free to pursue hers too. He was extremely supportive of her work. And she had come to like working in TV news over the past three years, but she still missed her old shows occasionally, her TV films and miniseries and specials. And more than once, she had talked about leaving the news and getting a production job on a series.

"And when they cancel it?" Steven always said. "Then what? You're on the unemployment line, you're back to square one. Stick with the news, sweetheart, it's never going to be canceled." He had a horror of losing jobs, being out of work, losing opportunities, or not following a stellar route right to the top. Steven always kept his eye on his goals, and his goals were always at the top. And they both knew he was going to make it.

The past two and a half years of marriage had been full for both of them. They had worked hard, done well, made some friends, he had traveled a lot in the past year, and the previous year, they had bought a really lovely condo. It was just the right size for them, a town house with a second bedroom they used as a den, a big bedroom upstairs, a living room, dining room, and a big kitchen. Adrian liked to putter in the tiny garden on the weekends. There was a pool for the entire complex to use, a tennis court, and a two-car garage for her MG, and his shiny new black Porsche. He still tried to get her to sell her car, but she never would. She had bought it used when she went to Stanford thirteen years before, and she still loved it. Adrian was someone who loved to hang on to old things, and Steven was someone who was always seeking what was newest. And yet, together they were a good team. He gave her an extra sense of drive and push that she might not have had to the same extent if she'd been on her own, and she softened his sharp edges just a little. Not enough for everyone. Her sister, Connie, and her brother-in-law, Charles, still hated him, and her parents had never come to love him. It had affected Adrian's relationship with them, and it pained her to realize at times how distant she had grown from them. But in spite of her love for them, she felt that she owed her principal allegiance to Steven. He was the man whose bed she shared, whose life she was helping to build, whose future she was forging. And no matter how much she loved them, they were her past, and he was her present and her future. Her parents understood it, too, they no longer asked when she and Steven were coming east. And they had even stopped nagging her in the past year about when she and Steven were going to have children. She had finally told Connie that they didn't want kids, and she was sure that her sister had passed the word on to her parents. Adrian and Steven's whole relationship seemed unnatural to them, in their eyes Steven and Adrian were two egocentric young hedonists living in the fast lane in California, and it was hopeless trying to explain a different viewpoint to them. It was easier just not to talk too often, and Adrian's parents no longer volunteered to come out for a visit.

But Adrian wasn't thinking of her parents as she took the Fairfax Avenue exit off the Santa Monica Freeway late that night. All she could think of was Steven. She knew how tired he was going to be, but she had bought a bottle of white wine, some cheese, and the makings of a fine omelet for him. And she was smiling as she slid the car into the garage next to his Porsche. He was home and she was only sorry she hadn't been able to pick him up at the airport. She had had to work the late shift as she often did, standing in for the producer of the late news, since she was his number one assistant. It was an interesting job, and she liked it, but there were times when it was also very wearing.

Her key turned easily in the lock, and she could see that all the lights were on as she opened the door, but at first she didn't see him.

"Hello! . . . anyone home? . . ." The stereo was on, and his suitcase was in the hall, but she didn't see his briefcase, and then she saw him, in the kitchen, on the phone, his handsome mane of almost jet-black hair full and slightly disheveled, his head bent as he took notes, and she suspected he was talking to his boss. He didn't even seem to see her as he wrote and talked, and she walked over, put her arms around him, and kissed him. He glanced down at her with a smile, and gently kissed her full on the lips, as he continued listening to his boss without missing a beat for a moment. And then he gently pushed her away as he went on talking.

"That's right . . . that's what I told him. They said they'd get back to us next week, but I think if we play hardball with them we'll get them to come around before that. Right . . . right . . . that's exactly what I think . . . fine . . . see you in the morning." And then, suddenly, she was in his arms, and he was holding her tight, and all was right with the world again. She was always happy when she was with him, always sure that she was exactly where she was meant to be. And as she kissed him all she could think of was how much she had missed him.

He kissed her long and hard and when he pulled away from her again, she was breathless. "My, my . . . it certainly is nice having you home again, Mr. Townsend."

"Can't say I mind seeing you myself." He smiled mischievously at her, holding her bottom in his two hands as he continued to hold her close to him. "Where've you been?"

"At work. I tried to get out of doing the eleven o'clock tonight but no one else was free. I stopped and got some food on the way home. Are you hungry?"

"Yes." He smiled happily, not thinking of what she had brought home in the brown bags. "As a matter of fact, I am." He flicked off the kitchen light just behind him, and Adrian laughed at him.

"That's not what I meant. I bought some wine, and . . ." He kissed her hard on the lips again.

"Later, Adrian . . . later. . . ." He led her quietly upstairs, his bags forgotten in the downstairs hall, her groceries abandoned on the kitchen floor, and he looked hungrily at her as she began peeling away her clothes and he turned up the stereo and pulled her down on the bed beside him.

CHAPTER

THEY BOTH LEFT FOR WORK AT THE SAME TIME THE NEXT day: It was a routine that went like clockwork every morning. Steven went for a run before work, and then he came back and rode his exercise bike while he shaved and watched the news, and Adrian made them a light breakfast. She had showered and dressed by then. And he showered and dressed while she cleaned up the kitchen and made the bed. On weekends she got him to help, but during the week he was too busy and rushed to be able to help her.

Adrian always watched the morning news, and as much of the *Today* show as she could get in before they left for work. If there was something of interest, they discussed it. But usually they didn't say much to each other in the morning. This morning was different, though. They had made love twice the night before, and Adrian was feeling chatty and affectionate as she kissed him and handed him a cup of coffee. He was still damp from his run, but even with his hair wet and his sweatshirt sticking to him, Steven Townsend was movie-star handsome. It was yet another thing that had set him apart while he was struggling to get out of Detroit and away from his parents. He had been too smart, too ambitious, and too good-looking for the life he'd been born to. And Adrian was striking, too, in her own way, but it was something she never thought of. She was too busy living her life to think about how she looked, except when she got dressed up to go out with Steven. But she had a clean, wholesome look and her natural beauty stood out in the world of artifice they lived in. But she was totally unaware of her own beauty, and it was rare for Steven to mention it to her. He was always preoccupied with other things, like his own life, and his own career. There were times when he scarcely even saw her.

"Anything special going on today?" He glanced at her casually over the newspaper as he ate his breakfast. She had warmed the blueberry muffins she'd bought the night before, and made him a heaping fresh fruit salad mixed in with yogurt.

"Not that I know of. I'll see what's happening when I go in. It didn't look like anything dramatic was happening on the morning news, but you never know. They could shoot the President while we're sitting here eating breakfast."

"Yeah. . . ." He was looking at the stock prices, and flipping through the business pages while she spoke. "You working late tonight?"

"Maybe. I won't know till this afternoon. A couple of people are out on vacation and we're short. I may even have to go in this weekend."

"I hope not. Did you remember the party tomorrow night at the Jameses'?"

Her eyes met his and she smiled at him. He could never quite believe that she remembered anything. No matter that she was the assistant producer of the news show on a major network. "Of course I remembered. Is it a big deal?"

He nodded, humorless when it came to his career, but it was something that she was used to. "Everybody who's anybody in advertising will be there. I just wanted to make sure you remembered." She nodded, and he looked at his watch and stood up. "I'm playing squash at six o'clock tonight. If you're working late, I won't come home for dinner. Just leave a message for me at the office."

"Yes, sir. Anything else I should know before we start the day and disappear into our separate worlds?"

He looked blank for a moment, trying to think, and then he shook his head and looked down at her, still sitting at the kitchen table. But his thoughts were already far from her. He was thinking about two new clients he wanted to approach, and a client he was planning to take away from a slightly more senior man at the agency where he worked. It was something he had done successfully before, with other accounts, and it was a modus operandi he was neither embarrassed about nor afraid of. The end always justified the means, it always had for him. Even sixteen years before when he'd aced his best friend out of the scholarship to UC Berkeley. The other boy had actually been more qualified, but Steven also knew that his friend had cheated on his very first SAT exam, and he had seen to it that the right people heard about it at the right time. No matter that his scores had been perfect ever since, and he had helped Steven prepare for every exam he'd taken junior and senior years. And they were best friends . . . but he *had* cheated after all . . . and they disqualified him. And Steven got the hell out of Detroit without ever looking back. He never heard from his friend again. And he had heard years before from his sister that Tom had dropped out of school and was pumping gas somewhere in the ghetto. Things worked out that way sometimes. Survival of the fittest. And Steven

Townsend was fit. In every possible way. He stood looking at Adrian for a moment, and then turned and raced upstairs to shower and change before he left for the office.

She was still in the kitchen when he came back down, impeccably dressed in a khaki suit, pale blue shirt, and blue and yellow tie. With his shining dark hair, he looked like a movie star again, or a man in an ad at the very least. It always jolted Adrian a little when she looked at him, he was so incredibly handsome.

"You're looking good, kid."

He looked pleased at the compliment, and looked her over as she stood up and picked up the tote bag she always took to work. It was a soft black leather Hermès bag she'd had for years, and like her ancient sports car, she loved it. She was wearing a navy wool skirt, a white silk blouse, and a soft white cashmere sweater knotted over her shoulder. She was wearing expensive black Italian loafers, and her whole look was of casual, understated, expensive elegance. It was a kind of casual, throwaway look, but when you looked again, it had style and whispered all the secret code words of good taste and breeding. She had a wonderful easy style, and as understated as she was, somehow everything about her still managed to be beautiful and striking. And as they left the house together, they were a handsome pair. He got in his Porsche as she climbed into the MG, and she laughed at the look on his face. It embarrassed him to be seen anywhere near her car and he had been threatening to make her use the open parking lot at the front of the complex.

"You're a snob!" She laughed at him and he shook his head and a moment later he was gone in a roar from the Porsche's powerful engine, while Adrian tied a scarf around her head, put her beloved old car into gear, and listened happily as it sputtered to life and she headed it in the direction of her office. The freeway was bumper-to-bumper by then and a few minutes later she wound up sitting in the car at a dead stand-still. She wondered how much better Steven had fared, and as she thought of him, she suddenly thought of something else, something that seldom happened to her. She was late. She should have had her period two days before, but she knew it didn't mean anything. With the odd hours she worked, and the constant stress, it wasn't unusual to be late, although admittedly it didn't happen to her very often. She made a mental note to think about it again in a few days, and with that, the traffic began moving again, and she stepped on the accelerator and headed for her office.

Everything was in total chaos when she arrived. The producer was out sick. Two of their prize cameramen had had a minor accident, and two of her least favorite reporters were having a heated argument two feet from her desk, and she finally wound up shouting at everyone, which took them all by surprise, since Adrian seldom lost her temper.

"For chrissake, how the hell is anyone supposed to get any work done around here? If you two want to beat on each other, go do it somewhere else." A senator had just gone down on a commuter plane and reporters at the crash site had just called in to say that there were no survivors. A major movie star had committed suicide during the night. And two of Hollywood's favorites had just announced that they were getting married. And an earthquake in Mexico had claimed nearly a thousand lives. It was going to be the kind of day that usually tried to give Adrian ulcers. But at least life was interesting for her, or at least that was what Steven said when she complained. Did she really want to live in fantasyland, working on miniseries, and specials about Hollywood ladies? No, but she would have loved to work on a successful prime-time series, and she knew she had enough production experience by now to do that. But she also knew she would never convince Steven that a job like that was worthy of her attention.

"Adrian?"

"Yeah?" For a minute she had let her mind drift to what wasn't and what might have been, and she didn't have time for that, not today at least. And it was also easy to figure out by then that she wasn't going to be having dinner that night with her husband. She asked someone to call and let him know and turned to the assistant who was begging for her attention. There had been a flood on the set and they were going to have to use an alternate studio, but everything was already set up, so there was no need to panic.

It was four o'clock before she ate lunch, and six before she even thought of calling Steven. But by then she knew he had left to play squash with his friends from work, and he knew she was working late anyway. And as she settled down for a long evening at work, she was suddenly struck by an odd feeling of loneliness. It was Friday night, and everyone was out, or at home, or with friends, or getting ready to go on dates, or maybe just curled up with a good book, and she was at work, listening to police reports of local homicides and fatal accidents, and reading telexes of tragedies worldwide. It seemed like a sad way to spend a Friday night, and then she felt foolish for the feeling.

"You're looking awfully gloomy tonight." Zelda, one of the production assistants, smiled at her as she brought Adrian a styrofoam cup of coffee. She was one of Adrian's favorites, she was always good for a laugh, and she was a character. She was older than Adrian, divorced frequently, and kind of a free spirit. She had bright red hair that sprang from her head like uncontrolled flames and an equally uncontrollable sense of humor.

"Just tired, I guess. Sometimes this place gets to me."

"At least we know you're still sane." Zelda smiled at her. She was a pretty woman, and Adrian guessed that she was about forty.

"Doesn't it ever get to you? Christ, the news is always so depressing."

"I never listen to it." She shrugged indifferently. "And most nights when I get out of here, I go dancing."

"I think you've got the right idea." Most nights, Adrian went home, and Steven was already sound asleep and snoring gently. But at least they had breakfast together in the morning, and there were always weekends.

Adrian struggled through her paperwork for the next four hours, and then she checked out the studio before the late news, chatted with the anchors, and read all the hottest stories. It was actually a pretty quiet night, and she could hardly wait to get home to Steven. She knew he was having dinner out with friends, but she was pretty sure he'd be home when she finished work. He seldom stayed out very late, unless there was something to be gained from it, like some important business with a client.

The late show went fine, predictably, and at eleven thirty-five she was on her way home on the Santa Monica Freeway. She walked in her front door at five minutes to midnight, and the bedroom lights were still on, and her heart leapt with glee as she took the stairs to their bedroom two at a time, and then she laughed when she saw him. Steven was sound asleep on his side of the bed, arms spread out like a boy, exhausted and relaxed after a hard day at the office followed by a lively game of squash and an early dinner. He was out for the count and no amount of rustling around the room would rouse him.

"Well, Prince Charming," Adrian whispered with a grin as she sat down next to him in her nightgown, "looks like it's a wrap, as they say in my business." She kissed him gently on the cheek and he never stirred as she turned off the light and curled up on her own side of the bed. And as she lay there, she thought about being late again, but she knew it was probably nothing.

CHAPTER

WHEN ADRIAN WOKE UP AT NINE-FIFTEEN, SHE COULD smell bacon cooking downstairs, and she could hear Steven clattering around in the kitchen. She smiled to herself as she rolled over in bed. She loved Saturdays, loved having him around, loved it when he brought her breakfast in bed and they made love afterward.

She could hear him coming up the stairs as she thought of it, he was humming to himself, banging the tray against the door as he came through, and she could hear the stereo downstairs playing Bruce Springsteen.

"Wake up, sleepyhead." He grinned down at her in their bed, and set the tray down beside her as she stretched and smiled in answer. He was a vision of handsome young manhood. His hair was still wet from the shower he'd taken before she woke up and he was wearing fresh white tennis clothes, his long, shapely legs were tanned, and from where she lay, Steven's shoulders looked enormous.

"You know, you're pretty cute, for a guy who can cook." She smiled up at him and propped herself up on one elbow.

"So are you, lazybones." He sat down next to her on the bed, and she laughed at him.

"You should have seen yourself passed out here last night."

"I had a tough day, and I was beat after we played squash." He looked faintly embarrassed and made it up to her by kissing her promisingly just as she took a bite of bacon.

"Are you playing tennis today?" she inquired. She knew him well. He loved competitive sports, especially squash and tennis.

"Yeah. But not until eleven-thirty." He glanced at his watch and smiled at her, and she laughed again, but before she could say anything, he had peeled off his tennis clothes and slipped into bed beside her.

"Now what's this all about, Mr. Townsend? Won't this weaken your tennis game?" She loved to tease him about his intense seriousness about his tennis.

"It might." He looked pensive and she laughed again. And then he turned to her with a sexy smile. "But it could just be that you're worth it."

"Could be? *Could* be? . . . You've got some nerve!" But he silenced her with a kiss, and a few minutes later they had both forgotten his tennis game, and half an hour later she was dozing contentedly in his arms, and he was gently stroking her shining black hair as it fell over her cheek and she purred at him. "Personally . . . I'd rather do that than play tennis any day. . . ." She opened one eye and reached up to kiss him.

"So would I." He stretched lazily, and an hour later he hated to get out of bed to go and shower again before he went to play with a man who lived in the complex and Steven knew only as "Harvey."

"Are you coming back for lunch?" she inquired, and he shouted back that he'd make himself a salad when he got back, and he reminded her again about going to the Jameses' party that night at seven. But it was going to be a tight squeeze for her. She had learned the night before that she was going to have to be at work for the evening news, and then go back to be there again for the late show. It would mean dressing for the party before she went to work, and then rushing back to meet Steven at home to go to the party, or maybe even meeting him there, and then leaving at a decent hour to get to work again. But she knew the party was important to him, and she was going to join him for it no matter how hectic it made her evening. She always tried never to let Steven down, and particularly not to let her work interfere with their home life. Unlike Steven, who traveled a great deal of the time, but that just made it easier for her to work late whenever she had to.

Steven was back, dripping wet, at two o'clock, and beaming at his victory. He had easily beaten Harvey. "He's fat and out of shape, and he admitted to me after the second set that he hasn't given up smoking. The poor bastard is lucky he didn't have a heart attack on the court."

"I hope you went easy on him," Adrian said from the kitchen, where she had just made lemonade for him, but they both knew that he probably hadn't.

"He didn't deserve it. He's really kind of a jerk." She had his salad ready, too, and she put both in front of him and told him she'd have to go to work before they went out, but he didn't seem to mind. He didn't even seem to mind it when she told him she had to go in for the late show. "That's okay. I can catch a ride home with someone else. You can take my car."

"I can even come back and pick you up." She looked apologetically at him. "I'm really sorry. If there weren't people out and the producer weren't sick. . . ."

"No problem. As long as you can make it for a while, that's fine."

She looked at him questioningly then as he ate the salad she had made for him. "Why is this party so important to you, sweetheart? Something big going on I don't know about?" Maybe another important promotion.

He looked mysterious for a moment and then he grinned at her. "If everything goes all right tonight, I might get the IMFAC account, or at least I'll get a shot at it. I got some inside information last week that they're unhappy with their current agency and they're looking around quietly. I gave them a call, and Mike was really excited about it. He might even let me fly out to Chicago on Monday to see them."

"My God, that's an enormous account." That was impressive, even for him. IMFAC was one of the biggest advertising accounts in the country.

"Yes, it is. I'll probably be gone all week, but I'm sure you'll agree it's worth it."

"It sure is." She sat back in her chair and looked at him. He was a remarkable man. At thirty-four, he just wasn't going to stop until he had gotten everything he wanted. But one had to admire him, particularly when one looked back at where he came from. She had tried to point that out to her parents over the years, but they seemed determined to ignore all his good qualities, and all they did was harp on the negative side of his ambitions. As though it were a crime to want to succeed, to get ahead. At least she didn't think so. He had a right to accomplish what he wanted to, didn't he? And he had a need to win. Sometimes she even felt sorry for him because that need was so acute in him. It really hurt him, almost physically, when he lost, even at tennis.

And Steven played tennis again later that afternoon. He was still playing when Adrian left for work, and she had promised to come back and pick him up at exactly seven. And when she did, he was waiting for her, handsome in a new blazer and white slacks, and a red tie she had bought him. He looked great and she told him so, and he told her she looked pretty too. She was wearing an emerald-green silk suit with matching shoes and she had just washed her hair and it shone like polished onyx. But she noticed as she slipped into the Porsche with him that he was nervous and distracted. But with an account the size of IMFAC on the line, it was easy to understand it.

She chatted easily with him about unimportant things on the drive to Beverly Hills and she was impressed when she saw the house. Mike James was Steven's boss, and his wife was one of the most expensive decorators in Beverly Hills. It was their housewarming, and she had been hearing for months about the endless multimillion-dollar renovations. But the results were impressive anyway, and there were easily two hundred people there when they walked in, and Adrian almost instantly lost Steven, and found herself wandering between one of the many bars and buffets, listening to snatches of conversation.

People talked about their kids, their marriages, their jobs, their trips, their houses.

Several people stopped and talked to Adrian, but she didn't know anyone there and so was in a quiet mood and didn't linger long in any group. And more than once she noticed, as she often did lately, that when people realized that she was married, they asked her if she had children. It made her feel strange sometimes, saying that she didn't. It was as though not having children was a kind of failure. No matter that she had an important job, and that she was only thirty-one. Women who had children looked proud of themselves, and lately Adrian had been wondering if she had missed something when she and Steven had decided never to have children. Nothing was written in stone, of course, and it wasn't as though their decision couldn't be changed, but she knew how strongly Steven felt about it, which was why she was beginning to feel a little flurry of panic each time she remembered that she was late. And day by day, she seemed to be getting later.

She had thought about buying an at-home test that afternoon, but it seemed a little premature, and there was no need to overreact just because she was a few days late . . . but what if she was pregnant? She stood alone, staring at the view, and a man stopped to chat with her and offered her a glass of champagne, but she really wasn't interested in talking to him. And after he left, she suddenly found herself thinking. What would happen if she really was going to have a baby? What would she say? What would Steven do? Would it really be so terrible? Or would it be wonderful? Could he be wrong about his vehement stance against children? Would he warm to the idea eventually? . . . and would she? Would it interfere with her work? Permanently end her career, or could she just go on doing what she did, after a maternity leave? Other women did. It didn't seem like the end of the world to other people. They seemed to have babies and work, it wasn't so disastrous, or was it? She wasn't sure. And as she thought about it, Steven suddenly appeared beside her.

"Done." He grinned.

"The deal?" She looked stunned. She had been so lost in her own thoughts, he had startled her when he suddenly turned up standing next to her, and she was almost afraid he could hear her thoughts or guess what she was thinking.

"No, I didn't make the deal yet. But Mike wants me to fly out to Chicago with him on Monday. We're going to have some very quiet meetings with them, discuss our philosophies, and theirs. And if everything goes all right, which it will, the following week I'll fly back out on my own and make the presentation."

"Wow! Steven, that's fabulous!" And he looked as though he thought so too when she kissed him. He allowed himself to have two drinks and he was still beaming from ear to ear when he walked her out to the car when she left for work, and he told her he'd have someone drop him off at home. He told her not to bother to come back to the party after work because he didn't think he'd stay long. And as she drove off, he waved, and went back to see his host again. For Steven, it had been a fabulous evening.

It had been less so for Adrian, and suddenly all she could think of, even in the midst of Steven's incredible opportunity, was whether or not she was pregnant. The idea tormented her all through the evening news, and she was still preoccupied on her way home, and then suddenly, with a quick swerve, she pulled into the curb and decided to stop at an all-night drugstore. Steven didn't have to know anything. She didn't have to say anything to him. But suddenly she wanted to know . . . and if not tonight . . . then sometime soon. If she bought the test now, she could do it anytime she felt brave enough. She could even do it while Steven was in Chicago.

She bought the kit and had the druggist put it in a brown paper bag that she shoved deep into her tote bag, and then she got back in the Porsche again, and drove back to their apartment.

Steven was home when she arrived, in bed, half asleep, but with a look of supreme bliss on his face. He was sure that he was on his way to Chicago to make the deal of a lifetime.

CHAPTER

AND IN HIS CONDOMINIUM, STARING OUT THE WINDOW INTO the darkness on Saturday night, William Thigpen looked anything but blissful. He had written for a while, bought Chinese takeout for himself, he had called his kids in New York, watched TV, and he was actually feeling rather lonely. It was one o'clock in the morning by then, and he decided to take a chance and call Sylvia in her room in Las Vegas. She might be back by then, and at worst, he could always leave a message. The phone rang half a dozen times, and when no one answered it, Bill waited for the message operator to come back on, and when he did, it was a man with a gravelly voice and he sounded half asleep and all he said was "Yeah?" as Bill waited.

"I want to leave a message for the party in 402," Bill said crisply.

"This is 402," the voice growled, "whaddya want?"

"I must have the wrong room, I'm sorry . . ." and then suddenly he wondered.

". . . you expecting a call from somewhere?" The gravelly voice asked someone in the distance, and there were hushed exchanges with a hand over the phone, and then suddenly Sylvia was on the phone, sounding very nervous. She would have been smarter not to take the call, but she hadn't figured that out, and she knew it was probably Bill calling from L.A.

"Hi . . . there's been a terrible mixup," she started to explain as Bill almost laughed at the absurdity of the situation. "They forgot to reserve half the rooms, and four of us are sharing." It was beautiful. It was a story worthy of his soap opera, and he was at the center of it, feeling as though he were watching someone else's life instead of his own.

"This is ridiculous . . . Sylvia, what the hell is going on?" He sounded like the irate lover, but the odd thing was that he didn't feel it. He felt stupid and as though he'd been had, but the truth was he wasn't even angry. All he felt was dumb and disappointed. They'd had something pleasant for a while, but it was more than obvious now that it was over.

"I . . . I'm really sorry, Bill . . . I can't explain it just now. But everything's gotten mixed up here . . . I . . ." She was crying and he felt like a complete fool just listening to her. He had caught her in the act and he was the one who wanted to apologize for being stupid.

"Why don't we talk about it when you get back?"

"Are you going to kick me off the show?" He felt sad for her as he listened. He wasn't that kind of man, and it hurt him that she didn't know that.

"That has nothing to do with this, Sylvia. These are two separate issues."

"Okay . . . I'm sorry . . . I'll be back Sunday night."

"Have a good time," he said softly, and hung up. It was over. It should never have started, but it had, because he was lazy and she had been convenient, and so goddam sexy. She was a knockout, there was no denying it, and now she was knocking out someone else. And for a minute, Bill found himself hoping that the man with the gravelly voice made her happier than he had. He had very little to give the women in his life. He had too little time for them, and even less interest in getting hurt, and opening himself up to the kind of pain he'd had when he lost Leslie and his children. These arrangements were always easy, but they usually ended like this, or some similar scene. Someone wanted to move on, and the party ended. And he had known for a while that she had wanted something he couldn't give her. Time. Real devotion. Maybe even love. But all he had to offer was kindness and some fun, while it lasted.

He thought about her for a while, as he stood looking out at the night sky, and then toasted her with a club soda, as he went to bed, thinking about his life. He felt lonely suddenly, and sad that it had ended like this, with a phone call to Las Vegas.

He lay awake for a long time that night, thinking of the women in his life in recent years, of how little they had really meant to him, how uninvolved they all really were, how meaningless their relationships, how casual their sex lives, and as he fell asleep, he found himself thinking longingly of Leslie for the first time in years, and the kind of relationship they had once shared. It seemed like several lifetimes ago, and it was. He doubted if he'd ever have that again. Maybe you only had that once, when you were young. Maybe you never got a second chance at the real thing, and maybe in the end, it didn't matter. He fell asleep finally, thinking not of Sylvia or his ex-wife . . . but of his boys, Adam and Tommy. In the end, they were all that mattered.

CHAPTER

••6••

SUNDAY FLEW BY IN A FLURRY OF PREPARATION FOR STE-
ven's trip, interspersed with tennis games, and Adrian never
touched the kit that sat hidden in her tote bag. She did his
laundry for him, made lunch for him and the three friends he
had played doubles with, and she said almost nothing to him,
but he seemed not to notice. And that night, they went to a
movie. She hardly heard anything that was said, and all she
could think about, as they sat in the dark reading the subtitles
on the Swedish film, was whether or not she was pregnant. It
was crazy, in the past two days it had become an obsession
with her, and yet she still wasn't that late. But for some reason,
she had an odd premonition. She didn't feel sick and her body
didn't seem to have changed, except in the ways it normally
did when she expected her period. Her breasts were slightly
enlarged, her body a little more bloated, she went to the
bathroom a little more frequently, but none of it indicated any

dire change. And yet, all she wanted now was for Steven to leave. She wanted him to leave the state so that she could find out in peace. She had to know, but she felt sure that if she did the test while he was around, somehow he would know what had happened. She didn't even dare do it after he had left for the airport on Monday. What if he came back? . . . if he had forgotten something . . . there she would be in her bathroom with a test tube full of bright blue water . . . if she was pregnant.

She still didn't really believe it could have happened to her, they were very careful almost all the time, but there had been one time . . . one time . . . almost three weeks before . . . three weeks . . . She thought about it all day while she was at work after Steven had left, and she rushed home after the six o'clock news, let herself into the house, ran upstairs, and set the kit up in her bathroom. She did everything it told her to do, and then she sat nervously, watching the alarm clock in her bedroom. She didn't even trust her wristwatch. If it turned blue, it meant . . . and it was a ten-minute wait . . . but within three minutes, the guessing game was over.

It was not a question of degree, there was no need to ask herself if the liquid in the vial had changed, if perhaps . . . or maybe . . . as she stared at it, it was so dark, and so bright, and so definite an answer that there was no question. She stood totally still, and then she sat down on the toilet lid to stare at the bright blue liquid in the vial. There was no doubt in her mind as she looked, she realized that no matter what Steven had or hadn't wanted, how careful they had been, or what they had said to each other over the years . . . in spite of all of that, as she sat staring at the vial, her eyes welling up slowly with unshed tears, there wasn't a moment's doubt. She was pregnant.

The only real question in her mind was what Steven was going to say. She was sure he was going to make a fuss, but how big a fuss, and how serious would he be, and would he really mean it? Would he change his mind eventually? Would he readjust to the idea of a child after all? Surely he couldn't have meant all the awful things he had said in the last three years. Surely, one small child couldn't make such a terrible difference. She had known about the pregnancy for five minutes, maybe less, and it was already a baby to her, and she was already arguing for its life, and she was praying that Steven would let her keep it. He couldn't force her to get rid of it, after all. And why would he want her to anyway? He was a reasonable man, and it was his baby. She sat in her bathroom and closed her eyes, as tears of fear rolled slowly down her cheeks. What was she going to do now? She was at the same time happy and sad, and terrified of what to say to her husband. He had always jokingly said that if she ever got pregnant and decided to keep it, he would leave her. But surely he didn't mean it . . . and if he did? . . . what would she do? She didn't want to lose him, of course, but how could she give up this baby?

It was a hellish week for her, spent agonizing over what to say to Steven when he got home, and each time he called with more exciting news of his meetings with IMFAC, Adrian sounded more and more confused, more distant, more distracted, until finally on Thursday night, he asked her what was wrong. She was hardly making sense and he was sure she hadn't listened to anything he'd said. The meetings had gone brilliantly, and he was returning to Los Angeles the next day, but he was going back to Chicago the following Tuesday.

"Adrian, are you okay?"

"Why?" Everything stopped as she said the word. What did he mean? Did he know? But how could he?

"I don't know. You've sounded funny all week. Are you feeling okay?"

"I'm fine . . . no . . . actually, I've been having terrible headaches. I think it's just stress . . . from work . . ." And in fact she had felt queasy once or twice, which she was sure was her imagination. But the pregnancy wasn't. She was sure of that. She had even done the test again, just to be absolutely certain.

Tears stung her eyes as she listened to him. She wanted him to come home now, so she could tell him. She wanted to get it over with, to be honest with him, so he could tell her everything would be okay, and she could relax and have their baby . . . baby . . . it was amazing . . . in a matter of days, her whole life had turned around, and all she could think of was this baby. She had always been perfectly content to give up the prospect of having children, for him, and now suddenly she was willing to turn her whole life upside down for an unknown baby. She was willing to change their apartment, their life-style, her job if need be, give up their den, their quiet nights, their independent freewheeling existence. She was still scared when she thought of it, still worried about what it would be like to finally be a mother, still desperately frightened that somehow she would make a botch of it, and yet in spite of all that, she knew she had to try it.

She wanted to go to the airport to meet his plane on Friday night, but in the end she had to work late, and she didn't see him until she got back to the apartment. He was unpacking his bags and watching TV, the stereo was on, and the whole place had come to life again now that Steven was home from Chicago. He was humming to himself when she walked in and he smiled when he saw her.

"Hi, there . . . where've you been?"

"At work, as usual." She grinned nervously, and slowly she approached him, but when he put his arms around her, she held him close, as though she might drown if she left him for an instant.

"Baby . . . what's wrong?" He had known something was

wrong all week, but he just couldn't put his finger on it. She looked all right to him now, and then suddenly, with a feeling of dismay, he wondered if she might have been fired and was embarrassed to tell him. Maybe with his own job going so well, she was just afraid to say it. And it was such a good job, too, he was really going to be sorry for her if she lost it. "Is it work? . . . is . . ." He stopped when he saw the look in her eyes. He didn't know what it was, but he knew instantly that something serious had happened. He pulled her down on the bed next to him with his arm around her, wanting to offer her all the support he could. He could afford to now, his own life was going so well, and Mike had already told him that he would get a huge promotion if the agency actually landed IMFAC. "What is it?"

Her eyes filled with tears as she looked up at him, and for a moment she couldn't bring herself to say the words. This should have been the happiest moment of their married life, and yet because of the things he had said to her in the past, this was instead their most frightening moment.

"Were you fired?"

She laughed through her tears as she shook her head at him. "No, unfortunately. Sometimes I think that might be a relief." But he didn't take her seriously. He knew how much she loved her job. It was a great job. He knew that.

"Are you sick?"

She shook her head more slowly this time, and her eyes locked on his with quiet desperation. "No, I'm not . . ." And then she took a quick breath and prayed that he would accept it. "I'm pregnant."

There was an endless silence in the room where she could hear her own heart pound and his breathing as he held her, and then suddenly he wrenched away and stood up to look down at her with quiet desperation. "You're not serious, are you, Adrian?"

Danielle Steel

"Yes, I am." She had known it would be a shock to him. It had been a shock to her, too, but it had been an honest error.

"Did you deceive me?"

She shook her head solemnly. "No, I didn't. It just happened."

"That's unfortunate." Something in his face turned to ice, and as Adrian looked at him, she felt awash with panic. "Are you sure?"

"Absolutely."

"That's too bad," he said quietly with a look of intense chagrin. "I'm sorry, Adrian. That's rotten luck."

"I wouldn't exactly call it luck," she said. "We had a little something to do with it, you know."

He nodded, feeling sorry for her, and himself. "I guess you'll have to take care of it next week." Her blood ran cold as she looked at him. It was that simple to him. *Take care of it.* But it wasn't that simple for her anymore as she stared at her husband.

"What does that mean?"

"You know what it means. We can't have a baby, for God's sake, you know that."

"Why not? Is there something I don't know about? Some terrible hereditary disease, are we planning a trip to the moon? Is there some reason why we can't have a baby?"

"Yes. A very good one." He looked adamant suddenly as they stood facing each other across their bedroom. "We agreed a long time ago that we didn't want to have kids. And I thought we both meant it."

"But why not? There's no real reason why we can't have kids." She looked at him pleadingly. "We both have good jobs. We have a good life. We could support a baby easily on our income."

"Do you have any idea how much children cost? Education, clothes, medical. And it wouldn't be fair to bring an unwanted child into our life. No, Adrian, it is not right." He looked terrified, even more so as he saw that he hadn't convinced her. She knew how extreme he was in his views because of the poverty of his own youth, but their life was entirely different.

"Money isn't everything. We have time and love and a nice home and each other. What more do you need than that?"

"The desire to have them," he said quietly, "and I don't have that. I never have. I don't want children, Adrian. I never have and I never will. I told you that before we got married, and if you turn on me now, I'm not going to stand still for it. You have to get rid of that . . ." He hesitated but only for an instant. ". . . the pregnancy." He refused to call it a baby.

"And what if I don't want to?"

"You'd be a fool if you didn't, Adrian. You have a shot at a great career yourself, if you set your mind to it, and there's no way you can do what you do and have a baby."

"I can take a leave-of-absence for six months and then go back. A lot of women do it."

"Yeah, and eventually they give up their careers, have two more kids and become housewives. And in the end, they hate themselves and their children for it." He was voicing the worst of her fears, but she still thought it was worth taking a chance and having the baby. She didn't want to give it up just because it was easier not having children. So what if they weren't millionaires? Why did everything have to be so goddam perfect? And why couldn't he understand what she was feeling?

"I think we ought to think about it for a while, before we do anything drastic that we might both regret later." She had friends who had had abortions and hated themselves for it, and admittedly, others who hadn't. But Steven didn't agree with her.

"Believe me, Adrian," he gentled his voice a little bit and took a step closer to her, "you won't regret it. When you think about it afterward, you'll be relieved. This thing could be a serious threat to our marriage." This "*thing*" was their baby. The baby she had come to love in the four days she had known of its existence.

"We don't have to let it be a threat to our marriage." Tears started to fill her eyes as she leaned against him. "Steven, please . . . don't make me do this . . . please. . . ."

"I'm not *making* you do anything." He sounded annoyed as he walked around their bedroom like a caged animal. He felt threatened to his very core, and deeply frightened. "I'm just telling you that this is a rotten piece of luck, and a bit of insanity to even consider going through with it. Our lives are at stake. For God's sake, do what you have to."

"Why do you have to see it that way? Why is a baby such a big threat?" She didn't understand why he felt so radical about it, she never had. He had always regarded children as if they were the threat of enemy invasion.

"You have no idea what kids can do to your life, Adrian. I do. I saw it in my own family. My parents never had anything. My mother had one lousy pair of shoes, one pair of shoes for my entire childhood. She made everything she could and then we used it till it fell apart, or the clothes fell off our backs. We didn't have books or dolls or toys. We didn't have anything, except poverty and each other." She felt sorry, and it must have been terrible, but it had nothing to do with the reality of their lives, and somehow he refused to understand that.

"I'm sorry that happened to you. But our children would never have to live like that. We both make healthy salaries and there's enough for us and a baby to live more than comfortably."

"That's what you think. What about school? What about college? Do you have any idea what Stanford costs these days?" And then, like a forlorn child, "What about our trip to Europe? We wouldn't be able to do anything like that any-

more. We'd have to give up everything. Are you really prepared to do that?"

"I don't understand why you see it in such extremes. And
even if we did have to make sacrifices, Steven, wouldn't it be
worth it?" He didn't answer her, but his eyes said it all. They
said clearly that to him it wouldn't. "And in any case, we're
not talking about planning to have kids at some future date.
We're talking about a baby that's already here. That's very
different." To her it was, anyway, but not to him. That much
was clear.

"We are not talking about a baby. We are talking about a
nothing. A spot of sperm that touched an egg the size of a
microscopic dot, and that dot is a microscopic possibility of
nothing. It's a question mark, a maybe, a possibility and nothing more, and it's a possibility we don't want. That's all you
have to think about. All you have to do is go to your doctor and
tell him you don't want it."

"And then what?" She felt anger boiling up inside of her as
she listened to him. "Then what, Steven? He just says, 'Okay
Adrian, you don't want the baby, no problem,' and he checks
it off in the 'no' box on a little list? Not exactly. He pulls it out of
me with a suction machine and scrapes my uterus with a
scalpel, and he kills our baby. That's what he does, Steven.
That's what 'tell him you don't want it' means. And the thing
is, I *do* want it, and you need to think of that too. This isn't just
your baby, it's mine too, it's *our* baby, whether you want it or
not. And I'm not going to just get rid of it because you say so."
She had started sobbing as she spoke to him, but Steven acted
as though he didn't hear her. He was so terrified that all he
could do was act like an ice man. He was literally frozen with
terror. And Adrian was overwhelmed with anguish.

"I see," he said icily as he looked at her with fresh distance.
"Are you telling me you won't get rid of it?"

"I'm not telling you anything yet. I'm just asking you to

think about it, and I'm telling you that I'd like to keep it." She had surprised herself by admitting that she wanted it. And asking him to keep it made it sound as though they were talking about a puppy and not their child, and it horrified her.

Steven nodded miserably, and took her hand and pulled her down on the bed next to him, and suddenly she could no longer control herself as he put his arms around her, and she went on sobbing.

All the shock and fear and tension and excitement of it bubbled up inside of her and exploded over the sides until she couldn't stop crying anymore, and she lay in his arms and sobbed as he held her.

"I'm sorry, baby . . . I'm sorry this happened to us . . . it'll be all right . . . you'll see . . . I'm sorry . . ." She wasn't even sure what he was saying to her, but she was glad he was holding her, and maybe he would change his mind after he thought about it for a little longer. She thought that he probably would, but it was so emotionally draining dealing with this resistance.

"I'm sorry too," she said finally, and he wiped the tears from her eyes and kissed her. He began to stroke her hair then, and kissed the tears on her eyelashes and cheeks, and then slowly he undid her blouse, and slid her shorts and her underwear down past her ankles. She lay naked beside him and he lay admiring her. She had a beautiful body, and in his opinion defiling it with a baby would have been a crime. She would never have been the same again and he knew it.

"I love you, Adrian," he said gently. He loved her too much to let her do something so desperately foolish. And he loved himself, and their life, and everything they had striven for and accomplished and acquired, and no one was ever going to jeopardize that, certainly not a baby.

He kissed her longingly, and she kissed him in return, thinking that he understood how she felt finally, and they made love to each other, quietly and gently. It was a time of feeling close to each other and putting their argument aside, as each one hoped that the other would come to understand their side, and afterward they lay in each other's arms and kissed again, feeling much closer.

It was the middle of the afternoon by the time they woke up the next day, and Steven suggested they take a swim, which they did, after they showered and had breakfast. Adrian was in a quiet mood, and she didn't say anything as they went out to the pool holding hands and feeling pensive. It was a pool shared by all the residents of the complex, but there was no one there today. It was a beautiful sunny May afternoon and people had gone to the beach, or to see friends, or they were just lying on their decks, out of sight, getting suntanned and most of the time, lying naked.

Steven swam laps, while Adrian swam for a little while and then lay in the sun and dozed. She didn't want to talk about the baby anymore, not now. She was hoping that eventually he would calm down and adjust, now that he knew. It had been a big adjustment for her, too, and she knew it would be an even bigger one for Steven.

"Ready to go in?" he asked finally, after five o'clock. They had barely spoken all afternoon and after their emotional debate of the night before, Adrian was still feeling exhausted.

They went inside quietly and after Adrian showered, Steven put the stereo on, and they listened to UB40 while she made dinner.

Adrian wanted to spend a quiet evening with him. They had a lot to think about, a lot to consider.

"Are you okay?" he asked as she made pasta and a big green salad.

"I'm okay. I'm just kind of tired," she said softly, and he nodded.

"You'll feel better next week when you get it taken care of."

She couldn't believe he had said what he just did, and she stared at him in amazement.

"How can you say a thing like that?" She looked horrified, and she realized suddenly that he wasn't reconsidering at all. He was as adamant as ever.

"Adrian, all it is right now is a physical problem. It's making you feel lousy, so fix it. That's all. You don't have to think of it as anything more than that." She couldn't believe how totally unemotional he was, how totally uninvolved with their baby.

"That's disgusting. It's a lot more than that, and you know it." She hadn't planned to mention it again that night, but now that he'd brought it up, she was going to discuss it. "It's our baby for God's sake." Tears filled her eyes again and she hated herself for it. She didn't normally cry, but he was pushing her to extremes, with his casual attitude about her having an abortion. "I'm not going to do it," she suddenly said as she left their dinner on the kitchen counter, and hurried upstairs to their bedroom, and it was over an hour later when he finally came upstairs to continue the conversation. She was lying on the bed and he sat down next to her and spoke very softly. "Adrian, you *have* to have an abortion," he said calmly. "If you value our marriage. If you don't do it, it'll ruin everything." As far as she could see, it would ruin it either way. If she didn't have the baby, she would always feel the loss, and if she did, Steven might never forgive her.

"I don't think I can." She spoke from deep in her pillow and she was being honest with him. The last thing she wanted was an abortion.

"I don't think you can not. It'll destroy our marriage and cost you your job if you don't have the abortion."

"I don't care about my job." And the truth was, compared to the baby she didn't. It was amazing how quickly the baby had come to be important to her.

"Of course you care about your job." To Steven, it seemed as though overnight she had become a different person.

"No, I don't . . . but I don't want to destroy us," she said sadly, turning over to face him.

"I can tell you one thing I do know for sure, Adrian, and that is that I don't want a baby."

"You might change your mind later. People do," she said hopefully, but he shook his head.

"I don't. I don't want kids. I never have, never will, and you used to think that was all right too. Didn't you?"

She hesitated and then admitted something to him she never had before. "I thought that maybe eventually . . . you might change your mind one day. I mean . . . if we really never had kids, then I suppose it would be all right. But in a case like this . . . I thought maybe . . . I don't know, Steven. I didn't ask for this. But now that it's here, how can you just sweep it from our lives without a second thought?" It was awful.

"Because the quality of our lives will be better if I do, and you're a lot more important to me than a baby."

"There's room for both," she pleaded, but he shook his head.

"Not in my life there isn't. There's room for you and no one else. And I don't want to compete with a baby for your attention. I don't think my parents said more than two words to each other in twenty years. They never had the time or the energy or the emotion. They were drained. There was nothing left of them when we grew up. They were like two used, finished, old dead people. Is that what you want?"

"One baby isn't going to do that," she said softly, pleading with him again, and clearly getting nowhere.

"I'm not willing to risk it, Adrian." he said, looking down at her. "Get rid of it." His voice trembled as he spoke to her, and he went back downstairs for a long time, just to get away from her, and the threat of the baby she carried within her.

She thought about it for a long time as she waited for Steven to come back upstairs, and she knew that if she gave up this baby, an important part of her very soul would be lost forever.

CHAPTER

..7..

SUNDAY AND MONDAY WERE A NIGHTMARE OF ARGUMENTS and recriminations between the two of them, and at six in the morning on Tuesday before Steven left, Adrian finally collapsed in hysterical sobs and agreed to do anything he wanted. She hadn't been to work in two days, and she didn't want to lose the husband she loved, even if it meant giving up their baby. She promised to take care of the abortion while he was gone, and that day all she did was lie in bed and sob until she went to see the doctor at four-thirty.

She had lain in bed all that afternoon with a feeling of dread that grew to blind terror by the time she was dressed, and she wanted to run away from all of it as she hurried out of the apartment. She wanted to run away from what was happening to her, from what she had to do, from what Steven expected of her, and what she felt she owed him if she valued their marriage.

"Adrian," the nurse called as she stood up, looking very nervous. She had worn black slacks and a black turtleneck shirt and black shoes, and with her white skin and dark hair, she looked unusually somber.

She led Adrian into a small room and told her to get undressed from the waist down and put on a gown. She had been there before but it had all seemed less ominous the other times when she'd been there for birth control advice or her annual checkups.

She sat on the exam table in her black silk shirt, with the blue paper gown covering the rest of her, and her bare feet tucked under her, and she looked like a little girl, as she tried to keep her mind off why she was there and what was going to happen. She kept reminding herself that she was doing this for Steven because she loved him.

The doctor came in finally, and he smiled as he glanced at her chart and recognized her. She was a nice girl, and he had always liked her.

"What can I do for you today, Mrs. Townsend?" He was a pleasant old-fashioned man, about the age of her own father.

"I . . ." She couldn't bring herself to say the words, and her eyes looked huge in her pale face as he watched her. "I came here . . . for an abortion." The words drifted away, spoken so softly, he could barely hear them.

"I see." He sat down on a small revolving stool, and glanced at her chart. She was married, thirty-one, in good health, none of it added up. Maybe the baby wasn't her husband's. "Any special reason?"

She nodded painfully. Everything about her told him that she didn't want to be there. The way she was curled up on the table, as though to protect herself from him, the way she shrank backward every time he went near her, the way she spoke, barely able to say the words. He had seen a lot of women in distress, women who would have done anything to get rid of babies they didn't want, but this girl was not one of them. He was willing to bet she didn't really want an abortion.

"My husband doesn't feel this is the right time for us to have children."

The doctor nodded again, as though he understood perfectly. "Is there any reason why he feels that way now, Adrian? Is he out of work? Is there a health problem?" He was looking for why this girl was there, and without a good reason he was not going to do the abortion. Legal or not, he still had a moral responsibility to his patients. But she was shaking her head to all of his questions.

"No, he just . . . he just doesn't feel this is the right time for children."

"Does he want children at all?" She hesitated, and then shook her head as her eyes brimmed with tears.

"No." It was the merest whisper. "I don't really think so. He was one of five children, and he had a very unhappy childhood. It's hard for him to understand that things could ever be different."

"I should think they could be. You have a fine job, and I suppose he must be fairly stable. Do you think he might change his mind in time?" She shook her head sadly as the tears rolled down her cheeks, and the doctor was quick to tell her something that he suspected might make her a little less nervous. "I'm not going to perform an abortion today, Adrian." He had switched to her first name as soon as he understood the gravity of the problem. This was no time for formality, she needed a friend, and he wanted to help her. "First, I want to make sure that you really are pregnant, and there isn't a mistake. Have you had a pregnancy test?" He assumed that she had or she wouldn't be there.

"Yes. I did it at home. Twice. And I'm two weeks late."

"That would make you four weeks pregnant the way we calculate it. And I'm sure you are, but we'll just check to see in a moment. And after that, I'd like you to go home and think about this, just to be sure. If you still feel you want to terminate the pregnancy after that, you can come back tomorrow. Does that sound reasonable to you?" She nodded, feeling both hysterical and numb. She felt as though the emotional trauma she was going through was going to kill her. But the doctor was gentle and kind, he confirmed what she already knew, told her to go home and think and try to talk it over again with her husband. He felt that since she felt so strongly about not wanting to abort, surely her husband would come around if she explained it to him. What he did not take into account was the fact that Steven was rabid on the subject. And when he called her that night, he sounded clearly annoyed that she hadn't already had the abortion.

"Why the hell didn't he do it today, for chrissake? What's the point of waiting?"

"He wants us to think about it before we do anything drastic. And maybe that's not such a bad idea." The realization of what she was going to do left her with a crushing feeling of depression. "When are you coming back?" she asked anxiously, but he seemed not to hear the panic in her voice as she asked him.

"Not till Friday. And Mike and I are playing tennis on Saturday morning. Maybe you and Nancy can join us afterward for a set of doubles." She couldn't believe what he was saying to her, either he was completely insensitive, or just plain stupid.

"I'm not sure I'll be playing tennis by then." The sarcasm in her voice was both obvious and brutal.

"Oh, that's right . . . I forgot." In ten seconds? How could he forget so soon? How could he let her do it in the first place?

"I think you should be thinking this over again too. Steven, it's not just my baby, it's yours too." But she could feel the walls go up even as she said the words.

"I told you how I feel about it, Adrian. I don't want to discuss it anymore. Just take care of it, dammit. I don't understand why you have to wait until tomorrow." She didn't answer him, crushed by the brutality of what he was saying. It was as though the baby was threatening him, and she had betrayed him by letting it happen, and now she had to fix it at all cost, no matter what it did to her to do that. "I'll call you tomorrow night." Adrian caught her breath as the tears stung her eyes.

"Why? Just to make sure I did it?" Her heart felt as though it were breaking as she said good-bye to him, thinking that in a few hours it would be too late to save their baby. And she lay in bed awake all night, crying and thinking of this child she would never know. The child she was sacrificing for her husband. She was still awake when the sun came up the next day, and she felt as though she were waiting for an execution. She had taken the week off from work, and all she had to do now was get back to the doctor's office and force herself to have the abortion.

As she dressed, she kept telling herself that at the last minute Steven would call and tell her not to do it. But he didn't. The house was still silent as she left and drove away in sandals, a denim skirt, and an old work shirt. And she arrived at the doctor's at nine o'clock, as she'd been told to, if she decided to go through with the abortion. She hadn't eaten or had anything to drink since the night before in case they had to administer an anesthetic. She was trembling and pale as she drove the MG along Wilshire Boulevard, and she arrived at the doctor's office five minutes early. She told the nurse that she was there, and sat down in the waiting room with her eyes closed, and a feeling in her heart that she knew she would never forget for the rest of her life, and for the first time in her life, she knew that she hated Steven. She had a frantic urge to call him, to find him wherever he was, and tell him he had to change his mind, but she knew that it was pointless.

The nurse stood in the doorway and called her name, and

smiled at her as she led her down the hallway. She put her in a slightly larger room, and this time she told her to take all her clothes off, put on the blue gown, and lie on the table. There was an ominous-looking machine standing by, and Adrian knew that it was the vacuum. She felt her throat go dry, and her lips seemed to stick together like dampened tissue paper. All she wanted was to get it over with and go home and try to forget about it, and she knew that for the rest of her life she would never again let herself get pregnant. And yet, part of her still wanted to keep this baby. It was insane, she was using all her inner strength just to get rid of it, and part of her still wanted to hold on to it no matter what happened or what Steven said, or how neurotic he was about his childhood.

"Adrian?" The doctor popped his head around the door, and looked at her with a gentle smile. "Are you all right?" She nodded, but no words came to mind as she stared at him in ill-concealed terror. He walked into the room, closed the door and spoke to her firmly. "Are you sure you want to do this?" She nodded again as tears sprang to her eyes, and then shook her head honestly. She was so confused and so terrified and so unhappy, and she didn't want to be here at all. She wanted to be at home with Steven, waiting for their baby. "You don't have to do this. You shouldn't do it if you don't want to. Your husband will adjust. A lot of husbands make a fuss like this at first, and they're the ones who are the most excited when the baby comes. I want you to really think about this before you do it."

"I can't," she croaked. "I just can't." She was sobbing openly as she sat on the table. "I can't do it."

"Neither can I." He smiled. "Go home, and tell your husband to buy himself a cigar and save it till, oh . . ." He checked her chart again. ". . . I'd say the beginning of January, and then we'll give him a nice fat baby. How does that sound to you, Adrian?"

"It sounds lovely." She smiled through her tears and the kindly old doctor put an arm around her shoulders. "Go home, Adrian. Have a good rest, and a good cry. It'll be all right. It's going to be just fine. And so will your husband." He patted her shoulder then, and left the room so she could get dressed and go home, with her baby. She smiled to herself as she dressed, and she cried, and she felt as though something wonderful had happened. She had been spared, and she wasn't even sure why, except that her doctor had been smart enough to know that she just couldn't do it.

She started to drive home, and she decided suddenly to go to the office instead. She felt better than she had in days, and she wanted to go to work and lose herself in the piles of papers on her desk. She drove to the studio with the wind blowing in her hair, and she took a deep breath and smiled to herself. Life was suddenly so sweet, and she was going to have a baby.

She walked into her office with a spring in her step but feeling as though she had run a ten-mile race. It had not exactly been an easy morning, or an easy few days, and she still had to deal with Steven when he got back from Chicago. But at least now she knew what she was doing. She felt more relaxed than she had in days and the crushing feeling of depression seemed to have lifted.

"Hi, Adrian." Zelda stuck her head in the door halfway through the morning. "Everything okay?"

"Fine. Why?" Adrian was looking distracted with a pencil stuck behind each ear, and it was unusual for her to come to work in old clothes and no makeup.

"Well, to be honest, you don't look so hot. You look as though you've been through the wringer," and she had. "Are you feeling okay?" Zelda was more observant than Adrian had realized. She was right. Things had been pretty awful.

"I had the flu." She smiled, grateful that Zelda had noticed. "But I'm okay now."

"I thought you were taking the week off." She was looking at her intensely, as though deciding whether or not to believe her when she said she was all right. But she seemed happy as she sat industriously amid the debris in her office.

"I decided I missed all this too much."

"You're nuts." Zelda smiled at her.

"Probably. Want to go out later for a sandwich?"

"Sure. I'd love to."

"Come by whenever you're ready."

"I'll do that." She disappeared again then, and Adrian went back to work, feeling better than she had in days. The idea of a baby still scared her a little bit, but it was something she thought she could get used to. It was better than the alternative. She knew she couldn't have lived with that, and she still resented Steven for trying to force her to do it. She wondered how they would ever recover from the emotional bruises they had inflicted on each other in the past few days, or if they would ever forget it. She went back to work then, and tried not to think about him. She would have to think of what she was going to say to him later.

CHAPTER

AND IN A STUDIO JUST DOWN THE HALL, BILL THIGPEN WAS sitting on a stool, talking to the director and groaning.

"What the hell do I know where she is? She checked out of her hotel room a week ago. I don't know who she's with. I don't know where she's gone. She's a grown woman and it's none of my business . . . until she starts screwing up my show. Now it's my business, but I still don't know where the hell she's gone to." Sylvia Stewart had not come back from Las Vegas the previous Sunday night. She had checked out of her room there on Monday morning, exactly nine days before, the hotel said, but she still hadn't come back to work, and feeling awkward about it, Bill had gone to her apartment to check, and she hadn't been back there either.

They had written alternate scripts for the past week, but it was getting pretty desperate without her.

And in a few more days they would have to replace her. And

Bill had just said as much to the director. By not calling in to at least explain to them what was going on, she was in clear violation of her contract.

"If she doesn't turn up before tomorrow's show, you've got to get me someone else," Bill was saying to the director and one of the assistant producers. They had already called one of the agencies earlier that day, but it wasn't going to be easy to replace her without upsetting their viewers.

"Did everyone get the new material today?" the director asked, frowning at what Bill had just handed him. It was a whole new script, and it was obvious that Bill had the writers working night and day in Sylvia's absence. It was a heroic piece of work, and it kept the story afloat while she was gone. There were so many dramas occurring on the show at the same time that so far it seemed plausible that Vaughn Williams had not been seen for nine days, but barely. She was still in jail, being held for the murder of the man her brother-in-law had killed nine days before, on a Friday.

Bill stayed in the studio till they went on the air, and watched the entire show, satisfied that everyone was handling the new plot turns and the new script well, and when it was over, after congratulating everyone, he went back to his office. It was half an hour later when his secretary buzzed him on the intercom, and told him there was someone to see him.

"Anyone I know? Or are we going to keep it a secret?" He was tired from his long nights of work, but he was pleased that things were going well. It was mostly due, he felt, to a tremendous cast, two terrific writers, and an outstanding director. "Who is it, Betsey?"

There was a long pause. "It's Miss Stewart."

"*Our* Miss Stewart? *The* Miss Stewart we've looked for all over the state of Nevada?" He raised his eyebrows with interest.

"The one and only."

"Please show her in. I can hardly wait to see her."

Sylvia walked in the moment Betsey opened the door. She came in like a frightened child, and she looked more beautiful than ever. Her long black hair hung down her back like Snow White's, and her eyes looking at him remorsefully seemed enormous. Bill stood up as she walked into the room, and stared at her as though he had just seen a vision.

"Where the hell have you been?" he asked ominously. And for a moment she didn't know what to expect, so she started to cry as she watched him. "We've been going crazy, calling all over Las Vegas. The kids from *My House* said they left you with some guy. We were going to call the Nevada police and report you missing." He had been genuinely worried about her for the past week, frightened by what might have happened to her.

She let out a sob and sat down on the couch as he handed her some tissues. "I'm sorry."

"You should be. A lot of people were worried about you." It was like talking to a child, and he was suddenly relieved that in at least one way she was no longer his problem. "Where were you?" Not that it really mattered now, as long as she was back, and unharmed. That was what had worried him. Some nasty things had been known to happen in Las Vegas. Particularly to girls who looked like Sylvia Stewart. Especially when they slept with strangers.

But she was staring at him now, and started to cry again. "I got married."

"You got *what*?" For once, he looked stunned. He had suspected everything but that as he had tried to figure out what might have happened to her. "To whom? The guy in your room the other night?"

She nodded and blew her nose again. "He's in the garment industry. From New Jersey."

"Oh my God." Bill sat down heavily next to her on the

couch, wondering if he had ever known her. "What ever made you do something like that?"

"I don't know. I just . . . you always work so hard . . . and I've been so lonely." Christ. She was twenty-three years old, drop-dead gorgeous, and she was crying about being lonely. Half the women in America would have given their right arm and more to look like her, and she had married a clothing manufacturer she didn't even know, and had spent a weekend with in Las Vegas. And Bill was suddenly wondering if it was his fault. Maybe if he hadn't neglected her, if he hadn't been so wrapped up in the show . . . it was a familiar refrain. In some ways, the chorus went all the way back to Leslie. But was he responsible for all of them? Was it really his fault? Why couldn't they adjust to the way he lived? Why did they have to run off and do something crazy? And now this foolish girl had married a total stranger. Bill looked at her in amazement.

"What are you going to do now, Sylvia?" He could hardly wait to hear.

"I don't know. Move to New Jersey next week, I guess. His name is Stanley, and he has to be back in Newark by Tuesday."

"I don't believe this." Bill laid his head back against the couch and started to laugh, and in a minute, he couldn't stop laughing. Betsey could even hear him from her desk outside his office, and she was relieved that he wasn't shouting. He seldom did, but she had figured that Sylvia's disappearance might just do it to him. "You and Stanley have to be back in Newark by Tuesday . . . is that it?"

"Well . . ." She looked suddenly uncomfortable. "Sort of. Except that I know I have a contract to do the show for another season." The truth was that she had figured he would kick her off the show after calling the other night, and in a panic she had married Stanley. She had no idea what she was getting, and yet he had been very sweet to her, and he had bought her a rather handsome diamond ring in Las Vegas, and promised to take care of her once they got to Newark. He had promised to get her a great modeling job, and if she wanted to she could do acting jobs in New York, like maybe even on commercials, or the soaps there. It was a whole new horizon opening up for her, and in some ways being married to a man in the garment industry in Newark wasn't a total miscast for Sylvia Stewart. "What am I going to do about my contract?" She looked pleadingly at Bill and he almost started to laugh again. It was all so absurd, he almost couldn't stand it. It was impossible to take it seriously. It was life imitating art in the extreme, and he wasn't crazy enough not to see the humor in it.

"You know what you're going to do about your contract, Sylvia? You're going to give me two more days, today and tomorrow, on the set, for old times' sake, and we're going to kill you off in the most dramatic scene you've ever seen on Friday. And after that, you're free to go. You can go home to Newark with Stanley and have ten babies as long as you name the first one after me. I'm releasing you from your contract."

"You are?" She looked astounded, and he grinned at her in amusement.

"Yes, I am. Because I'm a nice guy, and I gave you a hard time by working my ass off and not paying enough attention to you. I owe you, sweetheart. And this is the payback." He was just grateful she had turned up at all. It was going to allow them to tie it all up neatly. John was going to kill Vaughn on the show, because she had seen him murder the pusher. And the saga could continue from there, ad infinitum. "I'm sorry, baby," he said to her gently then, and he meant it. "I guess I'm not much of a catch these days. Never was, in fact. I'm married to this show."

"It's okay." Sylvia looked at him almost shyly. "You're not too mad at me? . . . for doing what I did . . . for getting married, I mean."

"Not if you'll be happy." And he meant it.

Her arrangement with Bill had been a passing thing, and they both knew it. It meant very little to either of them, as she had proven by spending the weekend with a stranger in Vegas, and Bill suspected correctly that that was exactly why she had gone there.

"Do I get to kiss the bride?" He stood up, and she stood up, too, still astounded that he had let her off so easily. She had expected him to be furious and to kick her off the show without releasing her from her contract. It would make it a lot easier for her to get work in New York if he let her go this way. And she turned up toward him now, ready for a passionate embrace, for old times' sake, but he kissed her gently on the cheek, and for an instant, he knew he was going to miss her. There had been a sweetness about her he liked, a kindness, and they had had fun together. She was familiar to him, and they were good friends, and now he was alone again. But it would be easier not to be involved with someone on the show. It was a mistake he wouldn't make again, a form of extreme self-indulgence. There was no woman in his life, and for the moment he wasn't even sure if he minded. "What are you going to do about your stuff at my place?"

"I guess I'd better pick it up." She had forgotten all about that. There wasn't much, but there was about a suitcase worth of clothes she had left in his closet.

"Want to go get it now?"

"Sure. I have to meet Stanley at the Beverly Wilshire at four o'clock. But I have plenty of time." There was something else implied in her voice, but he pretended not to notice. It was over for him now. She had done what she'd done and he bore her no malice, but he no longer wanted her either.

He left his office with her, and he was sure that everyone thought they were going back to his place for a quickie. But he only laughed and drove her to his apartment and helped her throw all her things into boxes. And then he drove her back to her apartment.

"Want to come up?" She looked at him sadly for a minute as she took the last of her boxes out of his woody, but he only shook his head. And a moment later, he drove off, and that chapter in his life was over.

CHAPTER

··9··

WHEN ADRIAN GOT HOME AFTER THE SIX O'CLOCK NEWS, the phone was ringing, and she grabbed it just as the message on her answering machine went on. She spoke into the phone hurriedly, turned off the machine, and answered, still juggling her handbag and the newspaper, and some things she'd bought at the drugstore on the way home, and everything stopped when she heard his voice. It was Steven.

"Are you all right?" He sounded anxious and tense, and she instantly realized why. "I've been calling you all afternoon. Why didn't you answer the phone?" He had been desperately worried about her all day and he had been calling since noon and only getting the machine. He was frantic by seven o'clock when she finally got in, and it had never dawned on him to call her office. Nor had she wanted to call him. She needed time to think about telling him she hadn't had the abortion.

"I wasn't here," she said almost remorsefully, realizing that she had to make a quick shift of gears. She had come to terms with everything that was going on in their lives early that morning. But he had no idea what she'd done, and he still assumed that she had had the abortion.

"Where were you? Did they keep you at the doctor's all day? Did something go wrong?" He sounded frantic and she felt sorry for him, but she was also angry. He had been willing to let her go through with the abortion all alone, and he had tried to tell her it was no big deal, which it was, or would have been. And now she was still mad at him for it.

"Nothing went wrong." There was a long pause, an endless silence, and she decided to tell him right away and not lead him on. "I didn't do it."

There was an instant of silent disbelief and then he exploded into the phone. "What? Why not? Was something wrong with you that he couldn't?"

"Yes," she said quietly as she sat down. She felt very old suddenly, and very tired, the emotions she had repressed all day suddenly rushed back at her and she felt drained as she listened to her husband. "Something was wrong. I didn't want to do it."

"So you chickened out?" He sounded horrified, and now he was furious, too, which upset her even more and made her even more angry.

"If you want to put it that way. I decided I wanted to have our child. Most people would be flattered by that, or pleased, or something a little more human." But they both knew he wasn't human on this subject.

"I don't happen to be one of them, Adrian. I'm not touched . . . or flattered . . . I think you're a fool. And I think you're doing it to try to get at me in some way, but I've got news for you, I'm not going to let you do it."

"What are you talking about? You sound like a crazy person. This isn't a vendetta, for chrissake . . . it's a baby . . . you know, small person, made by you and me, blue and pink, cries occasionally. Most people can adjust to that, they don't act as though their lives are being threatened by a Mafia hit man."

"Adrian, I'm not amused by your sense of humor."

"And I am even less so by your sense of values. What is wrong with you? How could you leave me like this and just expect me to go out and get an abortion? It isn't the minor procedure you think it is, it isn't 'nothing.' It's something. It's a big something . . . and one of the reasons I didn't want to do it is because I love you."

"That's bullshit and you know it." He sounded threatened and cornered and extremely frightened by everything she had just said to him, and Adrian realized they weren't going to solve it on the phone, and possibly not even in the near future. He was just going to have to calm down, and see that the baby wasn't going to ruin his life. But first, they were both going to have to stop being angry.

"Why don't we talk about this calmly when you come home?" she said sensibly, but he was irate now.

"There's nothing to talk about. Unless you come to your senses and get an abortion. I'm not going to discuss anything with you until you do. Is that clear?" He was screaming at her in the phone and he sounded like a madman.

"Steven, stop it! Get a grip on yourself!" She spoke to him like a child who was out of control, but he was beyond being able to calm down. In his hotel room in Chicago, he was shaking with fury.

"Don't tell me what to do, Adrian. You betrayed me!"

"I did not betray you." She almost laughed, he sounded so absurd, but the truth was, it wasn't funny. "It was an accident. I don't know how it happened or whose fault it was. It doesn't matter anymore. I'm not blaming you, or myself, or anyone. I just want to have the baby."

"You're out of your mind, and you don't know what you're

talking about." He sounded like someone she didn't know, as she closed her eyes and tried to stay calm.

"At least I'm not hysterical. Why don't you just forget about it and we'll talk about it when you get home."

"I have nothing more to say to you, until you take care of it."

"What's that supposed to mean?" She opened her eyes again. There was something odd in his voice that she had never heard before, a kind of chill that frightened her, and she had to remind herself that this was only Steven.

"It means exactly what it sounds like. It's me or the baby. Get rid of it. Now. Adrian, I want you to go back to the doctor tomorrow and get an abortion." A hand clutched her heart for a moment, and she wondered if he was serious, but she knew that he couldn't be. He couldn't make her choose between the baby or him, that was insane. And she knew he couldn't mean it.

"Sweetheart . . . please . . . don't be like this . . . I can't go back . . . I can't . . . I just can't do it."

"You have to." He sounded as though he were near tears and she wanted to put her arms around him and comfort him and tell him it was going to be all right. And one day, after the baby was born, he would laugh about how upset he had been at the beginning. But right now it was all he could think of. "Adrian, I don't want a baby."

"You don't have one yet. Why don't you just relax, and forget about it for a couple of days." She was feeling exhausted, but calmer about it ever since she had made her decision.

"I'm not going to relax until you get rid of it. I want you to have an abortion." She sat there in silence, listening to him, for the first time in almost three years unable to give him what he wanted. Unable, and unwilling to, which upset him even more. And she just couldn't promise him that she would do as he told her.

"Steven . . . please . . ." Tears suddenly welled up in her eyes again, for the first time since that morning. "I can't. Can't you understand that?"

"All I understand is what you're doing to me. You are viciously and maliciously refusing to consider my feelings." He remembered only too well how depressed his father got every time his mother had gotten pregnant again. He had held down two jobs for years, and finally he had three, until finally, mercifully, he was practically dead of cirrhosis. And by then all the children were gone anyway, and his life was over. "You don't care how I feel, Adrian. You don't give a damn about me. All you want is your goddam baby." He was crying now, and Adrian wondered what she had done. She just didn't understand it. He had said he might be willing to have children eventually, when they were "well set," but he had never said he hated them, he had never told her he absolutely wouldn't have them. "Well, you can have your baby, Adrian. You can have it . . . but you can't have me . . ." he sobbed into the phone, and she was crying too as she listened.

"Steven, please. . . ." But as she said the words he hung up, and the phone went dead as she held it. She couldn't believe how upset he had been, how frantic, and for the next two hours she tortured herself wondering if she should have the abortion. If it meant that much to him, if it threatened him so deeply, what right did she have to force him to have the baby? And yet what right did she have to kill the baby because a grown man couldn't cope with the prospect of being a father? Steven could adjust, he could learn to handle it, he would discover eventually that she didn't love him any less, perhaps she would love him more, and his life would not be over. She couldn't give the baby up, she reminded herself. She remembered again what it had been like going to the doctor and preparing to have the abortion, and she knew she just couldn't do it. She was going to have their baby, and Steven was just going to have to accept it. She would take full responsibility for it, all he had to do was sit back and relax and not let it make him completely crazy.

She was still telling herself that when she drove back to work at eleven o'clock. And when she got home after midnight she played back her machine to see if he had called, but he hadn't. And she was still upset about it the next day when she went to work and called his office and asked what plane he was coming in on, and it was perfect. He was due in at two o'clock, and she would have plenty of time to go to the airport and pick him up, and hopefully by that night everyone would have calmed down, and life could begin to get back to normal. As normal as it was going to be for a while anyway. Sooner or later they were going to have to make the ordinary adjustments to the fact that she was pregnant, the way other couples did, buying bassinets and building nurseries, and getting ready for their babies. Just the thought of it made her smile as she went back to work and forced herself not to think of Steven.

Everyone stood on the set and watched Sylvia get killed that afternoon. John visited her in jail, pretending to be her lawyer. "Vaughn" appeared to be utterly amazed when she saw him, and moments later, unseen by the guard who had left them alone in a holding cell, he had his hands around her neck, and she was dead. She made wonderful sounds as John strangled her. It was a great scene, and Bill was enormously pleased with all of them as he watched it. And then the moment came to say good-bye to Sylvia after they were off the air, and suddenly everyone was crying. She had been on the show for a year, and they were all going to miss her. She had been easy to work with, and even the other women liked her. The director had ordered champagne and they handed Bill a paper cup too, as he stood on the sidelines and watched as the soap opera seemed to become real, and Stanley stood there watching them all and feeling awkward. Eventually, Bill tried to slip away, but Sylvia saw him before he went and she went over to him quietly and said something no one else could hear, and he smiled and raised his glass to her, and then turned and raised it to Stanley.

"Good luck, you two. Have a great life in New Jersey. And don't forget to write," he teased Sylvia, and kissed her on the cheek as she started to cry again, knowing that she was taking a tremendous chance on Stanley. He had rented a white stretch limousine to take them from the studio to the airport. They were taking the red-eye to Newark that night, and her bags were already packed and in the car. She had already given up her apartment. She looked longingly at Bill as he left the set, and without looking back, he returned to his office. It had been a long week for him, but everything had ended well finally and he was actually going to take the weekend off, and take it easy. And as Bill drove home right after the show, Adrian was on the way to the airport. All she could think of was what she was going to say to Steven.

All Adrian saw as she watched Steven get off the plane was the look in his eyes when he saw her. He walked straight toward her without saying a word, his eyes full of hostility and questions.

"Why did you come here?" he shot at her, still furious after their conversation the night before.

"I wanted to pick you up," she answered gently. She tried to take his briefcase from him, to give him a hand, but he wouldn't let her.

"You didn't need to do that. I'd rather you hadn't."

"Come on, Steven . . . be fair . . ."

"Fair?" He stopped dead in his tracks in the middle of the

airport. "Fair? You're asking me to be *fair?* After what you're doing to me?"

"I'm not *doing* anything to you. I'm trying to do my best to cope with something that happened. It happened to *both* of us. And I just don't think it's fair to make me do something so upsetting."

"What you're doing is a lot worse." He started walking toward the exit as she followed him, wondering where he was going. She had left her car in the garage, and he was heading for the taxis.

"Steven, where are you going?" He was already outside the terminal, and he had just pulled open the door of a taxi. "What are you doing?" She was suddenly starting to panic. He was acting like someone she didn't know. And she was frightened by what it all meant. She couldn't understand it. "Steven . . ." The driver was watching them with obvious irritation.

"I'm going back to the apartment. . . ."

"So am I. That's why I came to the airport."

". . . to pick up my things. I rented a studio in a hotel until you come to your senses." He was blackmailing her. He was leaving her until she got rid of the baby.

"For chrissake . . . Steven . . . please . . ." But he slammed the door in her face, locked it, and gave the driver the address, and a moment later the cab pulled away from the curb and left her standing there, staring at them in disbelief, wondering where her life was going.

She couldn't believe what he was doing to her or that he would actually leave her. But when she got to the apartment, he had already packed three suitcases, two tennis rackets, his golf clubs, and a whole other suitcase full of papers.

"I don't believe you're doing this." She stared around her in utter disbelief. "You can't be serious."

"I am," he said coolly. "Very much so. Take as long as you want to make up your mind, you can call me at the office. I'll be back when you get rid of the baby."

"And if I don't?"

"I'll come back for the rest of my things when you let me know."

"Simple as that?" Something deep inside her was beginning to burn, but another part of her wanted to crawl into a hole and die, but the terror didn't show as she looked at her husband. "You're behaving like a complete lunatic. I hope you know that."

"I'm not aware of that. And as far as I'm concerned you have violated any basis of trust and decency in this marriage."

"By having our baby?"

"By going against something you know I feel deeply about." He sounded so uptight and so prim, she wanted to hit him.

"All right. I'm human. I changed. But I think we can do this. We have a lot to offer any child. And I think anyone else would think so, too, by any normal standards."

"I don't want a child."

"And I don't want an abortion just because you think you don't like children and you don't want it to interfere with your trip to Europe."

"That's a low blow." He looked highly insulted. "The trip to Europe has nothing to do with it. It's the entire picture. This baby will deprive us of a life-style we've worked our asses off for, and I'm not willing to give that up on a whim, or because you're too scared to get an abortion."

"I'm not too scared, goddammit," she screamed at him, "I *want the baby*. Haven't you figured that out yet?"

"All I've figured out is that you're doing this because you want to get at me." In his eyes, it was the final treason, the ultimate betrayal.

"Why would I do a thing like that?" she asked as he checked his closet again, to make sure he hadn't forgotten anything he wanted.

"I don't know," he responded. "I haven't figured that out yet."

"And you're really telling me that if I keep the baby, you're leaving me for good?" He nodded and looked her in the eye as he did, and all Adrian could do was shake her head, and sit down on the steps to the upstairs as he carried his bags out. "You're really leaving me, aren't you?" She started to cry again, and she sat on the stairs watching him wrestle with his bags, unable to believe he was really leaving her, but he was. After two and a half years of marriage, he was walking out on her because she was having his baby. It was difficult to believe, harder still to understand, but as she stared at him in disbelief, he carried the last of his suitcases to the car and came back to look at her from the doorway.

"Let me know what you decide." His eyes were like ice, his face perfectly calm as she sobbed and walked toward him.

"Please don't do this to me . . . I'll be good . . . I promise . . . I won't even let it cry . . . Steven, please . . . don't make me give it up . . . and don't leave me . . . I need you. . . ." She clung to him like a child and he took a step back as though she revolted him, and it only made her feel more panicked.

"Get hold of yourself, Adrian. You have a choice in this. It's up to you."

"No it's not." She was crying almost uncontrollably. "You're asking me to do something I can't do."

"You can do anything you want," he said coolly to her, and she turned on him then with a look of anger.

"So can you. You can adjust to it if you want to."

"That's the whole point," he said as he looked down at her, "I already told you, Adrian, I don't want to." He picked up his tennis rackets then, and with a last look at her, without another word, he closed the door behind him, as Adrian stood staring at the spot where he had been. It was hard to believe he had actually done this to her. He had left her.

CHAPTER
··10··

THERE WAS NO SMELL OF BACON WHEN SHE AWOKE THIS Saturday morning. No breakfast tray waiting for her. No omelet made by loving hands. There were no good smells, good sounds, friendly noises. There was nothing. Only silence. She was alone. And the realization hit her like a weight on her heart almost as soon as she woke up. She stirred in the bed, looking for him, and then just as suddenly she remembered. Steven had left her.

She had called in sick for the late news the night before. She had been too upset to go anywhere, and she had just lain on her bed and cried until she finally fell asleep with the lights on. She had woken up again at three a.m., peeled off her clothes, turned off the lights, and put on her nightgown, and now as she woke up, she felt like an alcoholic waking up from a two-week binge. Her eyes were swollen, her mouth was dry, her stomach was in her throat, and her whole body felt battered. It had been a hell of a night, a hell of a week. In fact, it had been a miserable ten days ever since she had discovered she was pregnant. And she still had the choice he had given her. She could still have the abortion and he would come back, but if she did, what would they have now? Mutual resentment and anger and eventually hatred. She knew that if she gave up the baby for him, she would eventually hate him, and if she didn't, he would always resent her. In one little week, they had managed to destroy what she had always considered a fairly decent marriage.

She lay in bed for a long time, thinking of him, and wondering what had made him do it. Obviously his memories of his childhood had been far worse than she had ever realized, and he had been truly traumatized, not just turned off, by the prospect of having children. It was not something that was going to change overnight, or maybe ever. And he would have had to want to change it very badly, which he didn't.

The phone rang then, and for a desperate moment, she prayed that it was Steven. He had come to his senses, changed his mind . . . he wanted her . . . and the baby. . . . She picked it up with a hopeful croak, and a crestfallen look. It was her mother. She called once every few months and Adrian never enjoyed speaking to her anymore. Their conversations had always centered around her sister's glowing deeds, which, as far as Adrian was concerned, were few, and unpleasant references to Steven. Most of all, her mother made not-so-veiled comments about Adrian's many failings. She hadn't called, hadn't come home for Christmas in years, had forgotten her father's birthday, her parents' anniversary, had moved to California, married someone they didn't like, and had compounded it by failing to have children. At least her mother had given up asking her if she and Steven had seen a doctor.

Adrian assured her now that everything was fine, wished her a belated happy Mother's Day from the week before, realizing that she had failed yet again, and told her mother that she'd been working so hard, she'd forgotten what day it was. Not to mention the fact that she had her own problems.

"How's Dad?" she managed to ask, only to be told that he was getting old, but that her brother-in-law had just bought a new Cadillac and what kind of car did Steven drive anyway? A Porsche? What was that? Oh, a *foreign* car, and did Adrian still drive that ridiculous little car she'd had in college? Her mother admitted to being shocked that Steven didn't buy her a decent car. Her sister had two cars now. A Mustang, and a Volvo. It was a conversation designed to irritate in every possible way, and it did. Adrian only said that everything was fine, and Steven was out playing tennis. It would have been nice having a mother she could talk to, someone whose shoulder she could cry on, someone who could bolster her spirits. But her mother was only interested in keeping score, and when she'd heard enough she told Adrian to give Steven her "best," and hung up without offering any comfort.

The phone rang again after that, but this time, Adrian didn't answer. She listened to her answering machine afterward, and discovered that it had been Zelda, but she wasn't sure she wanted to talk to her either. She wanted to be alone to lick her wounds, and the only person she really wanted to talk to was Steven. But he didn't call all day, and that night, Adrian sat alone, wearing his bathrobe and huddled in front of the television, feeling sorry for herself, and crying.

The phone rang again then, and she grabbed it without thinking. It was Zelda calling from work to ask her something, and she was quick to guess that something was wrong. Adrian sounded awful.

"Are you sick?"

"More or less . . ." she muttered, wishing she hadn't answered. She answered Zelda's questions about work and then

Zelda seemed to hesitate, wanting to ask her again if she was all right. Lately she had sensed that Adrian was troubled.

"Is there anything I can do for you, Adrian?"

"No . . . I . . ." Adrian was touched by her question. "I'm okay."

Zelda's voice was kind at the other end. "You don't sound it." And at her end, just listening to her, Adrian was crying.

"Yeah," she sniffed loudly into the phone, feeling foolish for falling apart so suddenly, but she just couldn't keep up the pretense anymore. It was all too hard, and too awful now that he had left her. She still couldn't believe he would do such a thing, and she wished that someone were there just to put his arms around her. "I guess I'm not okay after all." She laughed through her tears, choking on a sob, and Zelda couldn't help wondering what had happened. And then, Adrian decided to tell her. There was no one else to say anything to, and she and Zelda had always felt a comfortable rapport in the years they had worked together. "Steven and I . . . he . . . we . . . he left me . . ." The last words were barely more than a squeak while she started to cry all over again, and Zelda felt sorry for her. She knew how rough those things were. She had been through it before, which is why she only went out with young boys now. She wanted some fun, and some good times, but no more heartbreak and no headaches.

"I'm sorry, Adrian. I really am. Is there anything I can do?"

Adrian shook her head as the tears coursed down her cheeks. "No, I'll be okay." But when . . . and would he come back? She was praying that he'd come to his senses.

"Sure you will." Zelda encouraged her. "You know, no matter how much we think we can't live without them, we always can. Six months from now, you may even be glad that this happened." But Zelda's words only made her cry harder.

"I doubt that."

"Wait and see." She spoke convincingly, but Adrian knew

something she didn't. "Six months from now you may be having a hot romance with someone else you haven't even met yet."

And then suddenly, at her words, Adrian started to laugh. The image was comical at best. In six months, she would be more than seven months pregnant. "I doubt that." She blew her nose again and then sighed.

"How can you be so sure?"

And then Adrian looked serious again. "Because I'm having a baby." There was a moment's silence at the other end as Zelda absorbed what she had just said, and then there was a long, low whistle.

"That certainly puts a different light on things. Does he know?"

Adrian hesitated, but only for a fraction of a second. She needed to talk to someone, and Zelda was smart and wise, and Adrian knew she could trust her. "That's why he left. He doesn't want kids."

"He'll come back." Zelda sounded confident then. "He's just reacting. He's probably just scared." She was right. He was terrified, but Adrian wasn't totally convinced that he would ever come to his senses. She wanted him to, she wanted that more than anything, but it was hard to tell what he would do. He was the same man who had walked out on his family, and never looked back. In fact, she was certain that he'd never even missed them. Once he made up his mind, he was capable of severing a bond he had once cherished, if it suited his purpose.

"I hope you're right." Adrian sighed again, her breath catching on the remains of a sob, like a child who's been crying. And then she thought of something. "Don't say anything to anyone at work." She was far from ready to announce it. She wanted to settle things with Steven first. It would be simpler if he came back and things calmed down before she told anyone that she was having a baby, and she didn't want to get them nervous at work about whether or not she'd be leaving.

"I won't say a thing," Zelda was quick to reassure her. "What are you going to do? Quit or take a leave?"

"I don't know. I haven't figured that out yet. Take a leave, I guess." But what if Steven was gone? What if she was alone? How was she going to work *and* manage a baby? She hadn't even begun to figure that out yet. But whatever it took, she knew that she was going to do it.

"You've got time. And you're right. Don't say anything. You'll just get them nervous." And she had a good job, maybe even a great one. It was a job Zelda wouldn't have touched with a ten-foot pole, it had too much responsibility and too many headaches, but she knew that Adrian was good at it, and she had always thought that she liked it. In truth, the job had been Steven's idea, but Adrian had enjoyed it, too, even though she still longed at times for something a little more esoteric. Working with the news day after day was brutal sometimes, and they all knew it could be very depressing. They were too close to the horrors that man committed against man, and the tragedies inflicted by nature, and there was seldom an instance when they were cheered by a happy story. But there was the satisfaction of doing a job well, and Adrian did. They all knew that. "Just take it easy, Adrian. Try not to let all this bullshit get to you. The job will sort itself out eventually, the baby will come when it's ready to, and Steven will probably be back in two days with an armful of red roses and a present, wanting to pretend he never left you."

"I hope you're right." And as she hung up a few minutes later, so did Zelda. She wasn't sure what Steven would do. She had met him several times, and been impressed by him, but in her heart of hearts, she had never liked him. There was something cold and calculating about the man. He looked right through you, as though anxious to move on to someone else, and she had never thought he was as warm and decent as Adrian. There was something about Adrian that she had liked the minute she met her. And she was sorry for her now. It was rough being pregnant and having her husband walk out on her. It wasn't fair, Zelda fumed, and she didn't deserve it.

She didn't, but there was nothing she could do about it. She couldn't do anything to make him come back, or change his mind. And later that night Adrian sat in front of the TV, blinded by tears and crying. She fell asleep on the couch finally, and it was four o'clock when she woke up to the somber strains of the national anthem. She clicked off the TV, and turned over on the couch. She didn't want to go upstairs to their empty bed. It was just too depressing. And in the morning she woke up, as the first rays of sun streamed in through the windows. She could hear the birds chirping outside, and it was a beautiful day, but she felt as though there were an elephant sitting on her heart as she lay on the couch and thought about Steven. Why was he doing this to her? And to himself? Why was he depriving them both of something that had so much meaning? It was strange how after resigning herself to never having kids, now suddenly she was willing to sacrifice everything for this one. It was all strange, she thought to herself as she got up slowly, and sat on the couch, feeling as though she had been beaten by midgets. Every inch of her body hurt, and her eyes felt swollen from all the crying she'd done the night before. And when she went to the bathroom a minute later, she groaned when she looked in the mirror.

"No wonder he left you," she muttered at the image she saw, and tears filled her eyes again as she laughed. It was hopeless. All she did was cry. She washed her face and brushed her teeth, and then she brushed her hair and put on jeans and an old sweater of Steven's. It was a way of staying close to him. She could wear his clothes if she couldn't have him.

She made herself a piece of toast reluctantly, and she warmed coffee from the leftovers of the day before. It tasted awful, but she didn't really care. She only had a sip and then she sat staring into space, thinking of him again, and why he had left her. Her mind seemed to have only one theme, and when the phone rang, she jumped a foot, and ran to pick it up, breathless and excited . . . he was coming home . . . he had to be. Who else would call at eight o'clock on a Sunday morning? But when she answered it, the voice was Chinese, and he hung up as soon as he heard her. It was a wrong number.

She dragged around the apartment for the next hour, picking things up and putting them down, sorting out laundry, but most of it was his, and she started to cry again when she saw it. Nothing was easy to deal with anymore. Everything hurt, everything was a reminder of what had happened, and just being in the apartment without him suddenly seemed too painful. By nine o'clock she couldn't stand it anymore, and she decided to take a walk. She didn't know where to go, but she just wanted to go somewhere and get some air, and get away from his clothes and their things and the empty rooms that made her feel even more lonely. She picked up her keys, and closed the door behind her, walking toward the front of the complex. She hadn't picked up her mail in two days and she didn't really care. But it was something to do while she went out walking. She stopped at their mailbox and leaned against the wall, flipping through bills, and two letters for Steven. There was nothing for her, and she put it all back in the box, and walked slowly out to her car, thinking that maybe she'd go for a drive. She had left her car at the front of the complex the day before, and she noticed an old woody station wagon parked next to it, and as she approached she saw a man taking a bicycle out of it. He was hot and damp, and he looked as though he had been out for an early morning ride, as he turned and looked at her. He seemed to stare at her for a long moment, as though searching his mind, and then he smiled, and remembered exactly where he had seen her. He had a fantastic memory for things like that, useless details, faces he had once seen, and names of people he would never meet again. He didn't know hers because he had never known her name, but he remembered instantly that she was the pretty girl he had seen in the Safeway weeks before. And he remembered also that she was married.

"Hi, there," He set his bicycle down next to her, and she found herself looking into blue eyes that were direct and warm and friendly. She guessed him to be about forty or forty-one, and he had friendly, happy-looking little lines next to his eyes. He looked like someone who enjoyed his life and was at ease with himself and the people around him.

"Hello." Her voice seemed very small, and he noticed that she looked a little different than she had several weeks before. She looked tired and pale, and he wondered if she'd been working too hard, or maybe she'd been sick. And she seemed subdued, like someone who'd been through a lot. She had seemed bouncier somehow at the grocery store in the middle of the night, but in any case, she was still beautiful, and he was happy to see her.

"Do you live here?" He found himself wanting to talk to her, to find out something about her. It was odd that their paths had crossed again. Maybe their destinies were entwined, he teased himself, as he admired her. He would have liked nothing better, except, of course, he reminded himself silently as he smiled at her, that that would also mean having his destiny entwined with her husband's.

"Yes, we do." She smiled quietly. "We live in one of the town houses at the other end. I don't usually park here. But I've seen your car here before. It's great." She had admired it frequently, never knowing whom it belonged to.

"Thanks, I love it. I've seen yours here too," now that he realized it was hers. He had always liked the battered little MG whenever he noticed it, and now he realized that he had seen her at the complex once before, from the distance. She had been with a tall, handsome man with dark hair, and they had driven off in something boring like a Mercedes, or a Porsche. And he realized as he thought of it that that was probably her husband. They had made a handsome pair, but she'd made a much greater impression on him when he'd seen her alone at the Safeway. But women alone were more likely to spark some interest in him than handsome young couples. "It's nice to see you again," he said, feeling suddenly awkward with her, and then he laughed at himself. "Doesn't it make you feel like a kid again when you run into people like this? . . . Hi . . . I'm Bill . . . what's your name? . . . Gee, do you go to school here?" He put on a schoolboy voice and they both laughed because he was right. Married or not, she was a beautiful girl, and he was a man, and it was obvious to both of them that he liked her. "Which reminds me." He held a hand out to her, still holding onto his mountain bike with his other hand. "I'm Bill Thigpen, and we met about two weeks ago at the Safeway, around midnight. I tried to run you down with my cart and you dropped about fourteen rolls of paper towels."

She smiled at the memory and held her hand out to him. "I'm Adrian Townsend." She shook his hand with a small, solemn smile, thinking how odd it was to run into him again. She remembered him now, although only vaguely. And her whole life had changed since then. Everything . . . Hi, I'm Adrian Townsend, and my whole life has fallen apart . . . my husband left me . . . and I'm having a baby. . . . "It's nice to see you again." She was trying to be polite, but her eyes still looked so sad. Just looking at her made him want to put his arms around her. "Where do you ride your bike?" She struggled for something to say to him, he seemed to want to keep on talking.

"Oh . . . here and there . . . I drove down to Malibu this morning. It was really beautiful. Sometimes I just go down there to walk on the beach and clear my head if I've been working all night."

"Do you do that a lot?" She tried to sound interested, although she wasn't sure why. She just knew that he seemed like a nice guy and he was friendly and she didn't want to hurt his feelings. And there was something about him that made her just want to stand there, close to him, and talk about nothing. It was as though, standing near him, she would be safe for a little while, and nothing else terrible could happen to her. He had that kind of feeling about him, like someone who could take care of things, and as she spoke to him, he was intently watching her eyes. Something had happened to her in the past few weeks. He was sure of it. He had no idea what, but she had changed. She looked bruised. From within. And it made him sad for her.

"Yeah . . . I work late sometimes. Very late. And you? Do you always buy your groceries at midnight?"

She laughed at the question, but in fact she did, whenever she'd forgotten to buy something earlier. She liked shopping after the evening news. She was relaxed but still wide-awake from work, and the store was always empty. "Yes, sometimes I do. I finish work at eleven-thirty. I work on the late news . . . and the six o'clock. It's a good hour to go shopping."

He looked amused. "What network are you with?" She told him and he laughed again. Maybe their destinies really were entwined. "You know, we also work in the same building." Although he had never seen her there, his show was shot some three floors from her office. "I work on a soap opera about three floors from the newsroom."

"That's funny." She was amused by the coincidence, too, although less encouraged by it than he was. "Which show?"

"*A Life Worth Living.*" He said it noncommittally, trying not to give away the fact that *A Life* was his baby.

"That's a good one. I used to love watching it between jobs, before I went to work on the news."

"How long have you been there?" He was intrigued by her, and he loved standing there next to her. He could almost imagine that he smelled the shampoo in her hair. She looked so clean and bright and decent, and he suddenly found himself wondering stupid things, like whether or not she wore perfume, and if she did, what kind and if he'd like it.

"Three years," she answered him about how long she'd worked on the news. "I used to do specials, and two-hour movies. I'm in production. But then I got this chance to work on the news . . ." Her voice drifted off as though she still wasn't sure of it, and he wondered why.

"Do you like it?"

"Sometimes. It's pretty grim sometimes, and it gets to me." She shrugged as though apologizing for some intrinsic weakness.

"It would get to me too. I don't think I could do it. I'd much rather make it all up . . . murder and rape and incest. The good wholesome stuff America loves." He grinned again and leaned on his bike as she laughed and for an instant, barely more than that, she looked carefree and happy, the way she had the first time he'd seen her.

"Are you a writer?" She wasn't sure why she was asking him, but it was easy to talk to him and she had nothing else to do early on this Sunday morning.

"Yes, I am," he answered her. "But I don't write the show very often anymore. I just kibitz from the sidelines." She hadn't figured out that he was the originator of the show and he didn't want to tell her.

"It must be fun. I used to want to write, a long time ago, but I'm better at the production end." Or at least that was what Steven said, but as soon as she thought of him, her eyes got sad again, and as he watched her, Bill saw it.

"I'll bet you'd be fine at it, if you tried it. Most people think writing is a big mystery, like math, but it really isn't." But as he talked to her, he could almost see her drift away, back into her initial sadness. And for an instant, neither of them spoke as he watched her, and then she shook her head, forcing herself to think about writing again, to keep her mind off Steven.

"I don't think I could write." She looked at him so sadly then, he wanted to reach out to her and touch her.

"Maybe you should try it. It's a tremendous release sometimes . . ." for whatever all that is, roaming around inside you and making you sad. He sent all his good thoughts to her, but he couldn't say anything. They were strangers, after all, and he could hardly ask her what it was that was making her so unhappy.

She opened her car door then, and looked back up at him before she got into the MG. It was almost as though she was sorry to leave him, but she didn't know what else to say to him. The small talk was wearing thin, and she thought she should move on, but she didn't really want to. "See you again sometime . . ." she said quietly as he nodded.

"I hope so." He smiled, defying her wedding band, which was rare for him, but she was a rare girl. Without even knowing her, he knew that.

And as she drove away, he stood holding his mountain bike and watched her.

CHAPTER

••11••

Steven called her at home finally two days later before she left for work. By then, she was desperate to hear from him, and her spirits soared when she heard his voice, and then plummeted when he told her he needed his other razor.

"If you bring it in to work today, I'll pick it up sometime before work tomorrow morning. My good one just broke."

"I'm sorry to hear that." She tried to sound up, so he wouldn't know how depressed she had been. "How's the rest of you?"

"Fine." He sounded cool. "You?"

"I'm okay. I miss you."

"Apparently not enough. Unless something's happened I don't know about." He went right back to the same point. There was no compromise, no change, no sign of his relenting, and Adrian wondered suddenly if Zelda was wrong, and their marriage was actually over. It was difficult to believe, but so was his moving out because of the baby.

"I'm sorry you still feel that way, Steven. Do you want to come over this weekend and talk?"

"There's nothing to talk about, unless you've changed your mind." It was almost childish the way he kept insisting that she get an abortion, "or else."

"So now what? We live like this forever and I send you an announcement when the baby is born?" She was being face-tious, but he wasn't.

"Maybe so. I thought we should wait awhile, to see if you feel any differently in the next few weeks. And if you decide to . . . to go ahead . . . then I'll start looking for an apart-ment."

"You're serious, aren't you?" She still couldn't believe it.

"I am. And I think you know that. You know me well enough to know that I'm not going to play games for long, Adrian. Make up your mind and let me know so we can both get on with our lives. This isn't healthy for either of us." She couldn't believe it. He wanted to be notified as soon as possible so he could start dating and look for an apartment. She just couldn't believe it.

"It certainly isn't healthy. And it will certainly be interest-ing to explain to your son or daughter." But the barb didn't hit its mark. He didn't seem to care what she told them.

"Why don't we let it rest for a few weeks and you can let me know how you feel by then. I'm going to New York next week, and back to Chicago after that. In fact, I'm going to be travel-ing a lot in the next few weeks. Why don't we leave it until mid-June. That gives you a month to figure out what you want to do." She wanted to kill herself, that was what she wanted to do . . . or kill him . . . she didn't want to wait until June while he decided whether or not he wanted to divorce her.

"You're really ready to throw away two and half years over a temper tantrum?"

"Is that all you think it is? Then you don't understand very much, do you, Adrian? It's a question of life's goals, and yours and mine are apparently very different."

"You're right, I'm not willing to sell my soul, or my child, for a new stereo and a trip to Europe. This isn't a game show we're talking about. This is our lives, and our child. I keep saying that to you, but I don't really think you hear me."

"I hear you, Adrian. But I don't agree with what you're saying. I'll talk to you in a few weeks." And then, "Call me if you have a change of heart in the meantime."

"How will I find you?" And what if there was an emergency or if she needed him? He was still her next of kin on all her papers. That made her feel panicky too. Everything did. She felt totally abandoned.

"Call my office, they'll know where I am."

"Lucky them," she said sarcastically.

"Don't forget my razor."

"Yeah . . . sure . . ." He hung up then and she sat in her kitchen for a long time, thinking of what he had said, and wondering if she'd ever known him. She was beginning to doubt it.

She brought the razor to the office that day and the next day it was gone. He had picked it up that night and hadn't left so much as a note for her, but she didn't say anything about it to anyone. Not even Zelda. And she hadn't told anyone at work that Steven had left her. It was too embarrassing. And when they got back together in a few weeks, it would be less awkward if no one had known he'd been gone, except Zelda.

And when Zelda heard about the call, she assured Adrian that he would come to his senses in no time.

But in the meantime, the weekends were endless. He didn't call, and suddenly Adrian realized that she was so used to being with him that she didn't know what to do without him anymore. And Zelda had her own life to lead. She had a new twenty-four-year-old boyfriend, who was a model. And as concerned as she was about Adrian, she was busy with her own life, and Adrian didn't want to be a bother.

It was quiet while Adrian knew Steven was away, and in some ways it was restful. She stopped expecting to hear from him, or to run into him. She didn't lie in bed hoping he'd come to the apartment to pick something up, or turn up in her office to tell her that he'd been a fool and he was desperately sorry. She knew he was back in Chicago by then, and she hadn't heard from him in weeks, but maybe when he came back, they could finally sort things out and get back to the business of living.

In the meantime, she felt as though everything was on hold. She worked, she ate, she slept, she didn't go anywhere, she didn't go out. She didn't even go to a movie. She'd been back to see the doctor once, and he told her the pregnancy was progressing well, and everything was normal. Everything except the fact that her husband had left her, she thought to herself. But she was relieved that the baby was all right. It had come to mean everything to her now, it was all she had left . . . one tiny little being to love . . . a being who wasn't even born yet. She got so lonely once or twice, she was even tempted to call her parents, but she resisted the urge, and she had lunch at work with Zelda from time to time. At least she knew, and Adrian could talk about the baby.

She ran into Bill Thigpen at work, too, and now that they had officially met, they seemed to run into each other everywhere, in the elevator, the parking lot, and they had even run into each other again at the Safeway. She had run into him at the apartment complex, too, and he didn't tell her he had seen her husband leaving their town house several weeks before with a staggering amount of luggage. He knew he had to be going somewhere but he didn't ask where, and Adrian didn't mention it when they saw each other at the pool. Instead they talked for a long time about favorite books and movies they had loved, and he told her about his children. It was obvious that he was crazy about them and she was touched by the way he spoke about them.

"They must be very important to you."

"They are. They're the best thing in my life." He smiled at Adrian, admiring her as she put on more suntan oil. She looked happier than she had when he'd run into her before, and somehow more peaceful, but she still seemed very quiet. He wondered if she was always like that, or if she was just a little shy with strangers.

"You don't have kids, do you?" He assumed she hadn't, because he had never seen any with her, and she hadn't mentioned it, and she would have surely said something if she had children. Most people in the complex didn't. There were a few couples with newborns, but usually they moved out and bought larger homes after they had babies.

"No." She seemed to hesitate and he looked at her, wondering if there was more to the story. "No, we don't. I . . . we . . . we've both been pretty busy working."

He nodded, wondering what it would really be like to be friends with her. He hadn't been friends with a woman in a purely platonic way in a very long time, and in an odd way, there were times when she reminded him of Leslie. She had the same kind of seriousness and intensity, the same decent values about many things. And Bill found himself wondering more than once if he would like her husband. Maybe they could all be friends. All he had to do was forget that he thought she was sensational-looking and had a really sexy body.

He forced himself to look into her eyes then and discuss her future in the newsroom. It was one way to forget how she looked in her bathing suit, and the fact that he would have given anything to lean over and kiss her.

"When is your husband coming back?" he asked conversationally, and she looked startled by the question. She hadn't known that Bill knew he was gone. Maybe she'd said something, she thought, as she wondered.

"Pretty soon," she said quietly. "He's in Chicago." And when he came back, they were going to try and settle, once and for all, the matter of their marriage. It was no small thing, and she was both dreading his return and looking forward to it. She was dying to see him, but she was also dreading telling him that she had had no change of heart about the baby. The baby was part of her now, and it was going to stay that way, until it was born. And she knew Steven wasn't going to be happy to hear it.

She heard from Steven finally the second Monday in June, at nine o'clock, almost the moment she got to the office. Her secretary said he was on the line, and she pounced on it. She had waited almost a month for his call, and there were tears in her eyes when she heard his voice, she was so happy. But he didn't sound friendly. He asked how she was, and seemed to be asking pointedly about her health. She knew what he wanted to know and she decided to face it squarely.

"Steven, I'm still pregnant, and I'm going to stay that way."

"I thought so," and then, "I'm sorry to hear that." It was a cruel thing for him to say but it was honest. "You haven't changed your mind, then?"

She shook her head as the tears spilled from her eyes and rolled slowly down her cheeks. "No, I haven't. But I'd love to see you."

"I don't think that's such a good idea. It'll just confuse both of us." Why was he so afraid of her? Why was he doing this? She still didn't understand it.

"What's a little confusion between friends?" She laughed

through her tears, and tried to keep things light, but they just weren't.

"I'll move my things out in the next few weeks. I'll start looking for an apartment."

"Why? Why are you doing this? Why don't you come home for a while? Just try it." They had never had a problem getting along, never had fights, never had a problem adjusting when they were first married. Just this. Their baby. And suddenly it was all over.

"There's no point torturing ourselves, Adrian. You've made your decision, now let's just do our best to pick up the pieces and move on." He acted as though she had betrayed him, as though the fault was all hers and he had been decent and reasonable. She wondered if he was actually going to call a lawyer. "What do you want to do about the condo?" Their town house? What did he mean, what did she want to do with it? She was going to live there while she had their baby.

"I was planning to live there, do you have any objection?"

"Not now. But I will eventually. We should both get our money out of it, and then we can each buy something else, unless you want to buy my half from me," but they both knew she couldn't afford it.

"How soon do you want me to move?" He was putting her out on the street, and all because she was pregnant.

"There's no rush. I'll let you know if I want to make any moves in that direction. For the moment, I just want to rent." How nice. How wonderful for him. She felt sick as she listened to him. There was no fooling herself anymore. He was leaving her. It was over. Unless afterward . . . after the baby was born, he came back and realized how wrong he had been. There was always some small hope of that. She wouldn't believe he was really gone until he had seen their baby and then told her he didn't want it. She was willing to wait until then, no matter how neurotic he got in the meantime. And even if he divorced her, they could always get remarried later.

"Do whatever you want," she said calmly.

"I'll be by to get my things this weekend." In the end, he came the following week because he'd had the flu, and Adrian watched mournfully as he packed everything he owned into boxes.

It took him hours to pack it all, and he had rented a small truck that he'd brought with him, and a friend from the office to help him load it. And it was embarrassing for her just being there. She had been so happy to see him at first, but he had been cool and maintained his distance.

She went out for the afternoon when they loaded the truck and she just stayed in her car and drove so she didn't have to watch, or say good-bye to him again. She couldn't stand the pain of it anymore, and he seemed anxious to avoid her.

She went home after six o'clock, and she saw that the truck was gone. She let herself in, and her breath caught as she looked around. When he had said he was going to "take everything," he had meant it. He had taken everything that was technically his, everything he had owned before, and everything he had paid for, or given her even some of the money for, since they'd been married. She started to cry without meaning to. The couch and chairs were gone, the cocktail table, the stereo, the breakfast table, the kitchen chairs, every single thing that had once hung on the walls. There was not a single chair in the living room, and when she went upstairs the only thing left in the bedroom was their bed. All her clothes from the chest of drawers had been carefully folded and put in boxes. The chest itself was gone, as were all the lamps and the comfortable leather contour chair. All his toys and gadgets and devices. She no longer owned a television set, and when she went into the bathroom to blow her nose, she found that he had even taken her toothbrush. She started to laugh at the absurdity of it then. It was insane. He had taken everything. She had nothing left. It was all gone. All she had left was her bed and her clothes, the living room rug, a few odds and ends, which he'd carefully left on the floor, and the set of china she'd had when they were married, most of which was now broken.

There had been no discussion, no argument, no conversation about what belonged to whom, or who wanted what. He had simply taken all of it, because he had paid for most of it, and because he felt it was his and he had a right to. As she walked through the downstairs rooms again, she reached into the refrigerator for something to drink, and found that he had taken all the sodas. She started to laugh again then. There was nothing else she could do. And she was still looking around in amazement when the phone rang. It was Zelda.

"What's up?"

"Not much." Adrian looked around her ruefully. "In fact, absolutely nothing."

"What does that mean?" But she wasn't worried this time. Adrian sounded better than she had in a long time. She almost sounded happy for once. But she wasn't. She was just beyond being depressed anymore. It had all gone too far, and maybe all she could do was laugh now.

"Attila the Hun has been here. Plundering and looting."

"You've been robbed?" Zelda sounded horrified.

"You could call it that, I guess." Adrian laughed and sat down on the floor next to the phone. Life had become very simple. "Steven picked up the rest of his things today. He left me the rug and the bed, and he took everything else, including my toothbrush."

"Oh, my God. How could you let him do that?"

"What do you think I should have done? Gone after him with a shotgun? What am I supposed to do, fight for every dishtowel and hairpin? To hell with it. If he wants it all, he can have it." And if he ever came back, which she suspected he might one day, he would bring it all back anyway, not that it really mattered. She was beyond fighting over coffee tables and couches.

"Do you need anything?" Zelda asked sincerely, and Adrian could only laugh.

"Sure. Do you happen to have a vanload of tables and chairs, a couple of dozen dishes, some tablecloths, a chest of drawers, some towels . . . oh, and don't forget a toothbrush."

"I'm serious."

"So am I. It doesn't matter, Zelda. He wants to sell this place anyway." Zelda couldn't believe it, neither could Adrian. He had taken everything. But she had kept the only thing that mattered to her. Their baby.

She was in surprisingly good spirits in spite of everything and it was only the next day that it hit her. She lay by the pool for a long time, thinking of him, and wondering how their life had managed to fall apart so quickly. Something must have been wrong from the start, something essential must have always been missing, in him perhaps, if not in their marriage. She thought of the parents and siblings he had walked out on years before, the friend he had betrayed, with never a look back. Maybe there was a part of him that just didn't know how to love. Otherwise it wouldn't have been possible for everything to fall apart the way it had. It just couldn't have . . . but it had. In a matter of weeks, their marriage had ended. It depressed her to think about it now, but she had to face the fact that he was gone. She had to make a new life for herself, but she couldn't even begin to imagine how. She was thirty-one years old, she had been married for two and a half years, and she was pregnant. She was hardly dating material, and she didn't want to go out with anyone anyway. She didn't even want to admit to anyone that Steven had left her. She kept telling everyone that Steven was away. Because it hurt too much and it was too embarrassing to say that he had left her.

And when Bill Thigpen turned up at the pool that afternoon with a quizzical look and asked if they were moving out, she flinched visibly and said they were selling their furniture and buying everything new, but even to her something about the way she said it didn't sound convincing.

"It looked like great stuff," he said cautiously as he watched her as they lay by the pool. And there had been something about Steven's face that had reminded him of Leslie when she left him. But Adrian looked perfectly happy as she lay by the pool. She had a book in her hands, and she was holding it upside down as she felt her heart ache, thinking of Steven.

CHAPTER

··12··

THE WEEK THAT STEVEN MOVED OUT, ADRIAN FELT AS though she were in a dream. She got up, she went to work, she went home at night, and every night when she got there, she expected to find him. He would have come to his senses by then. He'd be mortified, apologetic, aghast at what he'd done, and they'd both laugh and go upstairs to bed and make up, and ten years hence he would tell their child how absurd he had been when she told him she was having a baby.

But when she got home at night, he wasn't there. He never called. And she sat on the floor of her living room at night, trying to read, or pretending to shuffle papers.

She had thought about buying new furniture as soon as he left. But she decided not to, in case he came back, which she still thought he would. And what was the point of having two sets of furniture for one apartment?

She kept the answering machine on most of the time, but

she listened to the calls when they came in. They were never Steven, but usually friends, or her office, and lately more often than not it was Zelda. But Adrian didn't feel like talking to her either. Her only concession to keeping her life afloat was going to work and coming home. She felt like a robot getting up and going to work every day, and then coming home, making herself something to eat, and going back for the eleven o'clock news. She felt as though she were on an endless treadmill. There was a blind look of pain in her eyes day after day, and it hurt Zelda to see her like that, but even she couldn't help her. She still couldn't believe what Steven had done, or that he really meant it. But when Adrian tried to call him, his secretary always said he was away, and Adrian wasn't sure if he was or not. There was still that panicky feeling of what would happen to her if she really needed him, but she didn't for the moment, and she knew she just had to sit tight until he came to his senses.

It was Friday of the Fourth of July weekend when she ran into Bill Thigpen at the Safeway again. She had just finished the late news, and she had realized that she had nothing in the house for the next day, and she was off for the whole weekend. He was juggling two carts, and they were filled with charcoal, two dozen steaks, several packages of hot dogs and some ground meat, buns, rolls, and an assortment of things that looked as though he was preparing a picnic.

"Hi," he said as they collided in the aisle where he was picking up two huge containers of ketchup. "I haven't seen you all week," he teased, and he realized as he saw her that he had missed her. There was something so fresh and appealing about her face that he liked just looking at her, and the intensity of her smile always warmed him. "How's the news?"

"The same. Wars, earthquakes, explosions, tidal waves, the usual stuff. How are things on *A Life*?" The thought that he was involved with a soap opera still amused her.

"Same as the news . . . wars . . . tidal waves . . . earth-quakes . . . explosions . . . divorce . . . illegitimacy . . . murder . . . the usual happy stuff. Maybe we're both really in the same business."

She smiled at him then. "Yours sounds like more fun."

"It is . . . sometimes . . ." He had been lonely since Sylvia left the show, but he had to admit that it was stupid. She had been fun to be with from time to time, and they had provided each other with something comfortable and easy. But the truth was that she didn't really improve the quality of his life, nor he hers, and she was better off with her clothing manufac-turer in New Jersey. She had sent a postcard to the cast after she'd left, rhapsodizing about the house Stanley had just bought her. And looking back, he felt foolish now, for being with her. He felt that way now about most of the women he'd gone out with. And he had decided to turn over a new leaf, to get involved only with women who really meant something to him, but the trouble was that most of the women he met just didn't. He met a lot of actresses through his work, a lot of women who just wanted to get laid in exchange for a great part, or an opportunity to appear on his show. They consid-ered it a fair exchange, and the attitude was hardly conducive to high romance. As a result, he hadn't been out with anyone in over a month, and he didn't really miss it. He missed having someone to talk to late at night, someone to bounce his ideas off for the show, someone to share his joys and sorrows with. But he hadn't had that with Sylvia anyway. In fact, he hadn't had that since Leslie.

"Are you coming to the barbecue tomorrow night?" he asked Adrian hopefully. He liked chatting with her, and he was curious about her husband. She had told him he was in advertising, but to Bill he looked more like an actor. But he hadn't seen him in almost two weeks, since he'd loaded all their furniture into a van and removed it. "The Fourth of July barbecue at our apartment complex is my biggest annual culinary moment. You really shouldn't miss it." He waved at the things in his cart and grinned at her. "I do it every year, previously by popular demand, nowadays out of habit. But I make a great steak." He smiled again. "Did you come last year?" He couldn't remember seeing them, although he knew he would have. He wouldn't have forgotten a girl who looked like her, or maybe he had just been distracted.

But she shook her head. "We usually go away. I think last year we were in La Jolla."

"Are you going away again?" He looked disappointed.

She shook her head. "No . . . I . . . Steven . . . my husband is out of town again. In Chicago." The words came out awkwardly, and Bill looked surprised.

"Over the Fourth of July? That's a bummer. What are you doing while he's gone?" He wasn't being fresh, he was just being friendly. They had enjoyed chatting by the pool several times. And he knew she was married, and he understood that.

"Nothing much," she said vaguely, looking nervous.

"Come to the barbecue, then. I'll fix you a famous steak à la Thigpen." She smiled at the look on his face, he looked so eager, and she really liked him.

"I . . . I'm having dinner with friends." She smiled, but her eyes were sad again and he saw it. "Maybe next year."

He nodded, and noticed the clock on the wall behind her. It was twelve-thirty at night, and they were chatting as though it were ten in the morning. "I guess I ought to get the rest of my stuff," he said regretfully. "Come by if you change your mind. Bring your friends. I've got enough for an army."

"I'll try." But she had no intention of going to the barbecue as she shopped for the rest of her groceries. She remembered seeing a sign-up sheet in her mail weeks before, but she had thrown it out. She had other things on her mind at that point, and she didn't regret it. The last thing she wanted was to hang around a bunch of lonely singles at the complex. She had her own life to lead, and she was not interested in cultivating new relationships, or dating. She was married, and all she had to do was wait for Steven to come to his senses. It was just a matter of time, she was sure of it. And when he came back, they could concentrate on having the baby. In the meantime, she had put that on a back burner too. She hardly ever thought of it. She had made her decision and gone ahead with the pregnancy, but now she put it out of her head as much as possible. And it was still easy to ignore for the moment, except for an occasional moment of queasiness, and an increased appetite the rest of the time, and some slight fatigue, she could just about forget that she was pregnant. Nothing showed, and she was only three months pregnant. And all she needed to think about was her work, and waiting for Steven. When he left, at first, she had told herself that it was all over, that he would never come back, and if he did, their relationship would be permanently damaged. But in the past two weeks, she had managed to convince herself that it was a temporary lapse, a moment of insanity in the otherwise healthy life of their marriage. She refused to believe that the fact that he never called, that he wouldn't take her calls whenever she called him, and that she hadn't heard from him since he'd removed everything he owned from their condo was a sign that he felt the marriage was truly over.

She caught a glimpse of Bill again in the checkout line, with three carts loaded to the brim trailing behind him. She carried her own meager purchases to the car, feeling sad again. She could fit a week's groceries into two bags now. Everything about her life seemed to have shrunk, ever since Steven had left her. And when she got home, the apartment seemed so ridiculously empty. She put her groceries in the fridge, turned off the lights, and went upstairs where the box spring and mattress still sat on her bedroom floor, and her clothes still sat in the boxes on the floor where Steven had left them. She lay in bed awake for a long time, thinking of him, and wondering what he was doing all weekend. She was tempted to call, to beg him to come home, to tell him she'd do anything . . . anything except an abortion. That wasn't the issue anymore. The issue was carrying on her life without a husband. It still surprised her to realize how lost she felt, how bereft and deserted. After two and a half years, she couldn't even re-member what she used to do with herself to keep amused before they were married. It was almost as though she had never lived alone before, as though there had never been a life before Steven.

It was after three when she finally fell asleep, and almost eleven when she woke up the next morning. It was the one thing she seemed to do easily now. She could sleep all day if she had the chance. The doctor said it was because of the baby. The baby. The idea of it still seemed unreal. The tiny being who had cost her her marriage. And yet she still wanted it. Somehow it still seemed worth it.

She got up and showered, and made herself some scrambled eggs at noon, and then she paid some bills and did her laundry. She looked around the empty living room and laughed. It was certainly easy keeping house these days. There was nothing to straighten out, or dust, no spots to worry about on the couch, no plants to water, he had taken those too. All she had to do was make her bed and vacuum. And at two-thirty, she went out to the pool, and saw Bill busily preparing for the barbecue. He was conferring with two other men Adrian had seen be-fore, and there were two women putting a big bowl of flowers on a long picnic table. This was obviously going to be an event, and she was almost sorry she wasn't going. She had nothing to do, and nowhere to go. Zelda was in Mexico with a friend, and all Adrian could think of to do was go to a movie.

She waved at him as she headed toward the pool, and lay

floating in the hot sun for a long time and then she lay down on one of the lounge chairs on her stomach. And he came and sat down next to her a little while later, looking happy but exhausted.

"Remind me not to do this next year," he said, as though they were old friends. But they were actually growing familiar just from running into each other regularly in all the same places. They lived and worked in the same place, and even bought their groceries at the same midnight market. "I say that every year." He lowered his voice conspiratorially. "These people drive me crazy."

She grinned as she looked at him. He was funny without meaning to be. And he looked wonderfully harassed, but he also looked as though he enjoyed it. "I'll bet you have fun doing it."

"Sure I do. Sherman probably had a hell of a good time with the march on Atlanta. But it was probably a lot simpler to orchestrate than this." He leaned closer to her so no one else would hear him. "The guys figure that maybe this year I should have bought lobster, they said I've done steak, burgers, and hot dogs for the last three years and it's getting old. The women think we should be having it catered. Christ, did you ever go to a catered picnic when you were a kid? I mean whoever heard of a catered hot dog for the Fourth of July?" He looked outraged and she laughed, the idea amused her. "Did you go to a Fourth of July picnic when you were growing up?"

She nodded. "We used to go to Cape Cod. When I was older we went to Martha's Vineyard. I loved it. There's nothing like that out here. That wonderful feeling of summer towns and perfect beaches and the kids you play with every summer and wait all year to see. It was great."

"Yeah." He smiled at his own memories. "We used to go to Coney Island. Ride the roller coaster and look at the fireworks.

My father would do a great barbecue at night on the beach. When I was older, they had a house on Long Island and my mom did a real picnic in the backyard. But I always thought the Coney Island days were better." He still had wonderful memories of the things he had done with his parents in his childhood. He had been an only child and he had been crazy about his parents.

"Do they still do that?"

"No." He shook his head, thinking about them, but the memories were all tinged with warm feelings now, the grief was gone. The shock of losing them was long over. He looked at Adrian, he liked what he saw in her eyes, liked the way her dark hair fell over her shoulders. "They died. After they got the house on Long Island. A long time ago . . ." Sixteen years. He'd been twenty-two when his father died, twenty-three when his mother died a year later. "I think I do this whole Fourth of July production because of them. Maybe it's my way of saying I remember." He smiled warmly at her. "It seems like most of us out here don't have families, we have girl- friends and kids and dogs and friends, but our aunts and uncles and parents and grandparents and cousins are all somewhere else. I mean, seriously, have you ever met anyone who grew up in L.A.? I mean someone normal, who doesn't look like Jean Harlow and is actually a guy who happens to be madly in love with his sister?" She laughed at him. He was so real, and so deep, and so solid, and at the same time he was lighthearted and funny. "Where are you from?"

She wanted to say L.A., but she didn't. "I'm from Connecti- cut. New London."

"I'm from New York. But I hardly ever get back there. Do you get back to Connecticut sometimes?"

"Not if I can help it." She grinned. "It stopped being fun right about the time they stopped going to Martha's Vineyard, when I went to college. My sister lives there, though." She and her kids and her incredibly boring husband. It was so hard to relate to any of them, and ever since she'd married Steven, she didn't even try. She knew she had to tell them about the baby one of these days, though, but she wanted to wait until Steven came home, after he came to his senses. It would be just too complicated to explain that she was pregnant and he was gone, let alone why, all of which was why she was trying to put the pregnancy out of her mind for the moment.

"It's too bad you can't make it tonight," he said forlornly. She nodded, embarrassed about the lie, but it was just easier not to go. She got in the pool and swam again, and he went back to his preparations for dinner, and a little while later he went back to his apartment to marinate the steaks. The barbecue sounded like a big production.

And at five o'clock she went back to her apartment and lay on the bed and tried to read. But she couldn't concentrate. Lately it was hard to do that most of the time, there were just too many things on her mind. And as she lay there, she could hear the sounds of the barbecue going on. At six o'clock people started to arrive. There were music and laughter, and she could hear what sounded like about fifty people. She went out on her deck after a while, where she could hear the noise and smell the food, but they couldn't see her, and she couldn't see them. But it all sounded very festive. There was the clinking of glasses, and someone was playing old Beatles albums and music from the sixties. It sounded like fun, and she was sorry she hadn't gone. But it was too awkward to explain why Steven wasn't there, even though she had said he was in Chicago on business. But it was embarrassing going out alone. She hadn't done it yet, and she wasn't ready to start. But smelling the food was making her desperately hungry. She finally went back downstairs and looked in her fridge, but nothing looked as good as what she smelled, and all of it was too much trouble to cook. She was suddenly dying for a hamburger. It was seven-thirty and she was absolutely starving. She hadn't eaten anything since breakfast, and she wondered if she could just slip into the group, grab something to eat, and disappear again. She could always write Bill Thigpen a check later for what she owed for participating in the dinner. There was no harm in that. It wasn't really like going out. It was just eating. Like going to a fast-food place, or Chinese takeout. She could even grab a hamburger and bring it back. She didn't have to hang around for the party.

She hurried upstairs again, looked in the mirror in her bathroom, combed her hair, pulled it back and tied it with a white satin ribbon, and then she slipped on a white lace Mexican dress she and Steven had bought on a trip to Acapulco. It was pretty and feminine and easy to wear, and hid the tiny bulge that didn't show but made it difficult to wear slacks or jeans now. But it still didn't show in her dresses. She put on silver sandals and big dangly silver earrings. She hesitated for just a moment before she went back downstairs. What if they all had dates, or if she didn't know anyone at all? But even if he had a date, at least she knew Bill Thigpen, and he was always easygoing and friendly. She went downstairs then, and a moment later, she was hovering at the edge of the crowd near one of the big picnic tables where the food was laid out. There were groups of people clustered everywhere, laughing and chatting and telling stories, some were sitting near the pool, with their plates on their laps, or drinking wine, or just relaxing and enjoying the party. Everyone looked as though they were having a good time, and standing at the barbecue in a red-and-white-striped shirt and white pants and a blue apron over them was Bill Thigpen.

Adrian hesitated, watching him, he was handing out steaks with a professional air, and chatting with everyone as they came and went, but he seemed to be alone, not that it really mattered. And she realized then that she didn't even know if he had a girlfriend, not that it really made any difference. But somehow she had assumed that he wasn't involved with anyone. He had always seemed so unencumbered. She walked slowly over to him, and his face broke into a broad smile as he saw her. He took it all in, the white lace dress, the shiny dark hair, her big blue eyes, she looked beautiful, and he was thrilled to see her. He felt like a kid, with a crush on a neighborhood girl. You didn't see her for weeks, and then suddenly you turn a corner, and there she is, looking gorgeous and you feel like a fool, stumbling all over yourself, and then she's gone again, and your whole world is over, until you meet again. Lately, he'd been beginning to feel as though his whole life, or the only worthwhile part of it, was just a series of chance meetings.

"Hi, there!" He blushed, and hoped she thought it was the heat of the barbecue. He wasn't sure why, but she was the first married woman he'd ever had a serious crush on. And it wasn't just that he liked looking at her. He liked talking to her too. The worst of it was that he liked everything about her. "Did you bring your friends?"

"They called at the last minute and said they couldn't make it." She told the lie with ease, and looked up at him happily as he watched her.

"I'm glad . . . I mean . . . yeah, actually, I am glad." And then he pointed to the meat he was cooking. "What can I do for you? Hot dog, hamburger, steak? I recommend the steaks myself." He tried to cover what he felt with ordinary pastimes, like cooking dinner. He really did feel like a kid every time he saw her. But so did she. And the funny thing was, all she wanted to do was talk to him. He was always so easy to be with and to talk to.

She had been dying for a hamburger a few minutes ago, but suddenly the steaks looked terrific. "I'll have a steak please. Rare."

"Coming right up. There's lots of other stuff over there on the table. Fourteen different kinds of salad, some kind of cold souffle, cheese, Nova Scotia salmon, I don't do anything with that stuff. I'm the barbecue specialist, but go take a look and by the time you get back, I'll have your steak for you." She did, and he noticed that she had piled her plate with the salads and shrimp and other things she had found at the buffet table. She had a healthy appetite, which was surprising, given how thin she was. She was obviously very athletic.

He put the steak on her plate, offered her some wine, which she declined, and she went to sit near the pool, and he hoped she'd still be there by the time he finished cooking. It was half an hour later when he finally decided he'd done his bit, everyone had been served, and most of the guests had had seconds. Another man, from a condo near his, offered to take over for him, and Bill gladly accepted and went to find Adrian, happily polishing off dessert, as she sat quietly by herself, listening to the people chatting around her.

"How was it? It couldn't have been too bad." The steak had disappeared, along with everything else she'd had on her plate. She looked embarrassed and laughed self-consciously.

"It was delicious. And I was starving."

"Good. I hate to cook for people who don't eat. Do you like to cook?" He was curious about her, what she was like, what she did, how happy she was with her husband. It shouldn't have mattered to him, but it did. He could hear alarm bells go off in his head, and he was telling himself to stop, but another, stronger, voice told him not to.

"Sometimes. I'm not very good. I don't have much time to cook." And no one to cook for. Now, at least. But Steven wasn't much of an eater anyway. He had always preferred just making a salad.

"Not if you do both shows on the evening news. Do you

come home between shows?" He wanted to know everything about her.

"Most of the time. Unless there's something really dramatic going on and I can't get out between shows. But generally I come home around seven and go back around ten or ten-thirty. Then I'm home again around midnight."

"I know." He smiled. That was usually when they ran into each other in the Safeway.

"You must keep pretty long hours too." She smiled. She was toying with the apple pie on her plate, embarrassed to devour it while he watched her.

"I do. Some nights I just sleep on the couch at the office." It made him great company, as any number of women would have been happy to tell her. "Our scripts change so fast some-times, it shifts everyone's position in the show. It's kind of a ripple effect, and sometimes it's difficult to keep up with. But it's fun too. You ought to see the show sometime." It sounded like fun to her and they talked about the show for a while, how it had started in New York ten years ago, and eventually he had moved it to California. "The hardest thing about coming out here was leaving my boys," he said quietly. "They're such great kids. And I really miss them." He had talked about them before, but there was still a lot about them she didn't know, just as there was about their father.

"Do you see them much?"

"Not as much as I'd like to. They come out for school vaca-tions through the year, and for about a month in the summer. They'll be here in two weeks." His whole face lit up as he said it, and it touched her to see it.

"What do you do with them when they're here?" Working the way he did, taking care of two young children couldn't be easy.

"I work like a fiend before they come, and then I take four weeks off. I go in once in a while just to keep an eye on things, but basically, much as I hate to admit it, the show does fine without me." He smiled almost sheepishly over the admission. "We go on a two-week camping trip, and we hang around here for about two weeks. And they love it. I could do without the camping trip. My idea of camping is a week at the Bel-Air Hotel. But it means a lot to them and they love getting grubby and uncomfortable and sleeping in the woods. Actually, we do that for about a week, and we stay at a hotel somewhere for the other week. Like the Ahwahnee in Yosemite, or we go up to Lake Tahoe. A week is about all I can handle in a tent and a sleeping bag, but it's good for us. It keeps me humble." He laughed, and Adrian finished her apple pie as she listened. They were nervous with each other this time, but it wasn't so much nervous as a kind of excitement. This was the first time they had been together, intentionally, in a social setting.

"How old are they?"

"Seven and ten. They're great kids. You'll see them here at the pool. They think California is all about swimming pools. It's a lot different than Great Neck, outside New York, where they live with their mother."

"Do they look like you?" Adrian asked with a smile, she could imagine him with two little teddy bear clones, just like him.

"I'm not sure. People say that the little guy does, but I think they both look like their mother." And then, nostalgically, "We had Adam right away. And it was rough. Leslie had to stop dancing, my wife was a dancer on Broadway then. And I was really struggling. There were times when I really thought we'd starve, but we never did. And the baby was the best thing that ever happened to us. I think that's one of the few things we still agree on. Adam and the show happened at about the same time. I always felt that it was providence sending us what we needed for him, and for us. The show has been good to me for a long time." He looked appreciative as he talked about it, as though he didn't really deserve it but had been very lucky, and he knew it. And it struck Adrian as she listened to him how different he was from Steven. His children meant a lot to him, and he was very modest about his success. The two men had very little in common. "What about you?" he asked her then. "Do you think you'll stay with the news?"

"I don't know." She had wondered about that, too, and maybe when she took her maternity leave, she would have time to think about what she wanted to do with the rest of her life, other than being a mother.

"I think about starting another show sometimes. But I never seem to have time to think about it, let alone do it. *A Life* is still a full-time commitment."

"Where do you get the ideas for it?" she asked, sipping at a glass of lemonade someone had poured her.

"God knows." He smiled. "Real life, my head. Anything that comes to mind and seems to fit. It's all about the kinds of things that happen in people's lives, all poured into one pot and stirred around. People do the damnedest things, and get into the most incredible situations." She nodded pensively. She knew exactly what he meant, and he was watching her expression. And when she looked up again, her eyes met his, and she looked as though she was about to say something, but she didn't.

The crowd was thinning by then, and people had come over to thank him several times. He seemed to know everyone, and he was always friendly and pleasant. She liked being with him and was surprised by how comfortable she was with him. She could imagine herself telling him almost anything. Almost. Except maybe about Steven. In some ways, she felt like a failure because he had left her.

"Would you like a drink?" he asked. He had been nursing the same glass of wine all night, and when she declined, he set it down, and poured himself a cup of coffee. "I don't drink very much," he explained. "If I do, I can't work all night."

"Neither can I." She smiled. There were several young couples sitting nearby, talking and laughing and holding hands, and she felt lonely as she watched them. It suddenly brought it home to her that she was alone again. After building her relationship with Steven for the last five years, she was alone, and there was no one to hold her and love her.

"So when is your husband coming back?" he said easily, almost sorry that he was. He was a lucky guy, and Bill still wished that Adrian wasn't married.

"Next week," she said noncommittally.

"And where is he again?"

"New York," she answered quickly, and suddenly something struck Bill as she said it.

He looked at her quizzically. "I thought you said he was in Chicago." He looked puzzled, and then backed off when he saw the look of panic on her face. Something had upset her terribly and he wasn't sure what it was, as she quickly changed the subject.

"This was a great idea," she said as she stood up, looking around nervously. "I had a wonderful time." She was leaving and he was desolate. He had frightened her off and he didn't want her to go. Without thinking, he reached out and took her hand, wanting to do anything to make her stay near him.

"Please don't go, Adrian . . . it's such a nice night, and it's so good being here, just talking to you." He looked very young and very vulnerable and it touched her heart the way he said it.

"I just thought . . . maybe . . . you had other plans . . . I didn't want to bore you . . ." She looked uncomfortable, but he still didn't know why, as she sat down again and he kept her hand in his own, wondering what he was doing. She was married, and he didn't need the heartbreak.

"You don't bore me. You're wonderful, and I'm having a terrific time. Tell me about you. What do you like to do? What's your favorite sport? What kind of music do you like?"

She laughed. No one had asked her that in years, but it was fun talking to him, as long as he didn't press her about Steven. "I like everything . . . classical . . . jazz . . . rock . . . country . . . I love Sting, the Beatles, U2, Mozart. I used to ski a lot when I was growing up, but I haven't in years. I love the beach . . . and hot chocolate . . . and dogs . . ." She laughed suddenly. "And red hair, I've always wanted red hair," and then suddenly she looked wistful. "And babies. I've always liked babies."

"So have I." He smiled at her, wishing that he could spend a lifetime with her instead of just an evening. "My boys were so cute when they were babies. I left when Tommy wasn't even a year old. It almost killed me." And there was the memory of real pain in his eyes as he said it. "I'd like you to meet them when they come out in a couple of weeks. Maybe we could all spend an evening together." He knew that if he and Adrian were going to be friends, he was going to have to make friends with her husband. It was the only relationship available to them, and he was willing to do that just to get to know her. And maybe her husband was nicer than he looked, although Bill considered it unlikely.

"I'd love to meet them sometime. When do you go on your camping trip?"

"In about two weeks." He smiled. "Actually, we're driving up to Lake Tahoe, via Santa Barbara, San Francisco, and the Napa Valley. Then we'll camp for five days when we get there."

"It sounds like a very civilized trip." She had expected something a lot more rugged.

"I have to do it that way. Too much fresh air comes as a shock to my system."

"Do you play tennis?" she asked hesitantly. It wasn't that she was comparing them, but she was curious. With Steven, it was almost a fixation.

"If you can call it that," he apologized. "I'm not very good."

"Neither am I." She laughed, longing for another piece of apple pie, but she didn't dare go and get it. He was going to think she was a real pig if she ate any more, but the whole dinner had been delicious. The "cleaning-up" crew was putting things away, and it had grown dark as they sat by the pool. The crowd had thinned out even more, but she was enjoying his company and she hated to leave, although she was beginning to think that she should. And then suddenly, high in the sky, the fireworks began. They were being set off in a park nearby and they were beautiful as everyone stopped and watched, and Adrian watched, too, like a delighted child, as Bill smiled at her. She was so beautiful, and so warm and so gentle. She looked like a little girl with her face turned up to the sky, but a very pretty one, and he had an overwhelming urge to kiss her. He had had that urge before, but it was becoming more acute each time he saw her.

The show went on for half an hour and exploded finally with a wild shower of red, white, and blue that went on and on and on, seemingly forever. And then the sky went dark again, with only the stars high above, and the black powder left from the fireworks and the little wisps of smoke falling slowly to earth, as Bill sat close to her and caught a whiff of her perfume. It was Chanel No. 19 and he liked it.

"Are you doing anything this weekend?" he asked hesitantly, not sure how proper it was for him even to ask her. But they could be friends after all. As long as he controlled himself, there was no real reason why they couldn't be together. "I thought maybe you'd like to go to the beach or something," since she had already told him that she liked beaches.

"I . . . well . . . I'm not sure . . . my husband might be

coming home . . ." She was embarrassed, and yet she wanted to go, and she wasn't sure how to handle the invitation.

"I thought he was in New York . . . or Chicago . . . until next week. I'm sure he wouldn't mind. I'm very respectable. And it's better than sitting around here all weekend, as long as you're not working. We could go down to Malibu, I have friends who let me use a house there. They live in New York, and they just keep the place for the hell of it. I keep an eye on it for them. You'd enjoy it."

"Okay." She smiled at him, not sure why she was doing it. But there was something irresistibly comfortable and appealing about the man, and she stood up then, and prepared to go back to her own apartment. "I'd like that."

"Does eleven sound about right?"

She nodded. It sounded perfect. But also a little scary. "I'll walk you back to your place." He had taken the apron off long since, and he looked nice as he walked her back to her town house. And when she got to her front door, she unlocked it carefully, and opened it just a crack without turning the light on. She didn't want him to see how empty her place was.

"Thanks a lot, Bill. I had a wonderful time. Thank you for inviting me tonight." It was a lot better than sitting at home, feeling sorry for herself and wondering what Steven was doing.

"I had a good time too." He smiled, feeling happy and relaxed and contented. "I'll come by tomorrow around eleven."

"That's all right. I can meet you at the pool."

"You don't need to do that. I'll pick you up here." He sounded firm and she looked nervous, as she prepared to leap through her front door before he could look inside it.

"Thanks again." She gave him a last look, and then suddenly disappeared, like an apparition. One minute she was standing in front of him, and the next, she was inside, and the door was closed, and he wasn't sure how she'd done it. It was one of the fastest good-byes he'd ever said, and he walked slowly back to his own place, smiling.

CHAPTER

••13••

Bill picked Adrian up the next day at precisely
eleven o'clock, and she was waiting outside when he came, in
jeans, a big floppy shirt, a sun hat, and sneakers. And she was
carrying a beach bag full of towels and creams and books and a
Frisbee, and he laughed when he saw her.

"You look about fourteen in that outfit." The shirt had been
Steven's, but she had always loved it, and it covered the fact
that her jeans were getting a little tight, but Bill seemed not to
notice as he watched her.

"Is that a compliment or a reproach?" she asked comfortably. She was completely at ease with him as she started to
follow him across the complex.

"A compliment. Definitely." And then he stopped, he had
forgotten something, as he turned to her. "Do you have any
sodas at your place? I'm fresh out." And everything was
closed. It was Sunday.

"Sure."

"Why don't we grab some, in case we get thirsty." She started back toward her place and he followed her, but when they got to her front door, she stopped, and glanced over her shoulder.

"I'll just run in and get them. Why don't you stay here with our stuff?" She acted as though she thought someone was going to run off with her beach bag.

"I'll come in and give you a hand."

"No, that's okay. The place is a mess. I haven't had a chance to clean since Steven left . . . the other day, I mean . . . when he went to New York . . ." Was it New York or Chicago, Bill wondered, but he didn't say anything, because it was obvious she didn't want him to go in, so he didn't.

"I'll wait for you here," he told her at the front door, feeling a little foolish. She left the front door unlatched, but closed so he couldn't see in. It was as though she was hiding something in her apartment. And a moment later, he heard a tremendous crash, and without thinking twice, he dashed inside to help her. She had dropped two soda bottles, and they had sprayed soda all over the kitchen. "Did you get hurt?" he was quick to ask with a worried glance, and she shook her head as he grabbed a towel and helped her clean the mess up.

"That was really stupid of me," she said. "I must have shaken them without noticing, and then I dropped them." It took them two minutes to clean it up, and he hadn't noticed anything unusual about the place, until she brought out more sodas and he realized there was no furniture in the kitchen. The place where a kitchen table might have been was empty and there was a lonesome stool sitting near a phone at the other end of the kitchen. And as they walked through the living room, it was almost eerie. There was no furniture anywhere, and there were marks on the walls where paintings had been, and then he remembered Steven loading furniture into a van almost two months before. She had said they were selling everything and buying new, but in the meantime, the apartment looked bare and depressing. But Bill didn't say anything, and she was quick to explain it. "We ordered a lot of new stuff. But you know what it's like. Everything is a ten- to twelve-week delivery. It'll be August before this place looks halfway decent again." In truth, she hadn't ordered anything. She was still expecting Steven to come home with the old stuff he'd taken with him.

"Of course. I know how that is." But something didn't ring true, and he wasn't sure what it was. Maybe they were too poor to buy furniture. Maybe it had all been repossessed. People in Hollywood lived like that. He had a lot of friends who did. And it was obvious that Adrian was embarrassed about something. "It's a nice, clean look," he teased. "And it's easy to take care of." She started to look embarrassed again and then he teased her gently. "Never mind. It'll look great when all the new things come." But in the meantime, it certainly didn't. The place looked somehow abandoned.

And as soon as they left, they both forgot about it, and they had a wonderful time at the beach. They stayed until after five when it started to get cool, talking about theater and books, and New York and Boston, and Europe. They talked about children and politics and the philosophies behind both soap operas and news shows, the kinds of things he liked to write, and the short stories she had written in college. They talked about everything and they were still talking as they drove back to the complex in his woody.

"I am in love with your car, by the way." He had admired her MG the first time he'd ever seen it.

She looked pleased at the compliment. "So am I. Everybody's been trying to get me to give it up for years, but I can't. I love it too much. It's part of me."

"So is my woody." He beamed. This was a woman who

understood what it was to love a car. This was a woman who understood many things, like caring and loss, and integrity and love and respect, and she even shared his passion for old movies. The only thing wrong with her, aside from her eating enough for two families, was the fact that she was married. But he had decided to ignore that and stop chafing about it, and just enjoy her friendship. It was rare for men and women to be friends, without expecting anything sexual out of it, and if they were able to have a real friendship, he was going to consider himself very lucky. "Do you want to have dinner on the way back? There's a great Mexican place in Santa Monica Canyon, if you want to try it." He treated her like an old pal, someone he had known and loved forever. "Or you know what, I've got a couple of those steaks left. Do you want to go back to my place and I'll cook you dinner?"

"We could cook them at my place." She had been about to say that she should probably go home, but there was no reason to, and she didn't really want to. It was a lonely Sunday night, and she was enjoying him too much to give it up just yet. And there was no real reason why she couldn't have dinner with him.

"I'm not exactly dying to eat them off the floor," Bill teased her. "Or is there more furniture I haven't seen yet?" Only her bed, but she didn't say that.

"Snob. Okay," she said playfully, feeling like a kid again, "let's go to your place." It had been years since she'd said that to a man. She and Steven had gone out for two years before they'd gotten married. And here she was, suddenly, five years later, having dinner at a man's apartment. But she had to admit, she didn't mind it. Bill Thigpen was terrific. He was smart, interesting, kind, and he gave her the impression of taking care of her, no matter what he did. He was always concerned if she was thirsty, hungry, wanted an ice cream, a soda, needed a hat, was warm enough, comfortable, happy, all the while keeping her amused with his stories about his soap opera, or the people he knew, or his two boys, Adam and Tommy.

And when she walked into his apartment, she saw yet another dimension. There were beautiful modern paintings on the walls, and some interesting sculptures he had collected in the course of his travels. The couches were leather and comfortable and well worn. The chairs, enormous and soft and inviting. And in the dining room there was a beautiful table he had found in an Italian monastery, a rug he had bought in Pakistan, and everywhere there were wonderful pictures of his children. There was a feeling of hominess about it that made you want to browse around, walls of books, a brick fireplace, and a beautifully designed large country kitchen. It looked more like a home than an apartment. He had a cozy den where he worked, with an old typewriter almost as old as his beloved Royal, and more books and a big cozy leather easy chair that was all beaten up and well loved and had been his father's. There was an attractive guest bedroom that looked as though it had never been used, done in beige wools, with a big sheepskin rug, and a modern four-poster, and there was a big colorful bedroom for the boys, with a bright red bunk bed that looked like a locomotive, and his own bedroom was just down the hall, all done in warm earth tones, and soft fabrics, with big sunny windows that looked out on a garden that Adrian hadn't even known existed in the complex. It was perfect. It was just like him. Handsome and warm and loving. And parts of it looked a little worn from the hands that had touched it. It was the kind of place where you wanted to stay a year, just to look around and get to know it, and it was in sharp contrast to the expensive sterility she had shared with Steven until he walked off with all of it, leaving her nothing but the bed and the carpet.

"Bill, this is gorgeous," she said in open admiration.

"I love it too," he admitted. "Did you see the kids' bed? I had it made by a guy in Newport Beach. He makes about two a year. I had a choice between that and a double-decker bus. Some English guy bought that, and I got the locomotive. I've always had a thing for trains. They're so great and old-fashioned and cozy." He sounded as though he were describing himself as Adrian smiled at him.

"I love it." No wonder he had laughed at her empty apartment. His had so much character and so much warmth. It was a great place to live or to work.

"I've been trying to talk myself into buying a house for years, but I hate moving and this is so comfortable. It works. And the boys love it."

"I can see why." He had given them the biggest room, even for the little time they spent with him, but to him, it was worth it.

"When they're older, I hope they spend more time here."

"I'm sure they will." Who wouldn't, with a father like him, and a home like this to come back to. It wasn't that the place was so big or so luxurious, it wasn't. But it was warm and inviting, and it was like a big hug just being there. Adrian felt it as she settled into the couch to look around, and then went out to the kitchen to help him with dinner. He had built most of the kitchen himself, and he was adept at cooking their dinner.

"What can't you do?"

"I'm rotten at sports. I told you, I'm terrible at tennis. I can't build a fire in the wilderness to save my life. Adam has to do it whenever we go camping. And I'm terrified of airplanes." It was a short list compared to what he could do.

"At least it's nice to know that you're human."

"What about you, Adrian? What aren't you good at?" It was always interesting to hear what people said about themselves.

And he asked her as he carefully chopped fresh basil for their salad.

"I'm not good at a lot of things. Skiing. I'm so-so at tennis, terrible at bridge. I'm lousy at games, I can never remember the rules, and I don't care if I win anyway. Computers, I hate computers." She thought seriously for a moment. "And compromising. I'm not good at compromising about what I believe in."

"I'd say that's a virtue, not a flaw, wouldn't you?"

"Sometimes," she said thoughtfully. "Sometimes it can cost you a lot." She was thinking about Steven. She had paid a high price for what she believed in.

"But isn't it worth it?" he said softly. "Wouldn't you rather pay a price and stick to what you believe? I always have." But he had ended up alone, too, not that he really minded.

"Sometimes it's hard to know what's the right thing to do."

"You do your best, kid. Give it your best shot, and hope that does the trick. And if the folks don't like it," he said, shrugging philosophically, "them's the breaks." Easily said. But she still couldn't believe what had happened as a result of her sticking to her guns with Steven. But it wasn't as though she'd had a choice. She couldn't have done otherwise. She just couldn't. There was no reason to. It was their baby, and she loved him. It made it impossible to get rid of it, on a whim, just because it frightened Steven. So she had lost him.

"Would you stick by what you believed in, no matter how someone else felt?" she inquired as they sat down to the big juicy steaks he had cooked while she watched him. She had set the table and made the salad dressing, but he had done everything else, and the dinner looked delicious. Steak, salad, garlic bread. And there were strawberries dipped in chocolate for dessert. "Would you hold your ground no matter what?"

"That depends. You mean at someone else's expense?"

"Maybe."

He puzzled over it for a minute, as she helped herself to the salad. "I think it would depend on how strongly I felt. Probably. If I really thought my integrity was at stake, or the integrity of the situation. Sometimes it doesn't matter how unpopular you get, you just can't deviate from what you believe in. I know, as one gets older one is supposed to get more moderate, and in some ways I have. I'm thirty-nine years old and I'm more tolerant than I used to be, but I still believe in taking stands about things I care about. It hasn't exactly won me a lot of gold stars, but on the other hand, my friends know I'm someone they can count on. That counts for something, I think."

"I think so too," she said softly.

"How does Steven feel about that?" He was getting curious about him. Adrian spoke of him very little, and he wondered how well they got along. He wondered how much they had in common. Just looking at them, they seemed very different.

"I think he feels strongly about his opinions too. He's not always very good about understanding other people's positions." It was a classic understatement.

"Is he good about adjusting to you?" Their marriage intrigued him. He wanted to get to know them both, since he couldn't have her to himself, much as he would have liked to.

"Not always. He's good at . . ." She groped for the words and then found them. "Parallel living is the best way I can describe it. He does what he wants to do, and he lets you do what you want without interfering." As long as he thought you were doing the right thing to get ahead. Like working in the newsroom.

"Does that work?"

It used to. It did. Until he moved right out of her life because he didn't like what she was doing. She took a breath as she tried to explain it to Bill Thigpen. "I think to make a marriage really work, you need more involvement than that, more intertwining, more interaction. It's not good enough to let each other be, you have to be something together." It made sense to him, and he had figured that out when he was married to Leslie. "But I only figured that out recently."

"The kicker is that that's the whole secret. A lot of people will just let you do your own thing. The trouble is, there are damn few people who want to do the same thing you do. I've never found one. Though I have to admit, I haven't looked very hard in the last few years. I haven't really had the time, or the inclination," Bill added.

"Why not?" She was intrigued by him too. He looked as though he would have enjoyed being married.

"I think I was scared. It hurt so much when Leslie and I broke up, and when she took the boys, I think I never really wanted to do that again. I never wanted to care enough to get that hurt, or have kids someone could take away from me just because the marriage didn't work out. It never seemed fair to me. Why should I lose my kids because the woman I'm with no longer loves me? So I've been careful." And lazy. He had purposely not looked for a serious relationship for a long time, telling himself he wasn't ready.

"Do you think she'll ever give the boys to you full-time, or more than for just a few visits a year?"

"I doubt it. She thinks she has a right to them, that they're hers, and she does me a big favor by sending them to me at all. But the truth is, I have as much right to be with them as she does. It's just bad luck that I happen to live in California. I could always go back to New York, to see more of them, but I always thought it would be even more difficult there. I don't want to be ten blocks away from them every night and wonder what they're doing. I want to wander in and out of the room when they're talking on the phone, doing their homework, hanging out with their friends. I want to stand there and get tears in my eyes when I watch them sleep at night. I want to be there when they're sick and throw up and have runny noses. I want to be there for the real stuff. Not just a few weeks of Disneyland and Lake Tahoe in the summer." He shrugged then, he had let her see what really mattered to him, and it really touched her. "But I guess this is all I get. So I make the best of it. And most of the time, I just accept what is, and I don't worry about it. I used to want to have more kids one day, so I could 'do it right' this time, but I think by now I've decided it's better this way. I don't want to go through all that heartbreak again, in case someone decides they don't really like me."

"Maybe next time you could keep the kids." She smiled sadly and he shook his head. He knew better than that.

"Maybe next time it would be smarter not to get married and have children." Which was what he'd done for years, but deep down he knew that wasn't the answer either. "What about you? You think you and Steven will have kids?" It was a rude question, but he was so comfortable with her that he dared to ask it.

She hesitated for a long time before answering, not sure what to tell him. For a moment, she almost wanted to tell him the truth, but she didn't. "Maybe. Not for a while. Steven is . . . a little nervous about children."

"Why?" That intrigued him. Bill thought they were one of the best things about marriage. But he had the benefit of experience, so he knew that.

"He had a difficult childhood. Dirt-poor parents. And Steven decided early on that kids were the root of all evil."

"Oh, dear. One of those. How does that sit with you?"

She sighed, and her eyes met Bill's. "It's not always easy. I'm hoping he'll come around eventually." Like by January maybe.

"Don't wait too long, Adrian. You'll be sorry if you do. Kids are the greatest joy in the world. Don't deprive yourself of that, if you can help it." To him not having children seemed like a real deprivation.

"I'll tell Steven you said so." She smiled, and Bill smiled back, wishing Steven in perdition. It would have been so nice if she were free. He reached out and touched her hand, not in a rude way, but a warm one.

"I've had a wonderful day, Adrian. I hope you know that."

"So have I." She smiled happily, and polished off the last of her steak, as Bill finished the salad.

"You know, for a skinny girl, you eat a lot." He was honest, but teasing, and they both laughed.

"I'm sorry. It must be all the fresh air." She knew exactly what it was, but she wasn't going to tell him.

"You're lucky, you can afford it." She had a beautiful figure, and he liked the fact that she obviously enjoyed his cooking.

They talked until about ten o'clock and she helped him clean up the kitchen, and then finally he walked her back to her place, carrying her beach bag. It was another beautiful night, with hardly any smog in evidence, and the stars bright above their heads. She hated to go back to work the next day. It was the Monday holiday of the three-day weekend, but she had said she would work because she had nothing else to do except wait for Steven to call. And they had their regular show to do, despite the long weekend. And so did Bill.

"Do you want to come by tomorrow?" Bill asked. "I should be in the office by eleven."

"It sounds like fun."

"We go on the air at one o'clock. Come on by if you've got a free minute. You can watch the show, tomorrow's a good one." She smiled at the prospect, and this time she was more relaxed as she unlocked the front door. He had already seen her empty apartment. There was nothing to hide from him anymore. Except the fact that Steven had left her two months before, and she was pregnant.

"Do you want to come in for a cup of coffee?" He was about to say no, and then decided he would, just to prolong the evening. She pulled up the stool and offered it to him as she made the coffee and then they went to sit in the living room with their cups. They sat on the floor because there was no-where else to sit. It was a far cry from his comfortable apartment.

He noticed as they sat that she didn't even have a TV or a radio, and then he noticed where there had obviously been stereo speakers. And it dawned on him suddenly that she wouldn't have sold them. There was absolutely nothing left in her place except the light fixtures and the doorknobs, a carpet in the living room, and an answering machine on the floor next to the telephone. Even the table the phone had been on was gone. It looked like a place someone had just emptied to move out of, and as he thought the words, he suddenly realized what must have happened. He looked at her as though he had spoken the words out loud, with a startled look, as the idea came to him, but he didn't dare ask her.

"So, tell me about your new things," he said, pretending to be casual, as he stood up and looked around. "What kind of stuff did you order?"

"Oh . . . just the usual stuff," she said vaguely, continuing to tell him about the politics of the newsroom, hoping to distract him.

"You know, your layout is so different than mine, the two places don't even look remotely related."

"I know. It's funny, isn't it? I noticed that, too, when I was at your place." She was smiling at him. She had had a beautiful day, and she was totally relaxed, even though she was a little bit tired.

"How much space do you have upstairs?"

"Just one bedroom and a bath," she answered easily. "We have another bedroom downstairs, but we never use it."

"Can I look?" He had let her wander all over his place and it would have seemed unfriendly not to let him do the same, so she hesitated but nodded, as he walked easily upstairs and asked her for another cup of coffee. And when she went into the kitchen to get it, he whipped like whirlwind through her bedroom. It was as empty as he had expected it would be, and within seconds he pulled open both closets, and looked through the bathroom cabinets, pawed through the boxes where she kept her clothes, and discovered what he had just figured out but she had never told him . . . unless his things were downstairs, and suddenly Bill wanted to know, but he didn't dare ask her. A sixth sense told him that there was a reason why Steven Townsend had loaded all their belongings into a van, and it wasn't because they were going to redo the apartment. Even their wedding picture in the silver frame now sat on the bedroom floor with the room's only lamp, because Steven had taken the dresser and all the tables.

"I like the layout," he said, as he came downstairs looking relaxed, his whirlwind tour having gone unobserved, and then he asked her if he could use the bathroom. There were two doors on the main floor, and he intentionally chose the one he suspected was a closet, pulled open the door and found it empty save for a handful of empty wooden suit hangers. And then he opened the right one, and closed it behind him as he walked into the bathroom. He opened all the cupboards as quietly as he could, and then flushed the toilet and ran the water. And as he sat down to coffee with her again, he watched her eyes for the answers to his questions. But there were none. She had said nothing to him. She had pretended for weeks that Steven was away on business, that he would be back in a few days, that everything was fine, although she had admitted over dinner that it wasn't always easy. She was a beautiful girl, and he knew she was married. She was still wearing her wedding ring. But he also knew one other thing, after going through every closet in the place. For whatever reason she chose not to disclose, Steven Townsend was no longer living with his wife, and when he had left, he had taken everything with him.

Bill thanked her after a little while, and told her he'd drop by the newsroom the next day. And he thought about her all the way back to his place on the other side of the complex, and he just couldn't figure it out. He was intrigued by her all over again. What was she doing? And why? Why was she pretending that everything was okay? Why hadn't she admitted that she was living alone? What was she hiding? And why? But as he thought of the empty closets again, Bill Thigpen was delighted.

CHAPTER
··14··

THE COMPLICATED PLOT TURNS HE WAS ABLE TO DEVISE were seemingly endless. And at the moment, Helen's husband, John, had recently been arrested for the murders of Helen's sister Vaughn, played by the late, great Sylvia before she moved to New Jersey, and a young drug pusher named Tim McCarthy. Vaughn's drug habit had been unveiled, her misdeeds as a call girl had come out and caused untold embarrassment, and a politician with whom she was involved, and for whom she had had an abortion years before, was about to become publicly disgraced when the entire scandal hit the papers. But even more important, the fact that Helen was pregnant was about to be unveiled on the show that week. And the real scandal was that the baby wasn't her husband's, a blessing in this case, but it would be the cause of untold guessing games in kitchens across the country for the next several months. Who was the baby's father? Eventually, John and

Helen's marriage would end in divorce when he wound up in prison serving a life sentence for the two murders, and the identity of Helen's baby's father would become known, but not for a long time. And Bill was going to have a lot of fun with it in the meantime.

And he was thinking about Adrian as he drove to work the next day, and why she hadn't told him that Steven had left her. It was not unlike one of his plots, although undoubtedly the reasons were a lot simpler. And there was always the possibility that he was wrong, he realized, but he didn't see how he could be. There wasn't a stitch of men's clothing in the house. No men's toiletries, no after-shave, not even a razor. He was absolutely sure of it after his brief investigation. But what was she hiding? And why hadn't she told him? He wondered if she was embarrassed, or if perhaps she just wasn't ready to go out yet.

He didn't have time to think about it once he got to work. One of the actors was sick, and the show's two principal writers were having a major battle, and it was almost noon before he had time to catch his breath, and he wanted to go to Adrian's show and pick her up to bring her on the set to watch their one o'clock airing.

And in her office, Adrian was coping with the discovery that a local senator's son had been wantonly kidnapped and murdered late the night before. It was a shocking case, and the family was devastated. The boy had been only nineteen, and the entire newsroom was depressed. And it made Adrian sick to see the tapes as they came in. He had been dumped on his parents' front steps with his throat cut.

She was busy assigning editors to work on what had come in, and reporters to speak to close family friends, when someone told her there was a call holding for her, but she didn't recognize the name when she picked it up, and she had no idea who it was. It was a man named Lawrence Allman.

"Yes?" She was in the middle of a dozen things and writing notes frantically as she waited to hear what he wanted.

"Mrs. Townsend?"

"Yes."

"Your husband asked me to call you." Her heart stopped as she heard the words.

"Has he been in an accident? Is he all right?"

He felt sorry for her as he listened to her reaction. This was not a woman who didn't give a damn about her husband, contrary to what Steven had said to Allman. "No, he's fine. I'm representing him. I'm an attorney." She looked confused as she listened to him. Why was a lawyer calling her and why had Steven told him to call her?

"Is something wrong?" For a moment he didn't know what to say to her. She seemed so totally unprepared for what was coming. He felt like a real heel for calling.

"I thought perhaps your husband might have said something to you. But I see that he hasn't." Or maybe she was playing games with him, but he doubted it. She didn't sound like that kind of person. "Your husband is filing for dissolution and he wanted me to work some things out with you, Mrs. Townsend." She felt as though she had been on a roller coaster all day and it had just stopped and pitched her right out of her seat, leaving her heart back about a dozen miles. She could hardly catch her breath as she listened to him. Steven was doing *what*?

"I'm sorry, I . . . I don't understand. What is this all about?"

"A dissolution, Mrs. Townsend." He spoke as gently as he could. He was a decent man and this wasn't his favorite case. Steven had not been totally reasonable when they had discussed this. "A divorce. Your husband wants a divorce."

"I . . . I see . . . Isn't this a little hasty?"

"I asked him if he would like counseling with you, but he insists that there are irreconcilable differences."

"Can I refuse? . . . the divorce, I mean . . ." She closed her eyes, trying not to cry into the phone, or the man would think she was a fool. She had to stay calm, but she was losing control just listening to him. She couldn't believe it. Steven wanted a divorce, and he wouldn't even talk to her about it. He had had a stranger call to tell her.

"No, you can't refuse," the attorney explained. "Those laws changed a long time ago. You or Mr. Townsend have the right to file for dissolution without the consent of your spouse." She couldn't believe what she was hearing, and there was more to come. "There are some additional papers Mr. Townsend would like you to be aware of."

"He wants to sell the condo, doesn't he?" There were tears brimming in her eyes as she listened to him, watching her whole world crumble around her.

"Well, yes. But he's willing to give you three months grace before you put it on the market, unless, of course, you'd like to buy him out, at fair market value." She felt nauseous as she stood in her office. He wanted a divorce. And he wanted to sell the condo. "But that isn't what I was referring to. Mr. Townsend is willing to be reasonable about the town house. I was referring . . ." He seemed to hesitate. He had tried to talk Steven out of it, but he could only assume that the baby's paternity was in question when Steven wouldn't listen to reason. "There are some other papers he's asked me to draw up. I'd like you to take a look at them."

"What exactly do they deal with?" She took a sharp breath and tried to regain her composure as she wiped the tears off her cheeks with trembling fingers.

"Your . . . uh . . . the baby. Mr. Townsend would like to renounce any parental rights antenatally. It seems a little premature and I must tell you, I've advised him against it. It's a highly unusual procedure. But he's adamant that that's what he wants. I've drawn up some papers in draft form, just for you to look at. They state simply that he renounces any claim to the baby. As a result, he would have no visiting rights, no claim to the child once it's born. It would not bear his name. You will be asked to resume your maiden name, as well as give it to the baby. His name would not appear on the birth certificate when it was born, and, of course . . . you and the child would have no legal or financial claim on Mr. Townsend. He wanted to offer some monetary remuneration for this, but I explained to him that according to California law, we couldn't do that. There must be no exchange of money in the renunciation of his parental rights, or it could later be declared invalid." She was crying openly by then and she didn't give a damn if the attorney heard her.

"What do you want from me? And why are you calling me today?" she sobbed. "This is a holiday, you aren't even supposed to be working." Steven had told him she would probably be at the station and it would be a good time to catch her, so he was calling from home. He felt like a complete louse telling her those things, but he had thought it would be worse if she had just opened her mail and found it all there. Steven had insisted he had no quarrel with her, she had been a good wife and they had been happy, he just didn't want the baby and she had refused to abort it. It seemed perfectly sensible to him. And Larry Allman wondered if Townsend was a little less than reasonable on this issue. But it wasn't his job to argue with him. He had tried to talk him into counseling, urged him to reconsider, and not to do anything about the termination of parental rights until after the baby came and he at least saw it. But Steven didn't want to hear it.

"Mrs. Townsend," Allman said quietly, "I'm really sorry. There's no pleasant way to advise you of all this. I thought that maybe a phone call . . ."

"It's not your fault," she sobbed, wishing that she could change the way Steven felt, but she knew that she couldn't. "Is he okay?" she asked, much to Allman's amazement.

"He's fine. Are you okay?" That seemed a lot more important.

She nodded as fresh tears rolled down her face. "I'm fine."

He smiled sadly at his end. "I'm sorry to say, you don't sound it."

"It's been a lousy day . . . the senator's son and now this." It was all so awful. And she had had such a nice weekend before this. "Do you suppose . . ." She felt stupid asking him, but she wanted to know if he thought Steven would change his mind once the baby was born, and maybe if he saw it. She still believed somehow that seeing it would change everything. After all, he was the baby's father. "You don't think he'll change his mind, do you? I mean . . . later . . ."

"He could. He's taking some awfully radical steps. Unduly so in some areas, but he seems determined to do this now, for his own peace of mind. He wants everything spelled out, and legally resolved."

"When will the divorce go through?" Not that it mattered anyway. What difference did it make? Except that it would have been nice to be married when she had the baby.

"Actually, he filed the petition two weeks ago. Which means that your divorce will be final . . . I'd say in mid-December." Wonderful. Two weeks before the baby. With no father's name on the birth certificate. It was great news. She certainly was glad he had called her.

"Is that all?"

"Yes, I . . . I'll be sending the papers out to you tomorrow."

"Thank you." She wiped her eyes again, and her hands were still shaking.

"We'll be in touch in a couple of months about the condo.

And, of course, any request for spousal support would be appropriate coming from your attorney."

"I don't have an attorney. And I don't want spousal support."

"I think you should seek the advice of counsel, Mrs. Townsend. You have a right to spousal support according to the laws of California." And he thought she'd be foolish if she didn't take it. He hated the case. And he would have liked to see her at least get some money out of Steven. He owed her something, for chrissake. And he had advised him of that himself. "We'll be in touch."

"Thank you." She listened as the phone clicked in her ear after he said good-bye, and she stood holding the receiver for a long time, as though a voice was going to tell her it was all a mistake, and they were just kidding. But they weren't kidding. Steven had filed for divorce, and he wanted papers saying that he was giving up his rights to the baby. It was the worst thing she had ever heard, and she stood shaking as she thought about it, wondering what she was going to do now. In truth, nothing had really changed. She still had the town house for a while, he still had all their furniture, and she still had the baby. But everything really had changed. She had no hope anymore, except a wild fantasy that eventually he would come back and fall head over heels in love with his baby. But even she knew that that was unlikely. What she had to face now was having the baby alone, keeping her job, finding a new home, and at least buying a couch to sit on. But more important, she had to face the fact that he was divorcing her, and legally, the baby would have no father. It was a stunning blow and her shoulders shook as she cried, as she finally put down the receiver. She had her back to the door, and she hadn't heard anyone walk into her office. And seeing only her back turned toward him, he hadn't realized that she was crying.

She turned slowly, her face awash with tears, and through the mist, she saw him. It was Bill Thigpen.

"Oh my God . . . I'm sorry . . . I didn't mean to . . . I guess this is a bad time." It was a mild understatement, and she tried to smile through her tears as she groped under her desk for a tissue.

"No . . . I . . . actually . . . it's fine . . ." And then she collapsed into a chair, crying again, as she buried her face in her hands. "No . . . it's awful." There was no way to explain it to him, and she didn't really want to. "It's just . . . I'm not . . . I can't . . ." She wasn't even making sense, as he walked over to her, and gently rubbed her shoulders.

"Take it easy, Adrian. It's going to be all right. Whatever it is, it'll get straightened out sooner or later." He wondered if she had gotten fired, or someone had died. She was shaking all over, and she looked green, she was so pale. For a moment, he wondered if she was going to faint. But he made her take a deep breath and handed her a glass of water, and a minute later, she looked better. "Looks like you've had a terrific morning." He looked down at her sympathetically and she tried to smile, but it was a meager effort.

"It's been quite a day." She blew her nose again, and looked at him with a mixture of embarrassment and appreciation. "First the senator's son is kidnapped and killed and we get five thousand miles of tape on it, with close-ups of his throat slit." She sobbed again, thinking of it. "And then . . ." She hesitated, looking up at Bill, debating whether or not to tell him. But there was no point to keeping it a secret anymore, and even if it was her fault, it hadn't been her decision. "And then . . . I got this stupid call from my husband's attorney." Her eyes filled with tears again and her voice trembled as she said it.

"Attorney? What's he calling you for? And today's a holiday anyway."

"That's what I said."

"What did he want?" Bill scowled, feeling protective of her.

She took a deep breath, clutching the tissue in her hand as she looked away. She couldn't face Bill as she said it. "He called to tell me that my husband . . ." her voice dropped so low, he could barely hear her. ". . . just filed for dissolution. Two weeks ago, actually."

For a moment, Bill was startled. But it was more the way she said it than the fact of it. It was her obvious anguish over it that touched him. He had actually figured out the night before that they were separated, and he was relieved now that it was out in the open. But he was sorry for her, she seemed to be taking it very hard, as though it was something she hadn't expected.

"Does that come as a shock to you, Adrian?" His voice was very gentle.

"Yes." She sighed and looked up at him, as he stood leaning against her desk, looking sympathetic. "I never really thought he'd do it. He said he would. But I didn't believe him."

"How long has this been going on?"

"About six weeks . . . maybe seven. . . . He moved his things out about three weeks ago. My things too." She smiled as they both thought of the empty apartment. "That doesn't matter to me. I just didn't think . . . I didn't want . . ."

"I understand. I felt that way when Leslie divorced me. I never wanted to get divorced. But all of a sudden she decided it was over. It doesn't seem fair when someone else makes the decision."

"That's kind of what he did." She started to cry again, and she felt embarrassed in front of Bill, but he seemed to take it very calmly. "I'm sorry . . . I'm a mess."

"You have a right to be. Can you go home and take the afternoon off? I'll drive you."

"I don't think I can. We have a special broadcast scheduled tonight before the news."

"Why didn't he call you himself?"

"I don't know." She looked depressed as she sat down at her desk, while he sat on the corner. "I guess he doesn't want to talk to me anymore."

"That's the hard part about getting a divorce when you don't have kids. At least when you have children, you have to talk to each other, until they grow up anyway. Sometimes it drives you nuts, but at least it's some kind of continued contact." She nodded, thinking that they did have a kid. Or at least she did. Steven had "renounced" it. "What do you think brought this on, do you know? Or is it none of my business?"

She smiled sadly. "I know. And it doesn't really matter. He took a position and so did I. I just couldn't do what he wanted, and I guess we each felt we were personally at stake, so we dug in our heels. And he won, I guess. Or we both lost. Something like that. He never gave me a chance once he made up his mind."

"He sounds like Leslie. But there was someone else involved at the time, and I didn't know it. Do you suppose he's involved with someone too?"

"Maybe. But I don't think so. I think this has to do with what he wants in life, and what he doesn't, and all of a sudden our paths became too divergent."

"That's a pretty brutal step to take over 'divergent paths.' " But people were strange and they did strange things. And they both knew it. "I was going to invite you over to the studio for a cup of coffee, but maybe now isn't the time." He was sorry for her, and he leaned over and touched her cheek with a gentle hand as he said it. "Maybe another time."

She nodded, feeling as though she had been beaten by Allman's words. "I've got to go back to work. We're putting together a special about the senator's family. The boy was on the football team at UCLA, a varsity star in high school, and he was very involved in public service. His girlfriend was the governor's niece. This thing is going to tear everyone's heart out." It had hers. And Steven had trampled what was left of it. She felt as though she had died just before lunchtime. "I'm going to be here until one o'clock in the morning, maybe two." And she already looked exhausted.

"Can you take a break? At least go out and get something to eat?"

"I doubt it. I'll come in late tomorrow." All she needed now was to lose the baby. But she couldn't even think of that now. She just had to get through the day, and then another day, and keep on going.

"I'm working late tonight too. We have a lot of new developments happening on the show. Murders, trials, divorces, illegitimate babies. The usual happy stuff. It ought to keep me pretty busy. And I want to make sure our writers get a bunch of scripts done before the boys come."

"Sounds like the story of my life." She smiled weakly, and he kissed her gently on the top of her head as he stood up and prepared to leave.

"Hang in there. I'll come by later. If you want anything, just let me know. Our studio kitchen is filled with food today, because all the restaurants around here are closed."

"Thanks, Bill." She looked at him gratefully, and he slipped out with a wave, as she sat staring out the window for a minute. It was a crazy world. Steven had walked out on her, and abandoned her and their baby. And someone had killed an innocent nineteen-year-old boy with a heart of gold and his life ahead of him, shattered in a single instant.

She went back to work then, and tried to forget her own problems, but she kept thinking of Bill and the amazing support he gave her.

The special she produced went on at five o'clock and was deeply moving, and even people in the newsroom cried as they watched it. They did the full six o'clock broadcast then, and after that, she watched some film to see what they were going to add to the special they were going to run at midnight. It was an endless day, and it was nine o'clock before she found the dinner that Bill had sent over for her. And at midnight, as she sat in the studio, watching the show, she saw him walk in and pointed to a chair next to her own. He sat down quietly and watched with her, obviously deeply moved by the program.

"What a stinking thing," he said as they went off the air. The senator had cried openly in front of the camera. And they had talked about God and His love for all of them, and their faith in Him, but it did little to change the heartbreak of what had happened. And then Bill looked at her. She looked even worse than she had earlier. The day had been endless. "How are you feeling?"

"Tired." The word didn't even begin to encompass what she felt, and he didn't want to intrude on her. But he wanted to help her. She looked too wiped out to even drive herself home, and he offered her a lift back to the complex.

"Why don't you let me take you home? You can always take a cab back here tomorrow. Just leave your car here. Or I can drive it for you if you want." But he didn't trust her on the road. She was so exhausted, she looked as though she might fall asleep at the wheel, and she didn't have the energy to argue with him.

"I'll leave my car here. And thank you for dinner, by the way." He seemed to think of everything, no matter how late he worked himself. They both signed out, and she groaned as she slid across the seat in the comfortable old woody. "Oh, God . . . I feel like I'm going to die."

"You might if you don't get some sleep." He slid behind the wheel, and she was too tired to even talk to him as they drove home on the Santa Monica Freeway. And when they got to the complex, he parked his car and walked her to her door without saying a word. And as soon as she opened the door, he looked at her earnestly as she turned toward him in the doorway. "Are you gonna be okay?"

She nodded, but she didn't look convincing. "I think so." But she had never felt sadder or lonelier in her life. She felt as though Steven had walked out on her all over again.

"Call if you need me. I'm not very far away." He touched her arm then and she smiled and then closed the door, feeling drained. She walked slowly upstairs without even turning on the light. She didn't want to see the bare walls and the empty rooms. And she walked across her bedroom and threw herself across the bed, and then she lay there sobbing, until she fell asleep, with all her clothes on, and Steven's baby inside her.

CHAPTER
··15··

FOR THE NEXT TWO WEEKS, ADRIAN FELT AS THOUGH SHE were in a dream. The papers Lawrence Allman had promised arrived. And she signed them in all the appropriate places. She checked the box that said she wanted no spousal support, and she agreed to put the town house on the market by the first of October. She said very little about it to Bill and he dropped by to see her at her office almost every day, but he didn't press her about going out. He sensed correctly that she was still too upset by the shock of the dissolution. A lot had been happening to her. Things had been wildly hectic at work, and he had his own hands full with changes in the scripts, and the fact that he was trying to clear his desk for his annual four-week vacation.

But he had nonetheless found the time to bring her to the set early one afternoon, and she had watched with fascination as they aired the show. It brought back memories of when she had worked on other shows. And afterward, he introduced her to everyone, and when they went back to his office, she admired his Emmys, and he showed her the program's current bible. In it, he had outlined the show's plot for the next several months, with alternate solutions to problems that might come up, and in a stack on his desk were tentative scripts that he still had to approve. He explained it all to her, and she found herself wishing she could work on a show like this, instead of the news, and as she read some of his notes, she made some very interesting comments.

"Why don't you help me with the bible sometime? . . . or some ideas for scripts? The writers would love a little help, they can always use fresh ideas. It's not easy coming up with five shows a week."

"I can imagine. . . ." And then she looked at him with excitement in her eyes. "Do you mean that, Bill? I mean about doing up some notes for ideas for the show?"

"Sure I do. Why not? You and I can kick some stuff around over dinner one night if you want. I'll give you some of the background material on the characters. You could have a ball." He looked as though he thought it was a great idea, and so did she, and they talked about it all the way back to the newsroom, and they talked about it again the next night when finally, two weeks after the Fourth of July barbecue, she agreed to go out to dinner.

It was a Saturday night, and they had run into each other at the pool early that morning. She looked better than she had in days, and she finally seemed to have absorbed the shock of everything that had happened. And she was still excited about seeing his show the day before. And as she talked about it, she looked prettier than ever.

"Can I interest you in a famous Thigpen steak tonight? Or how about something a little more glamorous, like dinner at Spago?" It was the favorite local hangout of anyone who was anyone in television and the movies. Wolfgang Puck had made it everyone's favorite place to eat, with delicious pasta and pizza and the miracles of nouvelle cuisine that he created.

Adrian had started to come to terms with the realities of her life in the last two weeks, and the prospect of an evening out sounded very appealing. And he had been incredibly patient with her. He had quietly kept an eye on her, without ever intruding. He had dropped by at work, sent food over late at night, offered her a ride once or twice, but never pressed the issue of a date or an evening that she obviously couldn't have coped with. And he had even recommended a lawyer who had taken her affairs in hand and already spoken several times with Lawrence Allman. But after two weeks of mourning and agonizing, she finally felt slightly more alive, and both of Bill's suggestions sounded delightful.

"Whichever you like." She smiled gratefully at him. He had become a good friend in such a short time.

"How about Spago?"

"That sounds great." She smiled, and they both went back to their own places to do the things they had to do, like laundry and paying bills again, a never-ending task, particularly now that Steven was no longer there to do it. Her salary covered everything, but lately she was trying to save as much money as she could for when she'd need it for the baby. Now that Steven wouldn't be contributing anything, she wanted to be a little more careful.

Bill picked her up at eight, and he was wearing khaki slacks, a white shirt, and a blue blazer, and she was wearing a dress that she'd had for years. It was a soft peachy-pink silk that flowed easily from the shoulders. They drove to Sunset chatting about work, and how hectic it had been for both of them in the past few weeks, and it was obvious how excited he was about the boys coming out on the following Wednesday. They were going to spend two days with him in town, and then they were embarking on their big adventure.

Bill ordered pizza made with warm duck, and she had cappelletti with fresh tomato and basil. And for dessert, they shared an enormous piece of chocolate cake, which came to the table drowning in delicious homemade whipped cream. As usual, she ate everything, and Bill teased her again about how well she ate, without apparently gaining weight, but as he said it, she looked a little nervous.

"I should be watching it more than I have been lately." He noticed that she was not pencil thin, but she was not overweight either. The only thing he did notice was that her chest seemed to be enlarging almost daily, but he still wasn't sure if that was due to inaccurate previous observation on his part. "I'm going to start eating nothing but salads."

"How depressing." He took a breath, pretending to suck in his own waistline, and he was solidly built, but he wasn't heavy either. "I'm going to be eating hamburgers and french fries at roadside fast-food places for the next two weeks, it'll be a miracle if I don't regress and wind up with teenage acne." They both laughed at the thought, and he looked at her strangely then. He had been wanting to ask her for weeks, ever since he had found out about Steven filing papers, but he didn't want to ask her too soon. And he wondered now if she was ready to hear it. "I have a funny question to ask you, Adrian." And as he said it, she looked suddenly panicked. "Don't get nervous. It's nothing intensely personal, and my feelings won't be hurt if you say no. I just thought I'd ask in case there's a chance I could talk you into it." He paused as though waiting for a drumroll. "What are the chances of your getting a week or two off from work?"

She suspected what he was going to ask, and she smiled, feeling very flattered. She knew how much his boys meant to him, and the fact that he would be willing to share them with her, or even introduce her to them meant a great deal to her. "It's not impossible. I have about four weeks coming. I was saving the time for a trip to Europe in October." A trip she was certainly not going to take now. She wasn't going anywhere, with anyone. And by then she would be six months pregnant.

"Do you think they'd let you off on fairly short notice? I was wondering if you would like to join us on our pilgrimage north. Any interest? If not, I'll respect your sanity, as well as your judgment. This will not be an easy trip. We are talking about being stuck in a car all day with two small boys, listening to them argue day and night, eating inedible food from one end of California to the other, and winding up in a sleeping bag on the hard ground at Lake Tahoe." But the truth was that he loved it and she knew that, and it was a real honor that he would ask her to join them.

"It sounds terrific." She smiled.

"Think you can get the time?"

"I don't know. I can ask." She wasn't sure what they'd say, but it was possible they would let her off, certainly for a week, if not two, and it sounded like just what she needed.

"If you can't get off for the first week, you could fly straight to Reno and join us at Lake Tahoe for the second. But the first part will be fun too. We're going to stop at the San Ysidro Ranch near Santa Barbara, stay in San Francisco at a funny old hotel we love, and then we're going to the Napa Valley. There are some great little inns, and I thought it would be a nice stop on the way to Lake Tahoe."

"It sounds wonderful." She smiled at him, relaxing for the first time in weeks. "You know, I really owe you an apology. I think I've been in shock for the past two weeks. Ever since I got that call from my husband's attorney." Her saying that brought up a question he'd been wanting to ask her.

"Why didn't you tell me what was happening before that?"

··181··

"I don't know, Bill. I was embarrassed, I guess. It's just . . . I just felt like such a failure when Steven left me." He nodded, he understood that, but it would have saved him some grief had she told him. For the first time in his life, he had actually been considering putting the make on a married woman, and he had been wrestling with himself for days. She could have spared him that, but it didn't matter now. And she looked a lot better. The shock had worn off, and he hadn't seen her cry since the first day. She was made of strong stuff. Much stronger than he even dreamed of.

"Anyway, what do you think about the trip? Do you think they'll let you off?"

"I'll ask them first thing on Monday morning. I think they might. Things are a little slow. And not too many people are out on vacation. Most people prefer the spring and fall, when it isn't so crowded."

"So would I, but I have to go when the boys are out here."

She looked at him, wondering how they would arrange it. She didn't want to sleep in the same room with him, but she didn't even know the boys, and they probably wouldn't welcome the idea of a strange woman sharing their room with them. It would be easy once they were in tents. But it was going to be a little more complicated when they were in hotels, unless she requested her own room and paid for it herself, which was what she was about to suggest to Bill when he started laughing.

"What's so funny?"

"You are. I can see the wheels turning in your head. Are you worried about the sleeping arrangements?"

"Yes." She grinned. "It's not that I don't trust you. I do, but . . ."

"Well, you shouldn't," he confessed. "I'm not sure I trust myself. But I also have a healthy fear of my ex-wife. We'll keep it very respectable. I promise. I'll probably sleep with the boys. I usually do, and they love it. And you can have my room."

"Wouldn't that be an inconvenience for you?"

"No," he said softly, "it would mean a lot to me to have you there. I'd love you to spend some time with me and the boys." He wanted to tell her more about how he felt, but he knew that this wasn't the time. She was still recovering from the blow dealt to her by Steven. And the headwaiter was anxiously waiting for their table. It was a busy Saturday night, and people were lined up all the way down the stairs and out the door. And as they left, she saw Zelda standing there, with the very young star of a TV show. He was a real catch, and Zelda had never looked happier or better. She caught a glimpse of Adrian with Bill and made a circle of her thumb and forefinger, indicating her approval, as Adrian laughed and followed him to the waiting woody. She thanked him for dinner then and turned to him with a serious look.

"I want to thank you for asking me to join you and the children. That really means a lot to me. I know how important they are to you, Bill."

"They are," he said, nodding, and then he turned to look at her more intensely. "And so are you. You're a very special person." She looked away, not sure what to say to him. She couldn't promise him anything. There was still far too much confusion in her own life. If Steven didn't want her with their baby, surely no one else would, and she knew that.

"I appreciate everything you've done for me." She looked away from him as they got into the car. She was thinking of how angry he would be when he found out about the baby, and she didn't want to mislead him.

"Is something wrong, Adrian?" He gently took her hand in his. They were still parked only a few feet from the restaurant and they hadn't moved, but he was worried about her suddenly. There were brief moments when she looked so unhappy and so worried. He knew it was probably the divorce doing it, but it made him sad for her and he wanted to help her through it.

"My life is a little complicated right now," she said cryptically, and he smiled.

"You sound like one of my characters on the show. In fact, I just wrote that line into a script yesterday. And you think you've got troubles. My character is pregnant with an illegitimate baby." The words almost made her choke and she tried to laugh as he started up the woody, but all she could do was smile weakly. Art imitating life again. Sometimes it happened a little too often.

They drove back to the complex then, and he invited her to his place for a cup of coffee. He had a fancy espresso machine, and they sat for a long time in his cozy kitchen.

"I always feel like I ought to look around for a last time before the boys come." He grinned. "From the moment they arrive till the moment they leave, this whole place is upside down, the television is constantly on, there are clothes in every chair, socks on every table, the bathrooms look like they've been hit by a bomb, and there's candy and gum all over everything I own. They're hopeless."

"It sounds happy." She smiled.

"That's a dangerous attitude." He smiled at her. From everything he had seen of her so far, he thought she was the perfect woman. And he had long since decided that Steven Townsend was either a bastard or a fool, but he had been crazy to let her go, much less divorce her. "I can't wait till you meet them."

"Neither can I," she said as she sipped her cappuccino.

"I really hope you can come on the trip."

"So do I." And she meant it. "If I can't, maybe I can fly to Lake Tahoe for a weekend."

"That would be nice. But I'd like a lot more than that." And he thought that two weeks with her and his sons would be absolutely blissful. It was the kind of life he had longed for for the last seven years, the kind of life he'd lost and thought he would never find again. But Adrian was a very special woman. In some ways, he was afraid of his feelings for her, and in other ways, he loved them.

He took her back to her place around twelve o'clock, and he felt like a teenager standing in her doorway. He was dying to get his hands on her, but he sensed instinctively that she wasn't ready. And Tahoe wasn't going to be the answer to his prayers either. He wouldn't dare make a pass at her while traveling with his children. They were just going to have to wait, or he was. He didn't even know if she was attracted to him, and he was afraid to find out too soon. There was always the possibility that he would scare her off. And she was grateful that he hadn't pressed her. She kissed him chastely on the cheek, and as he walked back to his place, his desire for her almost drove him crazy.

He took her for a drive the next day, and they went to the Ritz-Carlton in Laguna Niguel for Sunday lunch, and then they came back because he had to go to work. His work as usual helped him cope with his constant frustration. Sylvia had been gone for quite a while. And ever since Adrian had walked into his life, he hadn't wanted anyone else. But dreams of her were beginning to haunt him.

She appeared in his studio on Monday just before noon, with a broad grin on her face and a look of victory as he was coping with last-minute changes.

"I can come! They gave me two weeks off!" she announced with glee in a stage whisper that everyone heard, and then she laughed, and two of the actresses giggled. Bill looked at her with awe and delight and then asked her to stay while he finished what he had to do before they went on the air, and then he invited her to watch the show with him from the control booth.

It was an action-packed episode, filled with conflict and emotion. Helen had admitted that she was pregnant by then, but she wasn't telling anyone whose baby it was. John was in jail and the trial was coming up soon. And on the show, Helen made a call to an unknown man, threatening to kill herself if he told anyone that she was carrying his baby. The script was emotionally charged, and the woman who played Helen was an excellent actress. She'd been on the show for years, and she was one of *A Life'* s mainstays. But as Bill watched them perform, he turned to Adrian, pleased with the day's show and he was pleased to see the excitement in her eyes. She loved being around his show and everything about it.

"It's just a great show, Bill." It meant a lot to him that she liked it. And they were still talking about the show when they left the control booth. He introduced her to the actors she hadn't met yet, and she complimented "Helen" for a job well done, and then she went back to her office.

She had the trip to look forward to, and she could hardly wait to meet his kids. She just hoped, she thought with trepidation as she went back to work, that she would fit into her jeans until early August.

CHAPTER
··16··

THE BOYS ARRIVED TWO DAYS LATER, ON A WEDNESDAY AF-ternoon, and Bill went to pick them up at the airport. He had asked Adrian to come along, but she didn't want to crowd them. They didn't have any idea who she was, and they hadn't seen their father since Easter vacation. She had a doctor's appointment that day anyway. And it was the first time that she heard the baby's heartbeat. The doctor put the stetho-scope to her ears, and there was a small device like a micro-phone attached to the other end which he slid across her stomach. The first loud thumping she heard was her own, it was actually the placenta pumping blood to the baby. But beyond that, much more softly, and beating much faster than her own heart, was a smaller one, the tiny pat-pat-pat of the baby. She listened to it with a look of astonishment, and tears came to her eyes when she first heard it.

"Everything sounds fine to me," the doctor told her as she

sat up. Her blood pressure was fine, her weight was okay, too, though she had already gained quite a bit, and there was no denying now that her body was changing. There was an S curve to her suddenly, when she turned sideways in the mirror, and she was starting to wear her dresses a little looser, but so far, unless they knew, no one would have noticed that she was three and a half months pregnant. "Any problems, Adrian?" he asked. She hadn't seen him in a month, not since just before Steven had taken everything he owned out of the apartment and served her with papers.

"Nothing I've noticed," she said quietly. "I feel fine." She did most of the time, too, except now and then when she had a really long day at work, or a late night, then she felt absolutely exhausted.

"How's your husband adjusting to it now?" he inquired as he washed his hands. He fully expected Steven to come around and was sure he had by then. He had no idea what had happened in the last month, and Adrian didn't want to tell him. It was too embarrassing, and admitting that he was gone still gave her an overwhelming feeling of failure. She still hadn't told anyone at work, and the only one she had told, and sworn to secrecy, was Zelda. She insisted that Adrian was foolish not to tell people openly, that she had done nothing wrong, it was Steven who should be embarrassed, not Adrian. But Adrian still pretended to everyone that everything was fine, and claimed that he was doing a lot of traveling. She told her mother that, too, on the rare occasions when they spoke. And other than Zelda, she had told not a living soul about the baby.

"He's fine," Adrian said innocently. "He's away right now." As though the doctor would know he was gone. She stood up and pulled her dress down after the examination. All he did now was weigh her once a month, take her blood pressure; and listen to the baby's heartbeat. He had listened for it the previous month, but it had still been too early for him to hear it.

"Are you going away this summer at all?" he chatted pleasantly, and she was embarrassed about lying to him about Steven.

"We're going away in a few days. Camping at Lake Tahoe."

"Sounds like fun. Don't overdo in the altitude, take it easy a little bit. And if you drive there, stop every couple of hours and walk around, stretch your legs. You'll feel better." But so far she had had an uneventful pregnancy. Uneventful except for the fact that her husband was going to divorce her.

She went back to the office afterward, and as usual, there was a mountain of work for her to do. And she didn't hear from Bill, but she assumed that the boys had arrived safely. He called her in the newsroom late that night, just before the eleven o'clock news, the boys were in bed, and he sounded happy and exhausted.

"It's like having a whirlwind hit this place," he sighed happily, but they both knew he loved it.

"I'll bet they're happy to be here."

"I hope so. I sure am happy to have them. I'm bringing them to work tomorrow for a while, till they destroy the place. Adam is always fascinated by it, he thinks he wants to be a director when he grows up, but Tommy gets a little antsy. I thought maybe we could stop by and say hi, or take you to lunch if you have time. Depending on how your day runs. The boys would like to meet you."

"I can hardly wait to meet them." She smiled, but she was nervous about it too. The boys were so important to him that she was worried about what would happen if they didn't like her. Admittedly, she and Bill weren't deeply involved with each other, but she liked him a great deal, and she sensed that he liked her too. If nothing else, she hoped it was the start of a serious friendship. And there were overtones of something more, but something that, for the moment, due to her circumstances, neither of them had figured out how to handle. Too much had happened to her recently. Too much had gone on. Between the baby and Steven filing for divorce, she wasn't ready for a relationship. And yet, she was growing used to him. And she found that she needed him at unexpected times, and in some ways, she was afraid to need him as much as she might, if she let herself go completely.

"Do you want to come to the set after we air tomorrow, or should we just stop by at the newsroom?" he asked. He had told them about her, and they hadn't seemed surprised. They had met ladyfriends of his before, and they were used to it. They usually told him what they thought of them, and a couple of them had joined them on trips. But it was hard for him to explain to them that this one was different. This was a woman he respected and liked, someone he suspected he could love, but he didn't tell them any of that. He didn't want to scare them.

"I'll drop by the show. I want to see what you're doing to those poor people anyway. How's the one with the illegitimate baby?"

"Drinking too much, understandably. Everyone wants to know who the baby's father is. We've never gotten so much mail. It's amazing how that kind of thing fascinates the viewers. Dubious paternity seems to be an issue of interest to most of us. Or maybe it's just babies." He was hitting close to home again, and just hearing about it made her nervous. Her own baby's paternity was a cause of great concern to her, and she sighed as she realized that she had to get to the control booth.

"I'll see you tomorrow. Say hello to them for me."

"I will," he said, with something warm in his voice that was meant just for her, and she knew it. She was smiling to herself when she ran into Zelda on the way to the control booth.

"How's it going?" Zelda asked pointedly. She worried about

Adrian at times, but they were both too busy to talk to each other very often. Zelda asked her if she heard from Steven from time to time, and she was always horrified to hear that she didn't.

"It's okay." Adrian smiled. She knew Zelda wouldn't give away any of her secrets.

"I saw you with Bill Thigpen the other day." She was curious about that. She knew who he was, and how successful his show had been, and she wondered if anything was going to come of it between him and Adrian, but she suspected that Adrian was still deluding herself about Steven. "Is that anything?" she asked openly, and Adrian looked offended by her bluntness.

"Yes. A nice friendship." She hurried off to the control booth then, and at midnight she went home and fell into bed. She was too tired to even think, and she had a lot to do in the next two days before she left on vacation.

She went to Bill's studio again the next day, just in time to see the show air, and she watched in fascination as the woman who was supposedly pregnant sobbed, talking about her baby. Her husband was still in jail, and she was being blackmailed by a woman who allegedly knew who had fathered her baby. Her husband's trial had just begun, and Helen was still mourning the loss of her sister. It was easy to see why people got caught up in it. It was all so absurd, and so exaggerated, and yet it wasn't. It was exaggerated in just the way real life was, with all its unexpected quirks and turns and sudden disasters. People having accidents and getting killed and cheating on each other and losing jobs and having babies. There was a little more melodrama than in most lives, but not as much as one might have thought, Adrian mused, not if her own life was anything to judge by.

And as soon as she walked into the studio on silent feet, she saw the two boys, standing near Bill, watching the actors in fascination. Adam looked tall for his age, and he was standing quietly right next to his father, with sandy blond hair and big blue eyes, and long, long legs. He was wearing jeans and a T-shirt and high top sneakers. Tommy was wrapped around a chair in a cowboy shirt and a pair of chaps, with the exact same look on his face that Bill wore when he was concentrating on something. They looked almost like twins, except that one of them was much smaller. And just looking at Tommy made you want to run up and hug him. He had soft brown curls, and blue eyes that were even bigger than his brother's. He noticed her first, and stared at her with curiosity instead of watching the show. She smiled at him then, and waved, and he grinned, and tugged at his father's sleeve. He whispered something to Bill, and then Bill turned and saw her. He didn't walk over until they broke for a commercial and then he quickly introduced her before they had to be quiet again. Adam shook her hand with a serious air, Tommy grinned and asked if she was the one who was coming to Lake Tahoe. She only had time to whisper yes, and then found herself stroking his soft curls as she watched the rest of the show, but he didn't seem to mind it.

"That was good, Dad," Adam complimented him as soon as the show was over. And Bill introduced him to all the actors. He had met most of them before, but there were a few new faces, and it touched Adrian to see how proud of them Bill was. He was clearly a wonderful father.

Tommy was climbing on one of the cameras, while Adrian watched, and she noticed that he was keeping an eye on her while pretending not to. Eventually, they all went out to lunch, and over sandwiches, Tommy looked at her squarely.

"How long have you known my dad?" he inquired as Adam frowned at him.

"Tommy, stop that! It's not polite to ask questions."

"That's okay." She smiled at both of them, and tried to

remember. It depended when you started counting. From the first time in the supermarket, or from when they began to make friends. She wasn't sure which to tell them, and decided to go with the former. It made it look as though they had known each other a little longer. "A couple of months, I guess. Something like that."

"Do you go out with him a lot?" Tommy went on, as Adrian grinned and Adam shouted at him to stop.

"Sometimes. We're good friends." But he had spotted something of interest on her left hand, and he was staring at it as she ate her sandwich.

"Are you married?"

There was a long, long pause, and she avoided Bill's eyes. She wanted to be truthful with them, but this wasn't going to be easy.

"I am." She still wore her wedding ring. She couldn't bring herself to take it off. Bill had noticed it, too, but had never said anything, and wouldn't have had the courage of his younger son to ask her to explain it. And then, "I was," she corrected.

"Are you divorced?" This time Adam chimed in, curious about the line of questioning his brother had started.

"No, I'm not," she answered quietly. "But I will be."

"When?" His innocent questions went straight to her heart, but she did her best not to show it.

"Maybe around Christmas."

"Oh."

And then Tommy again. "Why do you still wear your wedding ring? My mom wears one like that," he volunteered, "only bigger, and it has a diamond." Adrian's was narrow and simple and she had always loved it.

"It sounds beautiful. I wear mine because . . . well, I guess I was just used to it." She had thought about taking it off in the past month, but couldn't bring herself to do it.

"Did you want to get divorced?" Adam asked then, and Bill

decided to step in and get her off the hook. Enough was enough.

"Hey, guys, give the lady a break. Tommy, pay attention to what you're doing or you're going to spill that soda." He rescued a can of root beer from him and looked at Adrian apologetically. He hadn't planned to subject her to the inquisition. "I think we owe Adrian an apology. Her private life is none of our business."

"I'm sorry." Adam looked at her remorsefully. At nearly ten, he knew better. But he'd gotten carried away with what his younger brother had started.

"That's all right. Sometimes it's better to ask about things instead of just wondering. I would have told you if I didn't want to answer." She didn't answer his question, though, about whether or not she had wanted the divorce. It was still too painful. "What about you?" She looked at the boys seriously. "Have either of you ever been married?" Adam grinned and Tommy guffawed. "Come on, I told you, now you tell me. What's the story?" She looked from one to the other as they both started to laugh and Tommy was the first to volunteer information.

"No, but Adam has a girlfriend. Her name is Jenny."

"It is *not!*" He looked annoyed and gave his brother a shove, as Adrian watched them.

"It is *too!*" Tommy defended his veracity. "He used to have a girlfriend named Carol, but she dumped him."

Adrian laughed at him, and looked at Adam kindly. "It happens to the best of us." She smiled. "And what about you?" She turned to Tommy. "Any girls we should know about? I mean, if we're going to be friends, you probably ought to tell me." They were the same principles they had applied to her, and she enjoyed teasing them a little bit, as Bill watched her. She was sweet and warm and open with them, just as she was with him. And he started to fall for her all over again. She was terrific.

They chatted through lunch, and Adrian hated to leave them and go back to the office. She invited them to come and visit the newsroom, but she didn't invite them to watch the show later that day. Some of the reels they had gotten in were just too grim, and she didn't want them to see that. But she showed them the studio and the editing rooms, and introduced them to everyone, including Zelda, who glanced at them, and their father, with interest. She questioned Adrian as soon as they'd left and she was back in her office.

"Could this be getting serious?"

"Not likely," Adrian said coolly. After all, Zelda knew she was pregnant. But she also knew that Steven had left her. "Under the circumstances."

"He could do worse." She looked pointedly at her friend. "Hell, nowadays there's no such thing as a virgin." Adrian laughed out loud at what she'd said. That was certainly one way to view it.

"I'll remember that if I ever feel the inclination to start dating." But that wasn't how she viewed her friendship with Bill Thigpen. She liked him a great deal, and if she thought about it, she had to admit that she was attracted to him, but she never felt as though that was the issue. They were just very comfortable with each other, and they had a lot in common. And she thought his kids were terrific. She was really getting excited about their trip now. And she was thrilled to have been asked to join them. It was going to be wonderful to get away on a vacation. She thought of dropping Steven a little note, to let him know where she'd be, and then she realized how ridiculous that was. He wasn't even speaking to her, and he had filed for divorce, he was hardly likely to try to reach her. And if he changed his mind and decided to come home, he would certainly call her office to find her. So she left a memo with Zelda and the manager of the newsroom with a list of the hotels Bill had given her. But she doubted very strongly that anyone would call her. And as she went back to her desk again, she thought of Adam and Tommy's questions over lunch about her wedding ring and her divorce, and whether or not she had wanted to divorce Steven. And then, as they got busy before the evening news, she forgot all about it.

She saw them again the next day, when they dropped by and Bill asked her if she had a sleeping bag. He had just discovered that he only had three and wanted to know if he should buy one.

"Gee, I don't," she said apologetically. She hadn't even thought of it, but he assured her it was no problem. And he had everything else. He told her to bring one decent dress for when they went out, and a warm jacket for the nights at Lake Tahoe.

"And that's it?" she teased. "Nothing else?"

"That's right." He smiled and stood close to her, enjoying the thrill of feeling her next to him. It was getting harder and harder to keep his distance. "Just a bathing suit and a pair of jeans."

"You're going to get awfully tired of me if that's all I bring," she warned, but Bill shook his head as he looked at her warmly.

"I doubt it."

"What about games? Is there anything you gentlemen like? Scrabble? Bingo? Cards?" She had already made a list to herself to pick up a few things to amuse them on the car trip. And Tommy immediately placed an order for comic books and a squirt gun.

"Never mind that!" Bill admonished them, and then they left again. They had some last-minute shopping to do too. They were leaving the next morning.

She packed that night when she went home after the evening news, and when she went back to do the late show, everything was ready and standing at the front door. Her two small bags looked strange in the empty apartment. It looked as though she was finally leaving too. The place was so depressing now that it was empty, and she thought about buying some furniture from time to time, but somehow she just couldn't bring herself to do it. It would make everything so final and there was always the possibility that Steven would come back with everything. And in any case, in a few months she was going to have to give up the apartment. But it wouldn't hurt anything to have a little furniture in the meantime. She just didn't have the time or the desire to buy it.

Bill called her right after the news, and they chatted for a few minutes about the trip. He sounded as excited as she felt. She felt like a kid going to camp for the first time, and for the first time in a long time, she felt really happy. Everything had been so difficult for the past two months, except the time she spent with Bill, that was always so different.

"I thought we'd leave around eight. That should get us to Santa Barbara by ten, and we'll have time for a ride or something before lunch. The boys are dying to go riding." It was the first time she thought of it, and she knew it was one of the few things she shouldn't do, and she wondered if Bill would be disappointed.

"I think I might just relax tomorrow while you gentlemen go riding."

"Don't you like horses, Adrian?" He seemed surprised. He'd been hoping to organize an overnight pack trip when they got to Lake Tahoe. But admittedly, if he couldn't, it wouldn't be a disaster either. He was pretty easygoing about their vacation.

"Not that much. And I'm not an absolutely marvelous rider."

"Neither are we. Well, see how you feel about it tomorrow.

And we'll pick you up at eight tomorrow morning." He could hardly wait, and neither could she, as she lay in bed thinking about it that night, and as she did, she ran a hand over her stomach. It was no longer quite so concave, and there was a subtle roundness that was beginning to protrude between her hipbones. And when she stood up, she could really feel it. Some of her clothes were beginning to feel tight, and she was wondering when people would start to notice. Everything would change for her then, including her relationship with Bill. She knew that there was no way he would want to go anywhere with her once it was obvious that she was pregnant. But at least for the moment, she could enjoy being with him, and she was really looking forward to the vacation. And there was no reason why he would suspect then, as long as she wore loose shirts over her jeans and sweatshirts and sweaters.

They picked her up at exactly eight-fifteen, and everything was ready. Bill picked up both her bags, and she carried a small tote bag with her makeup and toiletries, some snacks for all of them, and the games she had bought for his children.

Bill looked happy and relaxed, and he bent toward her as though he was about to kiss her when he arrived, and then remembered himself and backed away with a shy glance at her, and a look over his shoulder at the two children. He had rented a Wagoneer, and they were fully equipped for all aspects of their trip. The back was piled high with sleeping bags and equipment and valises.

"Is everybody ready?" he asked, beaming at her, as she smiled at him from the front seat next to him, and then glanced back at the two children.

"We are!" they responded in unison.

"Good! Then let's get this show on the road!" He put the car in drive, and they headed north on the freeway. Adam was wearing earphones and listening to a tape, and Tommy hummed to himself as he played with an assortment of little men and soldiers. And Bill and Adrian chatted easily in the front seat. It was just like being an ordinary family, off on their summer vacation, and as she thought of it, Adrian started to giggle. She had a big blue bow in her hair, and a pale blue sweatshirt on, and a pair of ancient jeans and sneakers, and Bill thought she looked like a kid herself as she sat next to him and laughed. "What's so funny?"

"Nothing. I love this. I feel like I'm playing a part in a sitcom."

"Better than a part in a soap." He grinned. "Then you'd have to be married to a man who drinks, with a daughter who had recently run away, and a son who was secretly gay, or you might even be pregnant by someone else, or fighting a fatal disease." He reeled off the possibilities, and although some of them were more apt than he knew, she was still smiling.

"This is a whole lot better."

"It sure is." He put the radio on, and they drove easily to Santa Barbara, and stopped at the San Ysidro Ranch just after ten-thirty. There was an adorable cottage waiting for them, with two bedrooms and two baths, and a cozy living room with a fireplace. It looked like a honeymoon cottage, and Bill put his things in the boys' room, as he had said he would, and gave Adrian the nicer of the two bedrooms.

"Are you sure?" she asked apologetically. She felt guilty taking the prettier room, but he insisted that he was happy sharing with the boys in the other. "I could sleep on the couch."

"Sure you could. Or on the floor. Why don't we do that in San Francisco?"

She laughed at him and helped the boys put their things away, and a few minutes later, Bill and the two boys went to inquire about hiring horses. She had begged off, saying that she would organize everything. They were staying there for two days. And when they got back, everything looked neat and tidy.

"You're a good organizer," he said, smiling.

"Thank you. How was your ride?"

"Lovely. You should have come. The horses are so tame, you could ride them with your eyes closed." Yes, but not with her baby.

"Maybe next time." He sensed that it was something she didn't want to do, so he didn't force it. They ordered lunch and then lay by the pool. But by midafternoon, the boys were bored and chafing for something to do, so Bill organized a game of tennis. It was a perfect match, they were all equally unskilled and laughed so hard they could hardly play at all. Their conclusion was that Adrian and Tommy won, but only by default, and only because Adam and Bill played even worse than their opponents.

They had dinner in the ranch dining room, and then brought the children back to the cottage to bathe and watch television before Bill put them to bed at nine o'clock and told them he didn't want to hear another word, which, of course, he did until almost eleven. They whispered and played, and Tommy came out in tears when he couldn't find the battered rabbit that he always slept with. Adam had hidden it under the bed, and Bill looked happy and tired when the boys finally fell asleep, and he and Adrian sat in the living room and talked in whispers in front of the fireplace.

"They're so cute," she said. She really admired the way he handled them, with more kindness than firmness, and a lot of common sense and love and reason.

"Especially when they're asleep," he agreed. He wanted to tell her she was cute, too, but he didn't dare. One of the children might have woken up and been listening. "Are you sure you won't go bonkers with two weeks of this?"

"Yes, and I'm going to be awfully lonely when I go home again."

"So will I, when they leave," he said pensively, "it's just brutal. It's always like a reminder of the bad old days when I first moved out here after Leslie left me. But at least now I get busy with the show and I readjust pretty quickly." And maybe this year he'd get lucky and get busy with her. He was hoping that would be the case, but he still wasn't sure what Adrian expected. Distance or closeness. He was never quite sure. Friendship, or romance, or both. He was still being extremely cautious so he didn't lose her. She seldom mentioned her husband anymore, but he knew that he was still very much on her mind, just from little things she said. And Adam had had a good point about her wedding band. Just exactly why did she wear it?

"I can't thank you enough for letting me come on this vacation."

"Don't worry. You'll hate me for it before it's over." He grinned, but they both knew that wasn't true. The boys were terrific.

"Is there anything special you want me to do? Stuff I can do to help you with them?"

"They'll let you know."

"I don't know much about kids," she said wistfully, but she was going to have to learn soon.

"They'll teach you everything you need to know. I think what means the most to them," he said thoughtfully as he sat back against the couch next to her, "is honesty. That means a lot to kids. Most kids have a lot of respect for straight shooters."

"So do I." It was something she had liked about him right since the beginning.

"I like that about you too," he said calmly, still speaking softly so they wouldn't wake the children. "There are a lot of things I like about you, Adrian." She was silent for a moment and then she nodded.

"I can't have been much fun in the past few weeks. My life has been kind of up in the air." That was the understatement of a lifetime.

"You seem to be handling it pretty well, all things considered. It's a bitch when you're not the one who wants a divorce. But sometimes I think those things happen for a reason. Maybe there's something better out there waiting for you . . . a situation that might make you a lot happier than your marriage to Steven." It was hard to imagine that, not that they had been so blissfully happy every moment of the day. But she had never questioned what they had. It just seemed right, and as though it was forever. "What did your parents say when he left?" He had already surmised that she wasn't close to them, but he imagined they would be pretty shocked in proper Boston.

She hesitated and then smiled, obviously slightly embarrassed. "I haven't told them."

"Are you serious?" She nodded. "Why?"

"I didn't want to upset them. And I thought that if he came back, it would just be less awkward not to have told them."

"That's one way to look at it. Do you think he will come back?" His heart did a flip as he asked the question.

She shook her head, unable to explain all the complicated ins and outs of the situation. Unwilling more than unable. She did not want to tell him that she was pregnant. "No, but there are some complicated little problems that make the whole thing difficult to explain to my parents." Maybe he was gay, Bill thought. That was a possibility he hadn't even considered. And he didn't want to pry and embarrass her further. That would have explained a lot, and she didn't appear to want to elaborate on the matter.

They chatted on for a while, and eventually they stood up

and said good night, as he looked longingly at her, and smiled as she waved and closed the door to her bedroom. She didn't lock the door that night, because she trusted him and knew she didn't need to. And she didn't wake up until the next day when she heard the boys listening to the television in the living room. It was eight o'clock in the morning. And by the time she came out, showered and fresh, in jeans, a pink shirt, and pink sneakers, Bill had already ordered her breakfast.

"Are pancakes and sausages okay?" he asked, glancing over the paper, as she groaned.

"Great. Except I'll be as big as a house before we ever get to Lake Tahoe." He already knew that she liked to eat, and he admired the fact that it didn't really show, except slightly around her middle.

"You can diet when we get back. I'll join you." He had sausages and eggs and toast and orange juice and coffee, and Adrian ate everything on her plate, and the boys devoured silver dollar pancakes. They went for another morning ride, and that afternoon they walked all over Santa Barbara. She bought the boys a kite, and they drove out to the beach after that to fly it. And they were all windblown and happy when they went back to the hotel for dinner. And that night the boys fell into bed exhausted, shortly after seven. She had forced them to take a bath, and they had growled at her, but Bill had seconded her suggestion.

"What kind of vacation is this anyway?" Tommy looked outraged as she answered.

"A clean one!" But they had forgiven her by the time they went to bed and she told them a long, long story. It was a story she remembered from when she was a little girl, about a boy who had gone far, far across the ocean and discovered a magic island. Her father had told it to her, and she embellished it for them, and they both fell asleep right after she told it.

"What did you do? Give them sleeping pills? I've never seen them conk out like that," he said admiringly.

"I think it was the kite and the beach and the bath, and the big dinner. I'm ready to fall asleep too," she laughed, as he poured them each a glass of wine. It had been a wonderful day, and even a call from the director of the show hadn't upset him. There was a minor problem that was easily resolved by phone, and he was totally relaxed as he sat next to her on the couch and they chatted about his children.

"Did you always know you'd like kids?" she asked.

"Hell, no." He laughed. "When I first heard Leslie was pregnant I was scared stiff. I didn't know one end of a baby from the other." She smiled at his answer. That's how Steven was, but he hadn't stood his ground to face it, he had run away, unlike Bill with Adam. She was still convinced that eventually he would have discovered it wasn't so bad . . . if he'd been willing to try . . . and he might still. . . . "You're good with kids, Adrian. You should have children one day. You'd be a wonderful mother."

"How do you know that?" she asked worriedly. "What if I weren't?" It was something she had worried about a lot lately.

"How does anyone know? You do your best. You can't do more than that."

"It's pretty scary."

He nodded his agreement. "But so is anything in life. How did you know you'd be any good at working on the news, or going to college, or being married? You tried it. That's all you can do."

"Yeah." She smiled ruefully. "And I wasn't so great at that."

"Bullshit, it sounds more to me like he blew it, you didn't. You didn't walk out on him. He did."

"He had his reasons."

"Probably. But at least you tried. You can't spend the rest of your life reproaching yourself or feeling guilty."

"Don't you?" she asked honestly. "Don't you feel somewhat responsible for the failure of your marriage?"

"Yes." He was equally honest. "But I know it wasn't entirely my fault. I worked too hard and I neglected my wife, but I loved her and I was a good husband, and I wouldn't have left her. So some of it is my fault, but not all of it. I don't feel nearly as responsible as I used to."

"That's encouraging. I still feel so damn guilty." She hesitated and then decided to tell him. ". . . And like such a failure."

"You're not. You just have to tell yourself that it didn't work. The next time it will be better," he said confidently, and this time she laughed.

"Oh, 'the next time.' What makes you think there'll be a 'next time'? I'm not that dumb . . . or that brave!" And besides, with a baby on her own, who would want her? She still couldn't envision a future with anyone except Steven. But Bill sat back and hooted at what she'd said to him.

"Are you serious? Do you really think this is it? At thirty-one, you think it's all over?" He looked more amused than sympathetic. "That's the silliest thing I've ever heard." Particularly for a woman who looked and thought and behaved the way she did. Any man in the world would have been lucky to share his life with her, and he would have been more than happy to try it.

"Well, you haven't done it again." She looked at him searchingly and he smiled.

"You're right. But I've never found the right woman." He had also been pretty careful not to.

"Why not?"

"Scared," he admitted to her. "Busy. Lazy. Not in the mood. A lot of reasons. Besides, I was older than you are when I got divorced. I already had two kids. And I knew I didn't want any more children. That took away some of my incentive to look for someone to marry."

"Why not? No more kids, I mean."

"I don't want to have kids and lose them again," he said, almost sadly. "Once is enough. I couldn't do this again. It tears my heart out every time they go back to New York. I wouldn't be willing to take that risk again now." She nodded, thinking that she understood it.

"It must be rough," she said sympathetically.

"It is. Rougher than you can imagine." And then he smiled tenderly at her, and for a moment she wanted to tell him about the baby.

"Sometimes life is more complicated than it looks," she said cryptically.

"That's for sure." He wondered what she meant but didn't press her. He had a feeling that more had happened with Steven than she was willing to tell him. Another woman, another man, some special kind of heartbreak or disappointment.

They talked for a long time that night, sitting close to each other, looking into the fire. It was a cool night and he had lit it early on and it was still burning. The children never stirred, and they were both tired, but neither of them seemed to want to leave the other. They seemed to have a myriad of things to talk about, experiences to relate, opinions to share, and as the night wore on, without thinking, Bill seemed to move closer to her. It was an expression of how he felt about her, and she didn't seem to object, and suddenly near midnight, he looked at her and couldn't remember what he'd been saying. All he could think of was how much he wanted her, and without thinking, he reached out and touched her face with both his hands, and murmuring her name, he gently kissed her. She hadn't been prepared for it, and she was totally surprised, yet she didn't push him away or move. And she found herself kissing him back, and then longing for him as he held her. And then finally, she pulled away and looked up at him sadly.

"Bill . . . don't . . ."

"I'm sorry," he said, but he wasn't. He had never been happier in his life, never wanted a woman more, never loved anyone as he loved her. He loved her with all the emptiness and longing of the past seven years, and all the tenderness and wisdom of his full forty. "I'm sorry, Adrian . . . I didn't mean to upset you. . . ."

She stood up slowly and walked across the room, as though she had to pull herself away physically so she wouldn't do something foolish. "You haven't upset me." She turned and looked at him regretfully. "It's just . . . I can't explain it . . . I don't want to cause you pain."

"Me?" He looked stunned. "How could you possibly cause me pain?" He walked toward her and took her hands in his own, looking deep into the blue eyes he already loved so dearly.

"Take my word for it. I have nothing to give anyone just now. Except headaches."

He smiled at her. "You make it sound very appealing." He wanted to kiss her again, but he forced himself not to.

"I'm serious." And she looked it. She was a lot more serious than he knew. She didn't want to burden anyone with the responsibility of her baby. If Steven didn't want it, then she had no right to burden anyone else with it, certainly not Bill, who had his life and his hands full with his own children. And he had already told her he didn't want more. This was her problem, and no one else's.

"I'm serious, too, Adrian. I didn't want to rush you, because I know the divorce has been a tremendous blow." He looked down at her and everything he felt for her seemed to pour through him. "Adrian . . . I love you. I know this sounds crazy, and it hasn't been long, but I do. I'm not going to press you, and if this is the wrong time, I'll wait . . . but give it a chance, please . . . give me a chance." He was whispering and then he couldn't stop himself from doing it again. He kissed her. And at first she tried to resist him, but only for a moment and then she melted into his arms again, knowing that she was falling in love with him too. But she couldn't. It wasn't fair. She was breathless and looked worried when he stopped and he only smiled and touched her lips with his fingers. "I'm a big boy. I can take care of myself. Don't worry about upsetting me. I can wait till you sort things out with Steven."

"But that's not fair to you."

"It's even less fair not to let this happen. We've been drawn to each other like magnets since we met. Call it kismet, destiny, fate, call it whatever you want. But I feel as though it was meant to be. And I don't want to lose that. You can't run away from it, and I'm not rushing you. I'll wait. Forever, if I have to." It was quite an offer and she was touched to her very soul. She felt the same way about him, but the baby changed everything for her. She had to give Steven a chance to come back, if he changed his mind. And she had to devote all her love and energies to the baby. And it wasn't fair to walk into Bill's life pregnant by her previous husband. It sounded too much like the bible for his show, and she almost groaned as she thought of trying to explain it. "I promise, I won't try to force anything. I won't even kiss you again while we're away if you don't want me to. I just want to be with you, and get to know you."

"Oh, Bill." She slipped into his arms again and he held her for a long time, and she wanted to stay there forever. He was everything she had always wanted, except that he wasn't her husband, or the baby's father. "I don't know what to say."

"Don't say anything. Just be patient with yourself, and with me. And give it time. And then we'll see. Maybe we'll discover that it's not right and it never will be. But at least let's give it a fair chance. Okay?" He looked down at her hopefully as she thought it over. "Please . . ."

"But you don't know . . . there's so much you don't know about me."

"What can it possibly be that's so terrible? You cheated on your husband? What terrible secrets are you hiding from me?" He was teasing her to lighten the moment, and she smiled. It wasn't a terrible secret, just a big one. A baby. "I can't believe that there's anything so awful lurking in your past, or even your present, that would change how I feel about you." She almost laughed at that, remembering how strongly Steven had felt about the baby. But this was not Steven, it was Bill, and she almost believed that he really loved her. But taking her on pregnant was asking too much of anyone, even Bill. She just couldn't do that. "Why don't we just let things ride for a while, relax, enjoy our holiday, and when we go home we can get serious about things, and talk everything over. Is that a deal? Shall we keep it light till then? And I'll behave myself. I promise." He held out his hand to shake hers and overcame, with difficulty, another overwhelming desire to kiss her. "Agreed?"

She shook his hand reluctantly and smiled. "You drive a hard bargain." But she was glad. For a moment, she had been tempted to go back to L.A. to get away from her own desire for him, but she was glad that she hadn't.

"And don't you forget it." He wagged a finger at her. "I play for keeps," he whispered as he turned off the lights, and a few minutes later, they both went to bed, with their own thoughts, and the memory of the passion that had almost been un- leashed between them. But they both knew it was there now, and even if they controlled it, sooner or later it would have to be dealt with. He was a serious man, Adrian knew, and a serious force to contend with.

CHAPTER

··17··

THEY DROVE TO SAN FRANCISCO THE NEXT DAY, AND THEY stopped in Carmel on the way, and browsed through the little shops, talking and laughing, and Adrian bought little odds and ends for the boys. But today, Bill was fairly quiet. He was thinking of the night before, and wondering what it was that she was so worried about, why it was that she was so certain he would reject her. He knew it had to do with her marriage, or her divorce, and he wondered what it was that she wouldn't tell him.

But by the time they reached San Francisco, he had relaxed again, and he was feeling better. They went to Fisherman's Wharf, rode the cable cars, visited Ghirardelli Square, and stopped at every possible tourist attraction. It was an exhausting two days, and Adrian looked pale when they finally headed for the Napa Valley.

"You okay?" Bill asked softly the morning they left. He was

driving, although she had offered to take a turn at the wheel, but he wanted her to relax and enjoy the drive through Sonoma. There were fields of wildflowers and vineyards, cows and sheep and horses grazing in fields, and beautiful tall trees that shaded them as the road turned, and they could see the hills in the distance. "You look tired." He was worried about her. She seemed to tire very easily, and she would grow pale, although she seldom complained about it. But she seemed healthy on the whole, she ate well, and she was always in excellent spirits. After their serious exchange on the second night of the trip, he had forced himself not to get too close to her, or tackle any serious subjects. She knew how he felt about her now, and he easily sensed that she felt the same, but he also knew that something was stopping her, and he wanted to give her plenty of time and space to resolve it. The one thing he was sure of was that he didn't want to lose her.

She was also wonderful with the boys, and they had never been happier with any of his friends. They teased her mercilessly, and Tommy loved to tickle her, and play with her hair and climb all over her just to let her know that he liked her. They were crazy about her, and they looked like a perfectly normal family as they made their way through the Napa Valley. They stayed at a cozy Victorian inn, visited several wineries, and drove slowly north, after a hot, sunny afternoon gliding in Calistoga. She wouldn't go gliding with them, but Bill didn't press the point, nor would she go in the hot-air balloon he rented to show the boys the rest of the Napa Valley at sunrise. She insisted that she hated heights and absolutely refused to do it, and he had a feeling there was more to it than that, but she wouldn't say what and he didn't want to ask her. The boys were disappointed that she wouldn't go, and she tried to make light of it. And then, without thinking any more about it, they headed for Lake Tahoe. She shared the driving with him, but she liked to stop every couple of hours to stretch her legs. She said she got too stiff if she drove for too long without stopping. So they stopped at the Nut Tree on the way up, and again at Placerville, and the boys had a great time riding the train at the Nut Tree.

They reached Lake Tahoe on Friday afternoon, and the mountain air was cool and beautiful, beneath a cameo-blue sky with little puffs of white cloud chasing each other across the mountains. It was perfect.

They easily found the campsite they had reserved, and Bill set up their tents. He had a larger one for him and the boys, and a smaller one he had bought especially for Adrian. He set thom up cido by cide, and Tommy announced he wanted to sleep with her, which was going to be very cozy, but she seemed very flattered. They had all been wonderful to her, and in some ways, she felt as though she didn't deserve it. She was driving herself nuts weighing everything, thinking of what they meant to her, and yet feeling that at some point she would have to pull back. She couldn't get involved with Bill, if she was going to have the baby. And yet, she couldn't seem to stay away from him. All she wanted to do was talk to him night and day, and look at him, and enjoy his company and feel his warmth somewhere near her. She kept finding herself standing next to him, brushing hands with him, wanting to feel his hands on her face again, and his lips on hers. And all she could do was look at him and wish that things were different. She didn't regret the baby inside her, but she found herself regretting that the baby wasn't his, wishing that life had dealt them a different hand, and she had never married Steven.

"What were you thinking about just then?" She had been standing still, staring into the woods, and he had been watching her. She had looked so sad that it worried him, like her occasional pallor.

"Nothing . . ." She didn't want to tell him. "Just dreaming."

"Yes, you were thinking about something. You looked so sad." He touched her hand for an instant and then pulled away. He had to keep reminding himself not to touch her, and it was anything but easy. He wanted to tell her again that he loved her, but he knew he had to wait, until she was ready to hear it.

He went on setting up the tents, and Adam helped him expertly. They did a very fine job, and then Adam and Adrian went to buy groceries while Bill and Tommy "set up camp." They were having a great time, and Adrian loved it. They bought steaks for Bill to barbecue, and hot dogs and marsh-mallows, and lots of good things for breakfast. Adrian was beginning to feel as though they were eating night and day, and she was becoming distinctly aware of her expanding waistline. In the week they had been gone, she had outgrown almost everything she had brought with her. It wasn't so much that she had put on weight, but suddenly her shape had changed radically, almost overnight, and their first night there she had to borrow one of Bill's big bulky sweaters. He didn't seem to mind, or to notice the reason for it, for which she was very grateful. She didn't want him to know, and she was still wondering how she was going to cut things off when they got home. It wasn't fair to continue tormenting him, or herself, and she couldn't begin a romance with him while she was pregnant. Maybe afterward, if they just stayed friends. Maybe then, if he knew about the baby, then maybe it would be fair . . . she thought about it constantly, and he could see that she was deeply troubled.

"You're doing it again," he whispered as they sat by the campfire that night, after a delicious dinner. The boys had sung songs until they fell asleep, and they were both in Bill's tent, but Tommy swore he was sleeping with Adrian the next night.

"Doing what?" she mused, sitting close to him and staring into the fire with a distant look. It had been a lovely evening.

"Thinking about something much too serious. Every now and then your eyes get sad. I wish you'd tell me what's bothering you." It upset him that she shut him out at times, yet most of the time they had never been closer.

"Nothing's bothering me." But she wasn't convincing and he wasn't convinced.

"I wish I believed you."

"I've never been happier." She looked him in the eye and he believed her, and yet he knew she was also preoccupied about something. She was worrying about the baby. How she would take care of it. What it would be like being all alone with it . . . giving birth with no one there to support her. As the baby grew, it became more real to her, and she was beginning to get worried. And she was afraid of losing Bill, and yet she knew she had to. It was inevitable once he knew, if not sooner. And suddenly, as she thought of all that, there were tears in her eyes, and Bill saw it, and without saying a word to her, he pulled her into his arms and held her.

"I'm right here for you, Adrian . . . I'm right here . . . for as long as you need me."

"Why are you so good to me?" she said through her tears. "I don't deserve this."

"Stop saying that."

She felt so guilty toward him. It wasn't fair misleading him and not telling him about the baby, and yet she couldn't. What could she tell him? That she was here on a camping trip with him and his children, and she was falling in love with him, and yet she was pregnant with Steven's baby? How could she? And then suddenly she was laughing through her tears at the absurdity of it all. It was a ridiculous situation.

"Where were you a few years ago anyway?" She laughed and he smiled in answer to her question.

"Making a fool of myself as usual. But better late than never." The trouble was that he was too late.

She nodded, and they sat that way for a long time, holding each other, and looking into the fire, but this time he didn't kiss her. He wanted to, but he didn't want to upset her.

He suggested they go to bed finally, and helped her into her tent, and then got into his sleeping bag in his, and a minute later he heard a noise, and she was standing next to him, looking worried.

"What's wrong? Are you okay?"

"Yeah," she whispered nervously, "I heard a noise over there." She pointed into the distance outside his tent. "Did you hear it?"

He shook his head, he had already been half asleep when she woke him. "No, it's nothing. Coyotes maybe."

"Do you think it could be a bear?"

He grinned at her, wanting to tell her it was ten of them and she'd better get in his sleeping bag to stay safe, but he didn't. "I don't think so. And the bears around here are pretty tame," despite an occasional disaster, but usually then the bears were teased, they seldom if ever attacked unprovoked, and she wasn't provoking anyone but him, standing there in her blue jeans and his sweater. "Do you want to sleep in here with us? It'll be a tight fit, but the boys will love it." She nodded, looking like a kid, and he smiled at her as she settled down in her own sleeping bag next to him, and she fell asleep, holding tightly to his hand as he lay next to her, and watched her.

CHAPTER
••18••

THE FOUR OF THEM WOKE UP IN THE TENT TOGETHER THE next day, and Tommy immediately took advantage of the situation to pounce on his father. He tickled him mercilessly, and then Adam and Bill turned the tables on Tommy. Adrian had to come to his rescue then, so Bill tickled her, while Adam assisted, and within moments they were a wild tangle of arms and legs and feet and squeals and hands that were tickling anything, anywhere on anyone, until Adrian finally begged them to stop, laughing so hard, she split the zipper on her blue jeans. Fortunately, she knew she had another pair, so she didn't panic. But she was laughing so hard, she could hardly walk, and so were the others as they all stumbled out into the sunshine. It was a nice way to wake up, and it was certainly a lot better than waking up in the empty silence of her now unfurnished apartment.

"How come you slept with us last night?" Adam asked as he stretched in the sunshine.

"She was afraid of being eaten by a bear," Bill explained matter-of-factly.

"I was not." She tried to cover up as he hooted and the kids grinned.

"You were too! Who showed up in our tent after we were all asleep and said she heard noises?"

"I thought you said it was coyotes."

"I did."

"All right, then, I was afraid of being eaten by a coyote." She laughed and they laughed with her, and as she organized breakfast with Adam's help, Bill announced plans to take everyone fishing right after breakfast.

"And we can eat whatever we catch for dinner tonight."

"Great. Who's cleaning?" Adam was quick to ask. He knew that game from previous camping trips with his father. He usually wound up cleaning the fish even when his father did have a girlfriend along, because they were always too squeamish.

"I'll tell you what," Bill suggested as Adrian lit the fire. "We each clean our own. Is that fair?"

"Perfectly," Adrian agreed with a broad grin, "because I've never caught anything in my life. I'll have a hot dog."

"No fair!" Adam complained, sniffing at the bacon she was cooking.

"Can we have corn bread?" Tommy inquired, it was one of his favorite things about camping. That and sharing a sleeping bag with his father. It was like sleeping with a big teddy bear who cuddled all night and kept you warm and toasty.

"I'll cook some tonight," Bill promised, looking up at the sky. It was a gorgeous day, and all was right with the world. He looked at Adrian over the boys' heads, and smiled at her, and she felt her heart turn to mush inside her.

"Why don't we go swimming today?" Adrian suggested as she fried her eggs. It was almost warm enough already, and in another hour it would be. It was freezing in the lake, but there was a lively river that ran a little distance behind where they were camping. They had seen it the day before, and there was a cascade of water running out of the mountains that made a sizable current to raft on.

"Let's go fishing first." It was Bill's suggestion, as she served him his breakfast and then served the children. But they agreed with Adrian, they wanted to go swimming, and fishing later.

"All right, all right. We'll go swimming, and then I'll buy the bait. And after lunch, we can get down to serious business. And whoever doesn't catch a fish will starve." He growled at them and they all laughed, as Adrian looked at him primly.

"Just don't forget my hot dog."

"Oh, no. You too. And don't tell me you're afraid of water." He was teasing her because she hadn't gone gliding or up in the balloon in the Napa Valley. But that was because of the baby, just like the horses she had avoided in Santa Barbara. The only thing was, he didn't know it.

"I am *not* afraid of water." She looked highly insulted at the suggestion, as she finished her eggs. She had just eaten yet another mammoth breakfast. But the mountain air made her ravenously hungry. "I was captain of the swimming team at Stanford, thank you very much. And I was a lifeguard for two summers."

"Can you dive real good?" Tommy inquired, highly impressed by her credentials.

"Pretty good." She smiled at him, tousling his hair with a gentle hand.

"Will you teach me when we get back to Dad's place?"

"Sure."

"Me too," Adam said quietly. He liked her a lot, and he

admired her even if she hadn't gone up in the hot-air balloon. "Dad taught me to dive last year, but I think I forgot over the winter."

"We'll get to work on it as soon as we get back." She cleaned up the breakfast things then, and they helped her. They rolled up their sleeping bags, and then took turns changing into their bathing suits, before zipping up their tents and going to the river. Adrian wore a T-shirt over her suit, which looked fine, even to Bill.

And they found a wonderful swimming hole full of other families and children and jumped in and out of it, laughing and teasing, and splashing water on each other. And in the distance, well beyond it and some rocks, were the rapids where people were rafting.

They played in the swimming hole for well over an hour, and then finally Bill got out and announced that he was driving to the store to buy bait and some supplies and he'd be back in a little while, and Adrian and the boys opted to stay in the swimming hole until he came back again. They were having a good time, and there was plenty of time for fishing later. He also wanted to look into renting a boat for them, and he had to go to the bait-and-tackle shop to do it.

"I'll meet you back at the campsite," he called out to Adrian with a wave as he disappeared across the clearing, and she turned back to the children. Tommy was having a wonderful time, and Adam was trying to dive underwater to see how deep it was, but she told him not to. The water wasn't clear and she couldn't tell if there were rocks and she didn't want him getting hurt, but he was very reasonable and listened to what she told him. She was explaining to him that it was never a good idea to dive where you didn't know exactly how deep it was, and she turned to explain the same thing to Tommy, and as she did, she realized that he was nowhere to be found. She began to panic as she looked for him, then she saw him on the rocks, watching the people in the rafts shooting the rapids in the river just beyond them. She called out to him, ready to scold him for leaving the swimming hole without telling her, and he didn't seem to hear her. She called him again, and then decided to get out and go get him. She asked Adam to get out and wait for her, and she got out and clambered over the rocks to go and get Tommy.

She called his name and Tommy turned and grinned mischievously at her, and she climbed over more rocks in her effort to reach him. He was standing on the riverbank and leaning as far forward as he could, as three rafts came racing past him. It looked like great fun to him, and he was planning to ask his father to rent a raft and take them rafting. It was a lot more fun than renting a rowboat and fishing in the middle of Lake Tahoe.

"Tommy! Come back here!" she called out to him, and Adam followed her over the rocks a little more slowly, annoyed that his brother had dragged them out of the swimming hole. But as he watched him, suddenly the smaller boy disappeared. He slipped right off the bank and into the turbulent water. "Tommy!" Adrian screamed at him. She had seen it, too, but he didn't hear her as he began moving swiftly downstream toward the rocks that were far down the river.

Adrian looked frantically for something to hold out to him, an oar, a pole, a limb from a tree, and at first there was nothing, and no one had yet seen what had happened. Adam came running toward her and he started to scream the boy's name, too, but all Adrian could see was a look of panic on Tommy's face as he was carried downstream, and suddenly two men realized what had happened.

"Get him! . . . Get the boy! . . ." one of them shouted to the people in the raft, but they couldn't hear over the roar of the water, and they didn't see the small figure in the blue bathing suit as he bobbed under the water. He was flailing wildly with his arms, but he kept going down and Adrian realized instantly that something terrible was about to happen. Adam was crying hysterically, and he started to jump in, but she grabbed at him and pushed him roughly aside, shouting at him as she pushed him away from the water.

"No! Adam, don't you go in there!" and as soon as she said the words she ran away from him, and as fast as she could, she ran along the river, sailing over rocks, and leaping over obstacles and trees and pushing away people in her path. She had never run so fast in her life and she knew that his life depended on it, and all along the riverbank people were screaming. They had seen him now. But everyone seemed to be helpless. Two men shoved an oar at him from one of the boats, but he was too small and too stunned to grab it, and he was pushed under the surface by the currents and disappeared again as Adrian continued to run without stopping for breath or for anything. She knew exactly what she was doing and where she was going, if only it wasn't too late by the time she got there. She could feel branches rip her legs, and something struck her hip, and her feet were numb from the sharp rocks, and her lungs screamed, but she could still see him, and then she dove, just before the rocks where the water was the roughest. She dove smoothly near the surface of the water, praying that she wouldn't hit anything and that she could catch him before it was too late. If she didn't, it would be all over, and no matter what it took, she knew she couldn't let that happen.

She was almost hit by an oar as she swam past, strong and swift and sure, battered by the currents, and in the distance she could hear people shouting, and from somewhere there was the whine of a siren. And then, as she was pushed down by the force of the water, suddenly she struck something hard, it hit her in the face, and she grabbed at it, and as she touched it, she knew she had him. It was Tommy. She pushed him to the surface, gasping for air herself, and the current dragged her down again, but she shoved him high above her head, trying to force him out of the water. He was sputtering and gasping, and swallowing water each time they went down, and he was fighting her with what strength he had, but she wouldn't loosen her grip on him and as the currents kept ripping at her, she kept pushing him upward, and then suddenly he was gone. She couldn't feel the weight of him anymore. He was somewhere and she couldn't find him, she was pressed down into a black hole, and she was falling into something very deep and very soft, and it was quiet there, as she continued falling.

CHAPTER

••19••

IT SOUNDED AS THOUGH THERE WERE SIRENS EVERYWHERE as Bill came back from the bait shop. He set his bag down outside the tent, and stretched his legs in the sun as he waited for them, and as he sat there, an ambulance roared past him. He had an odd feeling for just a moment as he watched it disappear, and then almost instinctively began walking toward the swimming hole where he had left Adrian and the children. And as he got there, he found Adam, running up and down on the riverbank, crying hysterically and waving his arms in the direction of the river.

"Oh my God . . ." Bill felt his whole body trembling as he ran to him, and several adults were already standing there trying to console him. Adam was calling Tommy's name and when he saw his father he ran to him. Bill clutched Adam to him and then pulled him away just as quickly. "What happened? What happened?" He shook him trying to calm him so he could understand, but Adam could only wave in the direction where the ambulance and two forestry jeeps now stood, and Bill left him and ran frantically toward them.

There was a huge crowd of people near them now, and people from the rafts were shouting something, just as Bill reached the spot where a cluster of rangers stood, several of them half in the water, and Bill saw them grab a small lump of flesh with a patch of bright blue, and he realized with horror that it was his son, unconscious and blue, and they laid him quickly on the ground, checked his breathing, and one of the men began breathing for him, as Bill sobbed, watching. He was dead . . . he had to be . . . people were staring in horror as Bill pushed past them to the boy and dropped to his knees next to the rangers.

"Please . . . oh . . . God . . . please . . . do something . . ." All he could think of was the boy, the baby he so dearly loved, and as he watched him, suddenly there was a terrible splutter and a cough and a explosion of water. He was still gray, but he moved, and a moment later, he opened his eyes and looked up at his father. He seemed a little dazed at first, and then he started to cry, as Bill leaned his face down next to his and sobbed as he held him. "Oh, baby . . . oh, baby . . . Tommy . . . I love you . . ."

"It . . . I . . ." He gagged again, and vomited what looked like gallons of water, but the paramedics were watching him closely and he was going to be all right. He looked bruised, and there was mud in his hair and there were scratches all over him, but he was alive. He kept looking at Bill frantically, and when he stopped vomiting he spoke, and Bill's heart almost stopped when he heard him. "Where's . . . Adrian?" Adrian. Oh my God. He turned, suddenly realizing that he hadn't seen her anywhere, and as he turned, he saw the men lifting her limp form from the water.

"Watch him!" Bill said to one of the men standing near the

boy, and in two strides he was next to her, but she looked dead. She was pale gray, and there was a terrible gash on one arm and one leg. But it was the look on her face that was so frightening. It reminded him of a highway accident he had seen once, and the woman had been dead in the car when he got there. "Oh my God . . . can you do anything?" he asked, but no one was listening to him. They were trying to resuscitate her, and there was no response from her.

"Is she your wife?" someone asked him quickly, as he started to shake his head, and then nodded. It was simpler than explaining the situation. "She saved the boy," the man explained. "He would have gone over the rocks in another minute. She kept him up near the surface till we got him, but I think she hit her head." And there was blood gushing from the cut on her arm. There was blood everywhere as Bill watched in horror.

"Is she breathing?" Bill asked as he stared at her. There were four men bending over her body, and tears rolled down his cheeks as he watched. She had died trying to save his son . . . she had saved him and . . . they were trying to resuscitate her, but nothing was happening. And suddenly the siren was on again, and two of the men shouted to the driver.

"We've got a heartbeat!" She gave a small gasp then, but she still looked terrible, as they continued to give her artificial respiration, and then they looked victoriously at Bill. "She's breathing on her own again. We're going to take her to the hospital. Do you want to ride with us?"

"Yes. Will she be all right?" he asked, as he looked frantically in the direction of where he had left Adam.

"We don't know yet. We don't know what kind of head injury she has, and she's lost a lot of blood from the wound in her arm. It's right near an artery. It's going to be close." He looked at Bill honestly, as he wound a tourniquet around her arm, and he was keeping pressure on it. Adam had just come running up to him, he was still crying and he clung to his father, as the paramedics lifted Tommy into the ambulance on a stretcher. Bill hopped in after him, and someone helped Adam in and handed him a blanket, as two of the paramedics lifted Adrian in. She was still deathly white, and there was an oxygen mask on her face. Bill knelt down beside her.

"Is she dead?" Adam asked in a voice full of grief, and Tommy just stared at her. There were still leaves in her hair, and one of the men was keeping pressure on her arm, as Bill shook his head in answer to Adam's question. She wasn't dead, but she was barely breathing.

They made it to the hospital in ten minutes flat, with Bill praying as he stroked her face and watched her. Twice he saw the paramedics checking her more closely, and he could see they didn't like what they saw, but there was a team waiting for them when they got to Truckee. Tommy was lifted out after that, and Adam climbed out of the ambulance. They all looked as though they were in shock, and an elderly nurse spoke quietly to Bill.

"I'll stay with the boys so you can be with your wife. They'll be fine. We'll find some warm clothes for them, and they want to keep an eye on the little one for a while anyway. They'll be fine." He nodded, and told them both he'd be back in a little while, and he pounded the pavement as he ran into the building where Adrian had been taken.

"Where is she?" he asked as soon as he was inside. They knew whom he meant, she was the most critically ill patient they had at the moment, and a nurse pointed to a pair of swinging doors almost at the same moment as he flew through them. He found himself inside a high-tech emergency room, and there seemed to be a thousand knobs and dials, a flood of bright lights, and a dozen people in green pajamas working on her still form. They seemed to be doing ten thousand things at once, and they were watching half a dozen monitors and reporting things in codes he didn't understand. It was like watching a science fiction movie. And inside he felt numb. He still couldn't understand what had happened. All he knew was that something terrible had happened to Tommy, and she had saved him, but at what price, and if she lived, he would be forever grateful. But for the moment that appeared to be less than likely. This woman whom he barely knew, the girl he had fallen in love with, was lying there like someone in a bad dream or a rotten movie.

"What's happening?" he asked them repeatedly, but they were too busy to answer. He saw them sew up her arm, start a blood transfusion, an IV, and administer an EKG, and still she was gray and unconscious. And he couldn't get near her. There were too many of them, and she was too injured, and there was too much they had to do to try to save her.

Finally, as he began to feel sick watching it all, one of the doctors took him aside and asked him if he would come outside for a few moments.

"Would you like to sit down?" He had noticed how desperate Bill looked, and Bill sank gratefully into a chair, thinking of what was happening in that room, the desperate fight for life that she appeared to be losing.

"What's happening?" he asked again, and this time he got the answers.

"As you obviously know, your wife almost drowned. She's taken a lot of water into her lungs, and she lost a great deal of blood from the cut on her arm. She hit an artery and that alone could have been fatal. There must have been something awfully sharp under the surface of the water. In addition, she appears to have sustained a considerable blow on the head. At first we were afraid of a fracture, but I think that's not the case. We think she's got a concussion, and of course things are complicated further by her condition."

"What condition?" He looked horrified and confused. Her

medical history was a complete mystery to him, and all he could think of were things like diabetes. "Will she be all right?"

"We don't know yet." He looked even more serious then as he looked at Bill. "And given the extent of her injuries, it's a distinct possibility that she could lose the baby." Bill stared at him in stupefaction as he said it.

"The baby?" He felt totally confused and like a complete fool.

"Of course," the doctor went on, assuming he was in shock and having trouble remembering anything after almost losing his son, and still being in danger of losing his pregnant wife. "She must be, what . . . four, four and a half months pregnant?"

"I . . . of course . . . I . . . I'm just so upset, I . . ." It was insanity, why was he pretending she was his wife? And why did he feel like this? Why did he actually feel as though she were his wife and this were his baby? And why in God's name hadn't she told him? He felt as though he had had yet another shock, as the doctor asked him to stay where he was. He was going back to check on Adrian again and he would report to Bill the moment there was any change in the situation.

He sat there alone for a long time, trying to absorb what had happened and what he had just heard, and for a long moment, he just couldn't. It was impossible to understand what had gone on, except suddenly little pieces of the puzzle began to fit into place . . . her enormous appetite . . . the fact that she looked as though she had gained a little weight since he first met her . . . but far more importantly, Steven's leaving her . . . but why, if she was having a baby? He had to be some kind of son of a bitch, Bill thought to himself. And that was also why she kept thinking he might be coming back, and why she still wore her wedding ring probably . . . and it was why she was loath to get into a relationship with him. Suddenly, it all made sense. Except now she might lose the baby. Four and a half months was serious . . . and she might die herself, which was a great deal more so. He felt as though his heart had just been torn out, as another doctor came slowly toward him. He looked ominous as Bill staredup at him, afraid of what he was going to tell him.

"We've done everything we can for her. She's breathing on her own, she's had a unit of blood. The concussion is severe but not necessarily fatal, there's no fracture of her skull . . . but we're just going to have to wait. She's still unconscious." And Bill knew that she could just slip into a coma and die. Those things happened sometimes. "There's no reason to expect permanent damage from this, if she survives. But the big question is, will she? We just don't have the answer to that yet."

"And the baby?" He felt a responsibility for the baby now too. For both of them. He wanted them both to live. He wanted both of them . . . or just her . . . anything . . . but please don't let them die. . . . He looked at the doctor, waiting to hear the answer to his question.

"The pregnancy is still viable. We have a monitor on her, and so far everything looks fine. We're still getting a fetal heartbeat."

"Thank God." Bill stood, waiting for more. But there was nothing more. Only time would tell what would happen. "May I see her?"

"Of course. We're going to leave her where she is, until we see what happens. She's still in an emergency unit. We'll move her to ICU later, if she improves." It was difficult to believe. A few hours earlier she'd been making bacon and eggs, and now suddenly she was on the brink of death, after saving Tommy.

"Is my boy all right?"

"I haven't seen him myself. But the last I heard, he and his brother were having lunch in the pediatric ward." He smiled at Bill. "I'd say he's going to be okay. He's a lucky boy. I understand that only her quick thinking and heroic maneuvers saved him. She's a very slight woman, it's amazing she was able to hold him up like that. She must have gashed her arm somehow in the process . . ." and hit her head . . . and almost drowned . . . and almost lost her baby . . . and she hadn't hesitated for an instant, even knowing that she was pregnant. He owed her everything. If she lived long enough for him to repay it.

He walked into the special emergency unit then, and sat down next to her. There seemed to be machines hooked to every part of her, and the oxygen mask obscured part of her face, but he gently took her hand in his own and kissed her fingers. The knuckles were cut and bruised, and there was still earth underneath her fingernails. She must have struggled ferociously to save him.

"Adrian . . ." he whispered to her still form. "I love you, sweetheart. I loved you the first time I ever saw you." He had decided that if he never got a chance to say it to her, he was going to say it all to her now, whether she heard him or not, and maybe she would hear him and it would make a difference. "I loved you right away, that first night in the supermarket, when I almost ran you down . . . do you remember that?" He smiled as tears ran down his face and he kissed her fingers again. "And I loved you the next time . . . when I saw you in the parking lot at the complex. Do you remember that? I think it was a Sunday morning . . . and at the pool at the apartment . . . I love you . . . I love everything about you . . . and the boys love you too . . . Adam and Tommy. They want you to get better too." He just went on talking to her, in his strong, gentle voice, and holding her hand carefully in his own. "And I love the baby too . . . that's right . . . and if you want that baby, so do I . . . I want you and the baby,

Adrian. Both of you . . . and the baby is going to be just fine
. . . the doctor said so." He watched her face then, he
thought he had seen her wince, but when he looked more
closely, he thought he had imagined it. She seemed as expres-
sionless as ever. He went on talking to her for a long time,
crooning her name, and telling her how much he loved her
and the baby. He rested his hand on the baby then, and felt
the small lump that he had never noticed before, that she had
never told him about, and he told the baby that he loved it,
and that it had better stick around, or it was going to make a
lot of people very unhappy. "That's right . . . you don't think
your mom has gone through all this in order to have you bail
out now, do you? So settle down and take it easy . . . right,
Adrian? You tell the baby to relax. . . ." And then he kissed
her gently on the cheek and talked to her some more, as one of
the nurses watched him from the doorway. She had never
seen anyone so distraught, and she had never heard anyone
talk to a woman like that. As she listened, she thought Adrian
was awfully lucky to have a man love her the way he did. And
as she watched, she saw something on the monitors that
caught her attention. She frowned and walked into the room,
and as she approached, Adrian turned toward Bill and opened
her eyes and then closed them. For an instant of sheer terror,
he thought she had just died, and he let out an almost animal
sound of grief, as he stood up and looked down at her again in
anguish. But as he did, she opened her eyes again, and the
nurse checked her vital signs and smiled down at her, and Bill
smiled at her as he was crying. He couldn't speak anymore.
She had taken his breath away, and he was so moved, he had
started to tremble.

"You're a very lucky girl," the nurse said to her. "Your little
boy is fine. I just gave him a Popsicle." She glanced at Bill
encouragingly. "And your husband has been right here talking to you ever since you got here." And then she remem-

bered as she glanced at the fetal monitor and back at Adrian again. "And your baby is fine too. Looks like everybody is going to be all right now. How are you feeling, Mrs. Thigpen?"

She fought to pull off the oxygen mask, and the nurse helped her to lift it. "Not so good," she croaked. They had pumped the water from her stomach and now she was hoarse and she felt desperately nauseous and viciously battered. The last thing she remembered was slipping into a soft warm place, when she had gotten the final blow on her head from a rock and started drowning.

"I'll bet you don't feel so good." The nurse smiled at her, and propped her head up a little bit. "You had quite a fight with a rock, and a whole lot of water. But they tell me you ran a race. You saved your little boy. You did!" She smiled at her, and Bill finally caught his breath, and looked at Adrian gratefully through his tears, still holding her hand tightly.

"Adrian, you saved Tommy." He started to cry harder then and leaned down and kissed her face. "Baby, you saved him."

"I'm so glad . . . I was so afraid . . . I couldn't have held him up for much longer . . ." Bill still remembered the limp body and the gray-blue face when they had snatched him from her just beneath the surface. "The current was terrible . . . and I was afraid I couldn't run fast enough . . ." There were tears in her eyes, but they were tears of relief and victory as she held fast to Bill's hand, and the nurse slipped quietly out of the room to report her improvement to the doctor. And then Bill leaned down and whispered to her.

"Why didn't you tell me about the baby?"

There was a long silence as she looked at him, grateful that he was there, her eyes full of the love for him that she'd been fighting almost since she met him. "I didn't think it was fair to you." She started to cry then as she said it and he kissed her gently and shook his head.

"It wouldn't have changed anything." He smiled then, and

sat down next to her, never taking his eyes off her. "It's a little unusual, I admit, but hell, to a guy who writes soap operas for a living, did you really think I couldn't understand it?" She smiled and then coughed, as he held her, and then laid her gently back down on the pillows. "Frankly, Adrian, I'm relieved. I was afraid that for you that appetite of yours was normal." She laughed again and then sighed, with a worried look.

"Is the baby really okay?"

"They say it's fine. I think you'll probably have to take it a little easy for a while. But babies are pretty sturdy." He remembered a bad fall Leslie had had when she was pregnant for the first time, and he had almost had a heart attack watching her stumble down a flight of stairs, but in the end, nothing had happened. And then he remembered something he wanted to ask Adrian. Something he now suspected. "Is that why Steven left you?" It was something he wanted to know now. It was inexcusable if it was true, and while she was unconscious, he had guessed that that was the reason for their separation.

And quietly, she nodded. "He never wanted children, and he gave me a choice. Him or the baby." She started to cry again, thinking of it, as she clung desperately to Bill now. "I tried . . . but I couldn't do it. I went to have an abortion, but I just couldn't. So he left me."

"What a nice guy he must be."

"He has very strong feelings about it," she tried to explain, and Bill looked at her ruefully.

"I'd say that was an understatement. The guy is divorcing you for having his baby. Does he realize it's his, or does he question that too?"

"No, he knows it's his. His lawyer sent me papers, he's filing for a termination of parental rights, so neither the child nor I can claim him as the father. In essence, the baby will be illegitimate," she said sadly.

"That's disgusting."

And then she sighed again. "But he may change his mind . . . maybe if he sees it." He realized then what the problem was. She was still hoping Steven would come back, for the baby, if nothing else. And then he asked her something else he wanted to know now.

"Adrian, are you still in love with him?" She hesitated for a long time, and then shook her head as she looked at Bill.

"No," she said quietly, "I'm not. But the baby has a right to its natural father."

"If he wanted you back, would you take him?"

"I might . . . for the baby's sake. . . ." She closed her eyes then. She felt nauseous and exhausted, and Bill was looking at her, saddened by what she had just told him, grateful for the honesty. It was one of the things he loved about her. He didn't think Steven would come back, not if he was filing papers renouncing the child, and divorcing her. The guy was obviously crazy. But it was equally obvious that she felt she owed him and the child something, a relationship they deserved, even if it meant giving something up herself. But she was that way. In trying to save Tommy, she had been willing to risk herself and her baby. She was an all-or-nothing kind of person. She lay there and closed her eyes then and for a while neither of them spoke and then she looked at Bill again, worried about what he was thinking. "Do you hate me?"

"Are you out of your mind? How can you say a thing like that? You just saved my child." And it had almost cost her her own life. He moved nearer to her again, and touched her bruised face with gentle fingers. "I love you, Adrian. This may not be the time or place to say it," he said softly, "but I love you. More than that, I'm in love with you. I have been for two months, maybe even three." He kissed her hand then and her fingers. He was afraid to hurt her if he really kissed her.

"You're not mad about the baby?" There were tears in her eyes as she asked him.

"How could I be mad about the baby? I think you're wonderful to do what you're doing. You're very courageous, and unbelievably strong, and a good, decent woman. And I think it's very special that you're having a baby." It was the first kind word anyone had said about her pregnancy, except Zelda, but she had taken so much abuse from Steven that in the face of Bill's kind words, she started to cry. And he gently wiped her eyes as she sobbed and tried to explain it all to him. She was feeling very emotional and terribly upset and suddenly the dam had broken after three months of having to apologize to her husband, and trying to cope with the pregnancy on her own.

"Just relax." She was getting too upset, and he was afraid of what it might do to her. She had already had a terrible shock to her system. "Everything's going to be fine. Okay?" He smoothed her hair off her face, and gently tucked her in. She looked like a battered child, and she was hiccuping like a little girl who'd been crying. "You're going to have your baby and it'll be beautiful." He leaned his face down to hers and carefully, carefully kissed her lips, and there were tears in his eyes too. "I love you, Adrian . . . I love you so much . . . you *and* the baby." And the beauty of it was that he meant it.

"How can you say that?" Steven had deserted her over this child, and now Bill, who barely knew her, was telling her he loved her. "It's not even your baby."

"I wish it were," he said honestly as he looked down at her. And then, he dared say to her exactly what he was feeling. "Maybe one day, if I'm very lucky, it will be." Fresh tears rolled down her cheeks then, and she didn't say a word, she just held his hand tightly in her own, and closed her eyes as she nodded. She dozed for a little while then, holding his hand, and he watched the monitors while she slept. The nurse came in a couple of times, and reassured him that everything was normal. He left for a little while eventually, to check on the boys. He found Tommy sleeping too. He was taking a nap, but he looked fine. They had put in a glucose IV, and they were checking his temperature regularly, but they said he could go home by the end of the afternoon. And Adam was watching old reruns of *Mork and Mindy.*

"How're you doing, sport?" Bill sat down next to him in the television room, and across the way he could see where Tommy was sleeping.

"How's Adrian?" he asked worriedly, but Bill looked so relieved, he knew she had to be okay. And a nurse had told him long before that his "mother" was much better. He hadn't corrected her, he was old enough to have figured out that it was simpler not to.

"She's sleeping, but she's better." He had been thinking all afternoon about what they ought to do. He didn't think she should travel right away, particularly in view of her pregnancy, but he also didn't think that she should be camping. What they needed was a week's holiday in a terrific hotel, some sun, and a lot of room service. "What do you say we stay in a hotel, instead of going back to camping?" He didn't want to disappoint the boys, but he had a responsibility to her now, too, particularly after what she had done for Tommy. The day could have ended in tragedy for all of them, and Bill was certain that if she hadn't been so quick to react, and relentless in her efforts to save the child, Tommy would no longer be with them. It was a debt he would owe her forever. But he had to think of Adam now, too, and he looked a little shaken. "Would you be very disappointed if this vacation wasn't too rugged?"

But Adam was quick to shake his head vehemently. "I'm

just glad they're both okay. You should have seen her, Dad. She ran like a blue streak once the current started taking him away. I guess she was trying to get downstream before he did, so she could stop him, but I couldn't figure it out then. And it worked. But it was so awful." He choked on the words as he said it. "They kept going under, and at first no one helped them. She just kept pushing him up, and the current right where they were, kept shoving her down again. And then she'd push him up again, and she'd go under. It was awful. . . ." He buried his face in Bill's chest, and he held his son for a long time.

"Tommy should never have left her in the first place. What in hell was he doing?"

"I think he must have been looking at the rafts or something. And he fell in while he was watching."

"We're going to have to talk about that when he wakes up." Eventually, he went over to check on the sleeping child, but his color looked good and his breathing and temperature were normal. He looked fine and there was hardly a scratch on him. It was hard to believe that this was the same child who had been blue only a few hours before. Bill knew that as long as he lived, he would never forget it.

He made some phone calls after that, and got a large suite in a deluxe hotel, and he went back to check on Adrian and talk to her doctor. She was still asleep, and they wanted her to stay that way for a while. She still had some repairing to do, and they thought she might be able to leave the hospital the next day if there were no further problems. They wanted to be sure she didn't develop pneumonia, or have complications with the baby. But so far, things seemed to be improving.

He told them he'd be back in a little while, and he went to tell Adam that, too, and then he got a ride back to their campsite, and he stood trembling as he looked around, thinking that only that morning, life had seemed so carefree and so simple. And now suddenly two of the people he loved had almost lost their lives . . . three, if he counted the baby. He had a sense of reverence and gratitude, and he was relieved when everything was packed and he drove to the hotel. They had set aside a beautiful two-bedroom suite, and he had already decided to sleep on the couch. He wanted to keep an eye on her at night, and be sure that he heard her if she called him. He would have preferred sleeping in the same room, but he was afraid it might upset the children.

And as soon as he dropped off their things, he went back to the hospital, and was startled to discover that it was six o'clock and the boys were eating dinner.

"Where've you been?" Tommy asked. They had taken out the IV, and he looked like his old self, as Adam told him to stop eating his mashed potatoes with his fingers. The children's ward was almost empty. There was a broken leg, a broken arm, a minor car accident that had required some stitches and observation for a concussion, and Tommy, having survived his dousing in the river. And most of the other children were older, and they were talking among themselves during dinner.

"I went to get a hotel room for all of us," Bill explained. "I checked on you all afternoon, but you were asleep all the time." He leaned over and kissed him and as he did he realized he was hungry. He hadn't eaten anything since the breakfast Adrian had fixed early that morning.

"Is Adrian okay?" Tommy's face clouded up with worry, but Bill nodded quickly.

"She's going to be fine. She was worried about you. She took kind of a beating trying to rescue you. Which reminds me, young man, what were you doing out of the swimming hole without the others?" The boy's eyes got huge in his face and brimmed over with tears. He knew exactly what part he had played in it, and he was old enough to know that it was his fault that he and Adrian had almost drowned, and he felt deeply remorseful.

"I'm sorry, Daddy . . . honest . . ."

"I know you are, Son."

"Can I see her yet?"

"Maybe tomorrow. She's pooped. Hopefully they'll let her out and we can take her back to the hotel with us."

"Can I go tonight?"

"We'll see." He would have liked to spend the night with Adrian, but he didn't want to leave the boys alone in the hotel, and even in the hospital, Tommy would have expected his father to sleep with him. And they had already said that Adam couldn't spend the night since he wasn't a patient. So Bill had no choice but to take them to the hotel, and come back for Adrian in the morning.

But she didn't seem to mind when he went back to see her. She was so exhausted from the perils of the day that she had barely woken up to talk to him before she was asleep again, and the nurse suggested that he leave her.

"She won't even know that you've gone, and I'll explain it to her when she wakes up," the nurse promised, "and if she wants to, she can always call you." He left the number of the hotel, and the hotel room, and he went back to get the boys, and an hour later they were jumping on the beds, and watching TV, and Tommy wanted to order chocolate ice cream from room service. It was difficult to believe that he had almost not survived the morning.

Bill gave him a bath and put them both to bed, and then he stretched out in the room that was to be hers, feeling completely exhausted. He couldn't remember a day in his entire life that had been as traumatic. And all he could think of was the hideous vision of their two bodies with the rangers and the paramedics struggling over them . . . the sirens . . . the sounds . . . the looks on their faces. He knew he would have nightmares about it for years, and as he thought of her, he found himself missing Adrian, and wanting to hold her close. There was so much he wanted to say to her now, so much for them to find out, to do together, to discover . . . and then there was the baby. He didn't even know exactly how pregnant she was. All he knew was what the doctor had guessed, but he had no idea when it was to be born. It was remarkable how suddenly a whole new being had come into his life . . . a whole new prospect of happiness for the future. He had loved her before, but now he knew that he loved her doubly. And as he thought about it, lying on her bed, the phone rang.

"Hello?" His voice was hoarse from just lying there, thinking of the emotions of the day, but he smiled as soon as he heard her voice. It was Adrian, calling from the hospital. She had woken up, and wondered where he was, and she was missing him, just as he was missing her. A whole new bond had formed between them since that morning.

"Where are you?"

"Here in your bed," he said, smiling, "wishing you were here with me." Given the chastity of their relationship, it seemed a rather forward thing to say, but he suspected she wouldn't mind after everything they'd been through. He almost felt as though they were married and she had just told him they were having a baby.

"Can you hear any bears?" she teased, she still sounded croaky, but a lot stronger.

"No bears and no coyotes." Given the price he had paid for the suite, with the view they had of the lake, there should only have been the sounds of minks and Rolls-Royces. "But it's lonely without you," he told her.

"It's lonely here too." She hated being in the hospital and she really missed him. "How are the boys?"

"Asleep, I hope. I put them to bed an hour ago. And if they

aren't asleep, I don't want to know it." He was almost as tired as she was. And then, with a tender smile, "How's the baby?"

"Okay, I guess." It embarrassed her a little bit talking to him about it. It was all so new to her. For all these months, she had pointedly ignored it, and now it was suddenly the focus of their attention. "It's all so strange. I'm not used to it yet."

"You will be eventually. When's it due, by the way?"

"The beginning of January. The tenth."

"Just in time for my fortieth birthday. My birthday is actually New Year's Day."

"That sounds like fun."

"So does the baby," he said softly. "It's been so long since I've even thought of little ones. It makes me think of when Adam and Tommy were small. They were so cute. And this one will be, too, if it looks like you." She couldn't believe what she was hearing. The man who had fathered it had left her in a fury, and this man, this almost total stranger, whom she had known for a mere three months, was excited about her baby. It made her feel so protected suddenly, and so happy and so much less lonely.

"Why are you being so good to me?" What did he want? And when was he going to hurt her? It just wasn't possible that he was this kind. Or was it?

"Because you deserve it."

And then suddenly, she laughed. "You're just using me as research for the show." And she laughed, too, remembering the absurdity of the parallel between the illegitimate pregnancy on the show, and her own baby.

"You certainly do keep things lively, Mrs. Townsend. Or should I call you by a different name?" He wasn't sure if she was going to change it.

"My maiden name is Adrian Thompson." And eventually she would have to go back to that, since the baby couldn't use

Townsend anyway, but that was all a long way off. "I can't wait until tomorrow. It's so depressing here."

"Wait till you see our hotel room."

"I can't wait." She felt as though she were about to leave on her honeymoon, except that she still had an IV tube in her arm, and they were still giving her oxygen through two tiny tubes just beneath her nose, and her face and hands and arms looked as though she had been in a cat fight, and she still remembered that some of the scratches had been inflicted by Tommy. It had been an incredible day, a miracle that had touched all of them, and they all felt more than a little awed by the happy outcome. And some good had come of it after all. Bill had found out about the baby. And he hadn't sent her away . . . and . . . she smiled to herself . . . he had even told her he loved her.

"I'll see you tomorrow. Now get some rest," he told her in a gentle whisper. It was late, and it seemed as though the whole world had gone quiet. "I'll miss you. . . ."

"I'll miss you too, darling, good night," she whispered from her hospital room in Truckee.

"And don't forget," he reminded her with a smile, "how much I love you."

CHAPTER

··20··

BILL PICKED ADRIAN UP AT THE HOSPITAL THE NEXT DAY, and he brought the boys with him. They brought flowers and balloons and a big THANK YOU sign that Tommy insisted on carrying himself, and as they helped her to the car, it looked like a jackpot at the casino. She was still pretty shaky when she was discharged, and they went straight to the hotel so she could rest. And Bill set her up with pillows in a chaise longue on their terrace. She was impressed by how fancy their quarters were, and she admitted to Bill confidentially that it was a lot nicer than camping. He laughed in answer and told her that some people would do anything to avoid sleeping in a tent, and she certainly had. In one day, she had managed to almost lose her life, save Tommy's, and admit to the fact that she was pregnant.

They ordered room service for lunch, and then Bill went out fishing with the boys. And they caught three and brought them back to the hotel kitchen to have them cleaned and cooked. It was the perfect arrangement.

"I love this kind of camping," Adrian announced as the trays came up eventually, supposedly with their fish, in delicate lemon butter sauces. Bill and the boys were convinced that they really were their fish, even though Adrian suspected that they weren't. They watched old movies on TV after that, and they all went to bed early. And all through the night, Adrian would wake up, thinking she heard sounds in her room, and it was always Bill, peering down at her, making sure she was all right and asking her if she needed anything. And she thanked him for it the next morning over breakfast.

"You don't have to worry about me. I'm fine."

"I just want to be sure. You just got out of the hospital yesterday." He was like a mother hen, but she thought it was terrific and she loved it.

"I feel great." But he noticed that when she wandered around the room, she still didn't have her old zip, and she didn't seem anxious to go out. In the end, it took four days for her to seem like herself again, and by then the vacation was almost over. But they had a lovely time, going for walks around the lake. They stayed away from the river, and the rapids, and the boys never repeated their request to go rafting.

They visited the state park at Sugar Pine Point instead, and were fascinated by it. And they went for a drive to Squaw Valley and took the ski lift to the top and then back again. And it was beautiful, and by the last night, Adrian and the boys were fast friends. It was as though they had always known her. They had called their mother long since, and told her all about Tommy's accident, and Adrian's heroics. And she had insisted on speaking to her and thanking Adrian herself. She sounded nice on the phone and she had cried copiously, just thinking of what might have happened.

"She sounds like a sweet person," Adrian said to Bill later. "And she sounds like she still likes you."

"I think she still does. I like her, too, even though we irritate the hell out of each other sometimes, when we don't agree about the boys. And her husband is kind of an uptight pain in the ass. He thinks that California is uncivilized, and devoid of culture, and he thinks pretty much the same thing about me because of the show. But I don't think Leslie lets him say much about it. At least that's what the boys say. But apparently the other two children are very, very proper. They're both girls and they're four and five and he has them playing concert piano and violin. I figure that can wait a few years." He grinned. "What do you think?"

"I agree with you." She smiled. "But Leslie sounds nice anyway."

"I think she was looking for someone completely different from me . . . or from what I was then . . . she wanted someone who spent a lot of time at home, who was very controlled, and not so compulsive, and maybe not so exuberant. And I think she got it."

"That's too bad," Adrian said without thinking, and then laughed. "I just meant that your way sounds better."

"Thank you." And with that, he leaned over where he was sitting and kissed her. And out of the corner of his eye, he saw Tommy giggle from across the room. And then he turned to Adrian again. For the past few days, his mind had been full of questions. "What happens when we go back, Adrian? To us, I mean?"

"I don't know." She looked him in the eye. She wanted to know, too, and she wasn't sure yet. "What do you want to happen?" She thought she knew, but she needed to take her clues from him, and then she needed to think about what she was going to do about Steven, if he ever turned up again. It wasn't fair to launch herself into a relationship with anyone, knowing full well that if he returned, she would go back to him. But she felt that she had an obligation to him, and the baby. But on the other hand, she couldn't sit around waiting for him for the rest of her life either. For the moment, he wouldn't even talk to her, and he was showing every possible sign of having deserted her permanently, and if that was the case, she had to go on living.

"What do I want to happen?" Bill thought about it for a minute. And then he smiled. "I want a happy ending, pre-ceded by a happy beginning. I think we're off to a good start, don't you?" She nodded. "And I want time with you, to go places and be together and do things, when we're not work-ing. And I want to get to know you. I think I already do, but I want to know more. I want you to know me. I want us to be . . . well," he said, groping for the words as he looked at her, "something very special." And then he smiled. "And in Janu-ary, I want," he almost gulped as he said the words, "to share the baby with you. It's a miracle, Adrian . . . and I'd like to share that with you, if I'm lucky enough, and you still need me."

"You're not the one who would be lucky," she said with tears in her eyes. "I would be. Why do you want to do all this for me?" she asked, still a little bit afraid, still puzzled. After all Steven had done to abandon her, it was so hard to believe she had found someone who wanted to stand by her.

"I want to do 'all this' because I love you," he said simply. "And I want you to know that this is a real departure for me. I haven't been seriously involved with anyone in years. Proba-bly not since the demise of my marriage. And I also swore to myself that I'd never have any more kids again . . . I don't want to fall in love with your child . . . and then lose it, if you leave me. But I'm willing to take that chance, if you're honest with me. And if that honesty is that you're reserving yourself for the possibility that Steven could come back when you have this kid, I've decided that I'm willing to take that chance for now. That's as straightforward as I know. I'm telling you that I'm willing to take the risk, and be there for you. Just don't forget to tell me what's going on, like you forgot to mention the pregnancy."

"I didn't forget," she explained, and he grinned.

"Yeah, I know. You just didn't mention it. A minor oversight. And how were you going to explain that one in a few months, after you'd eaten me out of house and home?" He loved teasing her, as she threw a napkin at him.

"I do *not* eat that much!"

"Yes, you do, but you should. The baby needs it."

But she grew serious then. "You're not scared to take the risk? What if he comes back? I owe him a life with his child, and I owe it to the baby."

"I disagree with you. I don't think you owe him anything, after the way he treated you, but if you do, I have to respect that. I just don't happen to think he'll come back. Anyone who'd go to the lengths of renouncing his parental rights, in a state where you can practically commit mass murder and still keep them, isn't planning to come back and be a daddy. But I could be wrong. I told you. I'm willing to take the risk. Because I love you." And as he said it, she got up from where she sat, and went to kiss him. She had been feeling better for the past two days, and there had been mounting passion in their occasional stolen kisses. She wondered what else was waiting for them once they got back to L.A., but as long as the boys were there, it was not an issue.

They spent their last night there quietly, chatting on the terrace and looking up at the stars and holding hands, and suddenly he laughed and he looked at her, feeling ridiculously happy. "Do you realize how crazy this is?" He grinned. "I'm in love with a woman who is four months pregnant. Do you have any idea how funny this is going to be when you can no longer see your feet? Talk about modern romance!" She started to laugh, too, and they just sat there and laughed about the absurdity of their situation. "I mean you could almost do this in the movies . . . guy meets girl in supermarket, falls madly in love with her, and they keep meeting. Girl is married, but husband walks out on her when he discovers that she is pregnant—with *his* baby. Guy from supermarket reappears, and they fall madly in love. Girl then staggers around with big belly, doing Fred Astaire–Ginger Rogers type dances with our hero. They get married. They have baby. And live happily ever after. Cute, isn't it? Maybe I should do it for the show. But it's much too simple. To do it for daytime TV, you would have to kill Steven, and the baby would really have to be someone else's, and then it would turn out that I was already married to your sister, or maybe I could turn out to be your father. That's a nice touch. I'll have to try to work that in somewhere." She was laughing at him then. And he was right. It was a ridiculous situation. But he had reminded himself of a more serious question. "When does your divorce become final, by the way? Before or after the baby?"

"Around the same time, I think. I'm not sure of the exact date."

"It might be nice if we could give Junior a name, other than Thompson," her maiden name, and she was touched by the way he said it. He was offering to marry her, if only to legitimize the baby, and she leaned over and kissed him for what he had just said.

"Bill, you don't have to do that."

"I know I don't. But I might want to by then. And so might you . . . if I play my cards right and get very lucky." He winked, and she lay back and looked at the stars again. She wished she had all the answers. But he was willing to leave an open door for her, and she couldn't ask for more than that. In fact, it was much more than she had ever dared to hope for.

She had envisioned herself alone and desperately lonely until the baby was born. It had never dawned on her that all of this would happen before she had the baby.

They left the lake the next day, and took their time driving down to L.A. They stopped in San Francisco again for one night, and then drove down Highway 5, and reached Los Angeles just in time for dinner. She made grilled cheese sandwiches at Bill's place while he got the boys ready for bed. And they ate dinner in their pajamas while Adrian told them silly stories about the newsroom, about the time a pig from a publicity stunt got loose and went berserk running all over the station, and the time there had been a food fight in the commissary that got so out of control, it took two weeks to scrape all the food off the ceiling. Adam particularly loved that story, and Bill grinned at her as she told it. They were all a little sorry to be home. And she particularly, as she had to go back to work the following morning. Bill was planning to take another two weeks off, so he could hang around with the boys, but she couldn't do that.

"Will we see you every day?" Tommy asked with worried eyes.

"I'll come by every night after work. I promise."

And then Adam. "Can we visit you at work?"

"Sure, but it's not much fun." And she was usually very busy, and Bill knew that. He suggested they go to Disneyland on the weekend and it gave Adrian something to look forward to as well. She was feeling depressed at not being with them every moment. She suddenly felt left out, and she was really sad when she helped put them to bed, and had finished reading them their favorite stories.

"I really hate to leave," she said quietly to Bill, after they had cleaned up the kitchen. She still hadn't been to her own place, and her bags were still in his hallway.

"Then don't. You can sleep in our guest room."

"The boys will think I'm a little strange. After all, I do have my own apartment to go to, and it's not exactly far away."

"So what. Pretend you lost your keys." He loved the idea, and so did she, and with a giggle, she agreed. And half an hour later, they were sitting on his couch, with her in her nightgown, and one of his bathrobes.

"This is fun," she laughed, he had just made a huge bowl of popcorn. "It's kind of like being a kid again, and staying over at a friend's house."

He smiled innocently at her. "They call it something else when you're as old as I am." After all, he was almost forty.

"Do they?" She walked right into it. "What?"

"I think they call it marriage." She fell silent then, and went on eating the popcorn, and when he came to sit down again, he smiled down at her. "It can be a happy thing, you know. Particularly between two people who know what they're doing, and happen to be very much in love. We might even qualify for both one day. We could even have a baby. Our own, I mean. Wouldn't that be something else?" He loved the idea of it suddenly, despite his many years of reservations. But he liked the idea of her baby, too, and he had been excited about it ever since he'd found out, and he kept telling her what she should be doing for the baby.

"What do you suppose the boys would say?"

"They'd be surprised certainly." He grinned at her, and handed her a mouthful of popcorn. "Kids don't think about things like that. You could wait until you're seven months pregnant before you tell them, and you'd still surprise them. They would just assume you were fat, until you told them something different."

"That's reasonable. That's what I thought, too . . . until I did the test."

"Were you surprised?" He was curious about that.

"More or less. Maybe less rather than more. But at the time I told myself that I was shocked. But I think maybe I wasn't. I was just scared about Steven's reaction."

"When did you tell him?"

"When he got back from a trip. And he wasn't exactly pleased." Which was a major understatement.

She slept in his guest room that night, and in the morning the boys came in and pounced on her with delight. They were thrilled that she had stayed, instead of being shocked. And they wanted her to stay every night, but she said she had to get back to her own apartment. In fact, she had to go back that morning, to get dressed for work, and Adam and Tommy went with her. They were surprised to see that she had no furniture, and Tommy looked around with obvious disapproval.

"Why do you live like that?" he asked. "You don't even have a couch!" To him that was minimal, and Adam was upset for her. He thought that maybe she was too poor to buy one, and he thought that Bill should have at least given her one, but she was quick to reassure them.

"My husband took all that stuff when he left," she explained.

"That was mean of him," Tommy said, and she didn't disagree with him.

"Why didn't you buy more?" Adam inquired.

"I haven't gotten around to it. He didn't leave very long ago."

"How long?" Tommy again.

"About two months . . . well, no . . . three, I guess."

"You'd better get some stuff," Thomas Thigpen advised her sternly.

"I'll do my best. Maybe before you come back again, I'll get this place looking decent." She went upstairs to dress for the office then, and when she came back downstairs Adam whistled. She was wearing a simple black linen dress, but it was well cut, and it showed off her legs. They were about all she had left of her figure.

"You know, you ought to go on a diet," Adam said. "My mom did. And she looks great. You could be really pretty if you lost some weight . . . I mean, you're pretty now . . . it's just that . . . you know, you'd just be better if you lost a little around the middle." She started to laugh at what they'd said, but then pretended to take it very seriously, just as Bill came to get them.

"Well, we've solved all my problems," she explained. "I need a couch, and I have to go on a diet." She could hardly keep a straight face, and he looked at her two young friends with dismay.

"Did you say that to Adrian?" he asked Tommy.

"No," she covered quickly for them, "we came to the conclusion together. And they happen to be right." Naturally she didn't tell them that she had to put the apartment on the market in two months, and she was going to have a baby.

She left for work then, and the day seemed endless without them. She was thrilled to come home that night, but she slept in her own apartment, because she thought Bill needed time alone with them, but she spent as much time with them as she could. And they had a wonderful time in Disneyland, and their last day together came too soon. Bill took all of them to Spago again as a special treat, but it was a mournful dinner. Bill and Adrian were so sad to see them go, and the boys were heartbroken to be leaving them. Both boys cried when they went to bed that night. And Adrian went to the airport with Bill the next day so he wouldn't be quite as lonely. And after they were gone, she felt as though someone had died, and he looked it. Their little faces had looked so sad, they had waved till the last moment when they got on the plane. And they had promised to call the minute they got home, and often after that, and Tommy had whispered thanks to her again for saving him as he left her. They had both kissed her good-bye, and she had cried as much as they had.

"I've never gotten used to it," Bill said as they walked back to the car. They had driven to the airport in his beloved woody. "It used to almost kill me when I said good-bye to them. And it still does." And when they got in his car, he turned to her and put his arms around her for comfort. But there was nothing she could say to take the hurt away, nothing she could do that would bring them back before Thanksgiving. "That's why I never wanted kids again. I never wanted to lose them." And yet . . . he was willing to share the baby with her . . . and give it back if she went back to Steven. Bill Thigpen was truly amazing.

CHAPTER

··21··

THE SILENCE IN BILL'S APARTMENT WAS DEAFENING WHEN they went back to it once the boys were gone. And Bill looked as though he'd lost his best friend, while Adrian tried desperately to distract him. She even volunteered to cook him dinner.

"Why don't you watch television, while I whip something up," she suggested, and he stared mindlessly at the tube, thinking about the boys, while she clattered around his kitchen. He was listening to her with one ear, and then finally he realized that she was dropping everything. First she dropped the metal mixing bowls, then there was the clatter of pans, the slamming of cupboards, and he started to smile to himself. Adrian was extremely capable everywhere, except in the kitchen.

"Do you need a hand in there?" he inquired above the din, and her voice came back sounding a little distracted.

"No, I'm fine. Where do you keep the vanilla?"

"What are you making?"

"Lasagna," she answered, dropping three more bowls and slamming the oven door again, and then he appeared, smiling broadly, in the kitchen doorway.

"I hate to tell you this, Adrian. But there's no vanilla in lasagna. Not in my recipe anyway. You must do something different." He looked highly amused and she looked completely flustered. She had every bowl, every pot, every baking pan, and what looked like every frying pan sitting on the counter, but he refrained from making comment.

"Oh, shut up," she said, glancing at the look on his face, and pushing the hair out of her eyes with her forearm. "I know there's no vanilla in lasagna. I'm making brownies. For dessert," she explained. "And a Caesar salad."

"It sounds lovely. Would you like a hand?"

"No, actually I'd like a cook." She grinned sheepishly. "How about a sandwich?" He was laughing by then, and walked into the kitchen and put his arms around her. He had never been alone with her, not really, not since the boys had arrived and he told her he loved her. The boys had been with him for a month, and a lot had happened in the time they'd been there.

"Would you like to go out?" he asked, enjoying the smell of her shining dark hair as he held her. "We could go to Spago." He was one of the few people who could get in almost anytime he wanted. He was one of Hollywood's elite, and most people would have killed to get into Spago. "Or I could cook for you. How about that?" He liked the idea of staying home with her, and he had been looking forward to a quiet evening. It was Saturday night, and all the restaurants in town would be too crowded.

"No," she said stubbornly, looking at the mess she had made. "I said I was going to cook you dinner, and I'm going to."

"How about if I help you? I'll be the sous-chef."

"Okay." She grinned mischievously at him. "Just tell me how you make lasagna." He laughed openly at her then, and started putting things away. And together they made a salad, and he grilled some steaks, and they chatted as they worked, about the boys, and the show, and the new season. He was less affected by the seasons than the evening shows, because his show didn't go into summer reruns, and it was live all year round. But he had to make it lively, and jazz it up to keep it fresh, and he was currently working on developing new subplots, and they had spent a lot of time talking about it together. He liked her ideas and she had given him some notes she had made, and he was impressed with them. And they were discussing them again when they sat down to dinner.

"I agree with you, Adrian." She had just made an interesting point. "But first we have to get Helen's baby born," he explained, countering her viewpoint. "But after that, I kind of like the idea of a kidnap. The baby disappears . . . it turns out that it's someone who hates John, and it has nothing to do with her, *or* . . ." He squinted while he thought, penciling it all in his head, "Or . . . it's actually the baby's natural father who takes it . . . there's a tremendous chase across numerous states and through all kinds of problems . . . and when we find him, and the baby, of course, then we know the identity of the baby's father." He looked pleased and she looked at him in fascination. She wondered how all these people constantly existed in his head, but she was just beginning to understand it.

"Who is the baby's father, by the way?"

"I haven't figured that out yet."

Adrian laughed at his answer. "She's already pregnant and you don't know who the father is? That's awful!"

"What can I tell you? This is modern romance."

"Extremely."

"Actually, I like the direction you suggested yesterday, because if I make it someone plausible and nice, whom the audience likes, we could get a lot of mileage out of it."

"What about Harry?" Adrian suggested.

"Harry?" Bill looked surprised, it was someone he would never have thought of. He was too obvious, and yet not obvious at all. He was the widower of Helen's best friend, but it was the perfect suggestion. With John in prison for life for two murders, it made sense to link Helen up with someone she could eventually marry. "That's a brilliant idea." And the actor who played him would be thrilled. His part had been dwindling for months, since the demise of his partner, and he was actually a very fine actor. "Adrian, you're a genius!"

"Yes," she smiled sweetly, "and a fabulous cook, don't you think?"

"Absolutely." He leaned over and kissed her with a broad grin. It was so much fun being with her, and so easy, and he loved the fact that she didn't resent the show, he was even getting the impression that she loved it. "Could you ever see yourself working on a show like this?" He had been thinking about it recently, when she started making such useful suggestions.

"I've never thought of it. I'm too busy dealing with rapes and murders and natural disasters in real life. But a soap would be a lot more fun. Why, are you recruiting?"

"I might be, at some point. Would you be interested?"

"Are you serious?" She looked at him, amazed, as he nodded. "I'd love it."

"So would I." He loved the idea of working close to her. But they both had a lot of other things to consider first, and she, above all, knew that. She was working on the divorce with the attorney he'd hired for her, and in January she was going to have the baby. She had already decided to take a leave of absence, but she hadn't told the newsroom yet. But maybe instead of going back to work at the news, she could go to work for Bill after the baby. It was certainly an intriguing idea. And as she thought of it as she sipped the cappuccino Bill had made, she realized that she really loved it. It was also a little scary combining their careers with their relationship, but maybe it would work. It *was* worth thinking about anyway. "Is there anything you can't do?" she asked admiringly, as she sat on a stool and watched him, thinking now nice it would be if they worked together.

"Yes," he said, with a gentle smile, leaning over to kiss her gently on the lips, "have babies. Speaking of which, how are you feeling?" It embarrassed her when he inquired about her health. She wasn't entirely ready to talk about the pregnancy with him, and yet he had been so sweet about it ever since he'd known it. But talking about it still seemed strange to her. It was her deepest, darkest secret.

"I'm fine," she reassured him. It was remarkable but she had had no lasting ill effects from her traumatic adventure at Lake Tahoe. She had seen the doctor as soon as she got home, and eventually the stitches in her arm had come out, but the scratches and bruises were gone, the concussion healed, the baby secure. It was truly amazing. The doctor could hardly believe it. He had told her that she was obviously carrying an astonishingly persistent baby, and Bill had been relieved to hear it. He acted as though the baby were his, and whenever he mentioned it, it touched her.

"Does it frighten you, Adrian? Being pregnant, I mean. I've always thought that it must be a little scary. It's so strange. You make love with someone, and this tiny seed grows into a little person, as though you swallowed it or something. And it grows and grows inside you until you look like you're going to pop, and then comes the hard part. You have to get it out. And that must really be scary. Psychologically, I mean. Physically, it all works out somehow. And the thing that always impressed me is that, as a man, you think—God, if I were in her shoes, I would never do this again—and two hours later a woman who just gave birth will tell you it wasn't so bad and she'd do it again in a minute. It's really very remarkable. Don't you think?"

"I do. It all seems a little strange to me. Especially since in my case I haven't had anyone to share it with, so most of the time it was like it wasn't even there. Only now, I'm beginning to realize that I can't ignore it for much longer and I'll have to face it." He handed her another cappuccino, and she stirred it and then sipped the froth of steamed milk, dusted with grated chocolate. He was definitely a much better chef than she was.

"Can you feel it moving yet?" She shook her head. "That's so wonderful when it happens. Life . . ." He sat down and looked at her lovingly. ". . . it's so miraculous, isn't it? I look at the boys, and I still think what a miracle they are, even as big as they are now, with shaggy hair, and ripped knees in their jeans and dirty sneakers. To me, they're gorgeous." It was part of why she had come to love him. He was so real and so good and so kind, and so serious about the things that were really important, like friendship and love and family and truth. She loved his values and what he stood for. Unlike Steven, who had run in the face of the challenge of their baby. He didn't want to give anything to anyone, which was the antithesis of everything Bill stood for. She still couldn't believe she had been lucky enough to meet him. He was putting their cups in the sink, when he turned to her with a shy smile, and their eyes met, and she felt herself pulled toward him. There was a magnetic quality about him that always drew her to him.

"Yes?" She knew he was going to ask her something, and he laughed at her clairvoyance.

"I was going to ask you a question, but I wasn't sure if I should."

"What about? Am I a virgin? Yes, actually I am."

"Thank God." He heaved a sigh of relief. "I hate women who aren't virgins."

"So do I."

He grinned. "In that case . . . would you like to spend the night? You can sleep in the guest room if you really want to."

It was silly, she had her own place just across the complex. But she was tempted to stay with him anyway. It was so lonely at her place, with only one lamp to light the room. There was no point, she kept telling herself, in buying furniture if she was going to sell the condo. And Bill's guest room was like a warm, cozy haven, just like him, a place where she could hide from the pressures of the world, and enjoy the warmth of his presence. "It seems a little silly, doesn't it?" she asked sheepishly. "I should probably go home."

"I just thought . . ." He looked sad for a moment. "It's going to be lonely without the boys tonight." She knew it would, and she wanted to be there for him. "We could make popcorn and watch old movies on TV."

"Sold. I accept." She smiled shyly at him. She loved being with him, but he pretended to look serious as he asked another question.

"From a marketing standpoint, would you mind telling me what swung your decision? Was it the popcorn or the old movies? Maybe I ought to know, just in case I want to convince you again someday."

She laughed easily at him. "It was the popcorn. And a free breakfast tomorrow morning."

"Who said anything about breakfast?" he teased with a blank stare.

"Be nice, or I'll make you lasagna . . . with vanilla!"

"I was afraid of that. *The Vanilla Virgin,* now there's a great title for a new show . . . or maybe just one episode . . . what do you think?" He turned and stood very close to her as they walked into the living room and her voice was very soft as she answered.

"I think you're wonderful."

He put his arms around her again and kissed her gently on the neck. "I'm glad to hear it . . . I think I love you. . . ." But she knew she loved him. She had known it for weeks, ever since she had woken up in the hospital in Truckee, and he told her he loved her and her baby. And it was odd talking about it with him now. He seemed to know so much more about pregnancy and babies than she did. It was comforting in a way, and she was coming to depend on him, and love the idea of having him near her. "What do you say we watch TV in my room tonight?" he inquired. He had a huge set in his room, and he and the boys used to pile into his bed at night and watch it. She had joined them several times, on nights when she was staying in the guest room, but it was different now that they were gone, and it was a little strange at first, getting on his bed with him, and being there alone with him, but she had to admit that she loved it.

She settled back against the cushions on the bed, and he flicked the television on with the remote, and then left the room to make the popcorn, and she didn't follow. She sat there, thinking about him, about how much he meant to her, and how drawn to him she was. It was odd feeling sexual about a man who wasn't your husband when you were almost five months pregnant. But she did. She was extremely attracted to him, and not entirely sure how to show it.

"Popcorn!" he announced, arriving moments later with a huge metal bowl from the kitchen. The popcorn was still hot and it was buttered and salted to perfection.

"This is terrific," she grinned, cuddling next to him as he flipped the dial via the remote to a channel that showed only old movies. There was an old Cary Grant movie on, and Adrian insisted that he leave it. "I love this," she smiled happily, nibbling at the popcorn, and he moved closer to her and gently kissed her.

"So do I," he said, and he really meant it. She was his best friend, and there was more to it as well. He found that he couldn't stop kissing her, as she nibbled at the popcorn and pretended to watch the movie. She was lying back against the pillows on his bed, her vision of the television obscured, and she found that she didn't care, as she kissed him back, and a passion rose in her that she had never known, as he whispered to her, "Are you on the pill?" and then she started to laugh and kissed him again.

"Yes, I am," she whispered back. There was humor and love and laughter between them, but they both grew more serious again as their passion rose, and the romance of Cary Grant was forgotten. He set the bowl of popcorn down, and turned off the light and turned to her again. She was so beautiful, and so sexy and so gentle. She was still wearing the free-flowing peach dress she had worn to take the boys to the airport, and he unbuttoned it slowly, as she slipped searching hands under his sweater. Their lips touched and parted and touched again, and he seemed to be devouring her with kisses, and finally, they lay naked in each other's arms and he forgot himself and all caution as they joined and made love as her body hummed beneath his hands, and the two of them became one, and they seemed to lie together for hours, bringing each other ecstasy and pleasure.

Neither of them had any idea what time it was when they finally lay side by side, kissing still, and whispering in the darkness.

"You're so beautiful," he said, and then touched her face with his hands again, and let his fingers trace slowly downward. She had a lovely body, and even now it was easy to see how slim and lithe she must be when she wasn't pregnant. "Are you all right?" He was suddenly afraid he might have hurt her or the baby. For a moment, he had forgotten all about it, but she only smiled and kissed his neck and his lips, touching his powerful chest with her hands. He made her feel happy and safe and protected.

"You're wonderful." Her eyes shone with her love for him, and as he looked at her, mesmerized by her, his hands felt the soft roundness of her belly, and then she frowned suddenly and looked at him oddly. "Did you do that?"

"What?"

"I don't know . . . something . . . I'm not sure what it was . . ." It had felt like a flutter and at first she thought it was his hands, but they hadn't moved, and then suddenly they both knew what it was at the same moment. She had felt the baby move for the first time. It was as though the baby had finally come alive from their loving. It was his baby now, and theirs, because he wanted it, and he loved her.

"Let me feel it." He put his hands on her again, but he couldn't feel anything, and then for an instant he thought he did, but it was still very small, and the movements were so slight, they were hard to feel. He pulled her close to him instead, feeling the swell of her against him, and then holding her full breasts in his hands. He loved everything about her. It was odd getting to know her this way, in a state of transition. This was the only way he knew her, and he felt bound to the baby somehow, as though it were his too. It seemed so much a part of her, and he wanted to share it with her.

He covered her carefully with his sheets and the blanket and they lay there together, snuggling, whispering, talking, dreaming, and talking about the baby.

"It's so funny," he confessed, vaguely hearing the voice of Cary Grant somewhere in the distance. They had forgotten all about the popcorn and the movie. "I feel as though the baby is part of me now. I don't know . . . it brings back all kinds of familiar feelings and memories, all that excitement I felt before Adam and Tommy were born . . . I find myself thinking about buying a crib, helping you set up the room, being there when it's born, and then I have to remind myself to go slow . . . that it isn't mine . . ." he said regretfully. But he wanted it to be. Even though he had just made love to her for the first time, he wanted that very badly.

"I was so lost before you came along. I was so lonely." She looked at him with serious eyes, worried about what he felt. "You really don't mind about the baby? I feel so fat and ugly sometimes."

He chuckled softly in the bed they had made theirs. "That, my love, is going to get a lot worse before it gets better. You are going to blow up like a balloon, and I'm going to love it. You're going to be so big and cute, and we're going to have such a good time with the baby."

"Silly." She winced at the thought of becoming enormous. It was something she hadn't really thought about and almost dreaded. Her thighs already felt twice the size they had been two months before, and her breasts seemed huge compared to what they normally were. She was usually very small, and suddenly she was very full-busted. All the changes seemed so strange and foreign to her, and yet at the same time, she was excited about the baby. And she could hardly believe that he was too. It was a miracle beyond belief that she had found him.

"It seems poetic justice somehow," he said, grinning as he sat up in bed and looked down at her, "that I should get involved with a woman who is four and a half months pregnant. I have been involved with more anorexic models and bulemic actresses than anyone deserves in one lifetime, and suddenly here I am with a woman I love, in full bloom, and any minute you're not going to be able to see your sneakers."

"You're terrifying me. Is there anyway to avoid turning into a blimp?" she asked with worried eyes, and he leaned down and kissed her again.

"Absolutely none. It's a beautiful gift. Just enjoy it."

"But will you still love me when I'm huge?" It was a familiar wail to any man whose wife had been pregnant.

"Of course. Wouldn't you love me if I were the one with a baby inside me?"

She laughed at the idea, but he made it sound so natural that it didn't seem so frightening suddenly. He did that with everything. With Bill, everything became normal and easy and simple. "Yes, I would." She smiled up at him, cozy in his bed.

"Then that answers the question, doesn't it? You're beautiful pregnant. Maybe you should be worrying about whether or not you'll turn me on when you're skinny. We know what you do to me when you're like this." He grinned evilly, and she laughed. She felt totally at ease with him, and loved as she never had been in her life. And the beauty of it was that she loved him, too, more than she had ever loved anyone . . . even Steven. Steven had never been this good to her, or this kind, or this wise, or this sensitive to her needs, and fears, and moods. There was no doubt in her mind. She was a lucky woman and William Thigpen was a rare person. "You drive me wild with desire, Adrian," he teased, growling at her, as he pretended to attack her again, but gently.

"Never mind that," she laughed. "Where's my popcorn?"

"You have no heart." He leaned over and handed it to her. "Only stomach." He kissed her loudly on her bottom then, and went to get them both a bottle of club soda, knowing before she said it that she was thirsty.

"You read my mind, do you know that?"

"It comes with the package." He was dying to make love to her again, but he was afraid to overdo it and hurt the baby. He was willing to be patient and love her carefully for the next four and a half months. It seemed a small price to pay for the miracle of a baby, and the gift of sharing that with her. He helped himself to some of the popcorn, turned up the TV, and looked over at her. He felt as though they belonged to each other now, as though they were one, and had always been married. It was impossible to believe that she was married to someone else, and carrying another man's baby. A man who wanted neither Adrian nor the baby.

The phone rang as Adrian was drifting off to sleep, nestled next to him, while he watched the television and glanced at her occasionally with a warm smile, and a hand on her shoulder. It was Tommy and Adam safely arrived in New York, and calling to tell him.

"How was the trip?"

"Great!" Tommy said. The stewardess let him have three hot dogs. Bill had ordered special meals for them in L.A. He always did, it was just one of the many things he thought of. "How's Adrian? Is she there?" he asked hopefully, and Bill looked down at her and nodded.

"Yeah. We're watching TV and eating popcorn and we really miss you guys. It was really sad here after you left." He was always honest with them, too, about how he felt. "We can hardly wait for Thanksgiving." He was already using *we* to describe himself and Adrian. There was no doubt in his mind that they would still be together by then. Only then, they would have to say something to the boys about the baby. He would leave it to Adrian to decide what she wanted to tell them. And as he thought of it, he put a hand on her stomach again to see if he could feel the baby. He felt possessive about it now that he had been closer to it, and felt her body joined to his. He had never felt closer to any woman.

Adam got on the phone then and told him about the movie they'd seen on the plane. Something about the war in Vietnam, and it sounded upsetting to him, but Adam seemed to have loved it. He asked to speak to Adrian then, and Bill gently nudged her and put his hand over the receiver.

"It's Adam, sweetheart. He wants to talk to you."

"Okay." She reached for the phone with a sleepy smile, but when she spoke to him she made an effort to sound normal. "Hi, Adam. How was the trip? Any cute girls?"

He guffawed at the question. She had been the first to realize that he was becoming interested in girls, and spent a lot of time in the bathroom combing his hair with assorted products. "Not really. Just one, in the seat behind us."

"Did you get her number?" Adrian teased, but he was serious when he answered.

"Yeah. She lives in Connecticut. Her dad is a pilot."

"Too bad you weren't interested in her . . . much . . ." They both laughed, and a minute later she talked to Tommy, and told them both how much they missed them. "Your dad and I were sitting here all sad and lonely tonight. Even the popcorn isn't the same without you."

"Thanks a lot." Bill pretended to pout, and listened to the animated conversation between the three of them with pleasure. She was wonderful to his kids, and he would never forget her saving Tommy's life, and nearly losing her own and her baby's. He had never been so frightened as when he'd seen that little lifeless body, and then hers . . . he shuddered when he thought of it.

She handed the phone back to him then, and he chatted with the boys for a few minutes and then let them go so they could spend time with their mother. She hadn't seen them in a month and Bill knew she'd be anxious to see them.

"They sound so close, but they're so far away," Adrian said sadly. Three months seemed an interminable wait to see them again, and she wondered how he stood it, particularly with no other family in California. It wasn't as though he was remarried and had other children. And even that might not have made a difference. Adam and Tommy were special and unique, and she knew now just how much he missed them. "It seems like an awfully long time till Thanksgiving."

"Now you know what it's like, or a little bit anyway," he said seriously, as he climbed back into bed with her and turned off the TV. "That's why I never wanted other children. I never wanted anyone to do that to me again. To take them away, to deprive me of them. No matter how decent Leslie is, they still live with her and only spend six weeks a year with me, if I'm lucky, maybe seven. It's lousy."

"I understand," she said gently. And she did. And she knew him well enough now to know how much it hurt him. And then, unprompted, she spoke up in the darkness. "I would never do that to you, Bill."

"How do you know that? No one can ever be sure. And look at you . . . you still feel an obligation to Steven. If he comes back after the baby is born, what happens to us? You don't know the answer to that either." He sounded angry and unhappy for just a moment, but it was only because he loved her, and was missing his children.

"No, I don't know the answer to that. But I would never hurt you." She knew that now. She didn't know what she'd do if Steven came back, and Bill was right, she did feel an obligation to her husband. But she felt something more now, too, a bond to Bill, a tie that had formed, that night perhaps when they were making love, or maybe it had happened more slowly, in the past few months when they became friends. But something had happened to bind them together, and she knew she'd never just walk out on him . . . or take away something or someone he loved. She was sure of it . . . or at least she hoped not. "I love you, Bill," she said softly, thinking of him, and the boys, and the baby.

"I love you too," he whispered back, thinking only of her, and as he did, his desire for her got the best of him again and he ran smooth hands slowly over her flesh, until she was panting with desire, and he made love to her again. It was a long, happy night, and they were still entangled in each other's bodies when they awoke in the morning.

She opened one eye, and was happily startled when she saw him. For a moment, she had thought it was a dream. But it wasn't, he was still asleep, and softly snoring. But he woke a few minutes later as she stretched, and shifted the weight of his leg on her a little.

"Is that you?" he growled sleepily, "or have I died and gone to heaven?" He smiled blissfully with his eyes closed in the morning sunlight.

"It's me. But is it you?" she whispered happily. It had been the most beautiful night of her life, the perfect honeymoon, in spite of being pregnant.

"It's me . . . are you still a virgin?" he teased, and she grinned.

"I don't think so."

"Good. Let's just hope you don't get pregnant."

"Don't worry. I'm on the pill." They were giggling and cuddling, and lying as close as they could in the rumpled bed they had slept in.

"I'm relieved to hear it . . . are you going to make me lasagna for breakfast?" He stretched and grinned as she nodded.

"With vanilla."

"Perfect. That's just the way I like it." And then he turned over on his stomach, and lifted his head to kiss her on the lips. "I have a better idea. You relax, and I'll make you breakfast. What would you like? Waffles or pancakes?"

"Shouldn't I be on some kind of diet?" She was feeling guilty. They did nothing but eat all the time, but she wasn't really getting fat, except for her stomach. The baby somehow seemed to absorb it.

"You can worry about that later. What's your pleasure?"

"You." And she demonstrated that amply to him before

breakfast, much to his delight. It was two hours later before they discussed breakfast again, and this time he made scrambled eggs and bacon and steaming, strong coffee. And they sat eating breakfast in the kitchen, in matching silk dressing gowns that were both his, reading the Sunday paper.

"This is the perfect way to spend a Sunday morning," she announced, and he grinned over at her, he had been reading the entertainment section.

"I agree with you entirely." It was absolutely perfect.

They showered and dressed afterward, and went for a drive in her MG, which Bill loved to drive. And they stopped in Malibu for a long walk on the beach, and at sunset they drove slowly home with the top down and the wind in their faces. They looked happy and relaxed and young, and the world seemed to be theirs. They stopped at the supermarket where they had met, and then they went back to his place and made dinner. He poured champagne for both of them before they ate, to celebrate their union.

"To the marriage of two hearts . . . with a third to come," he smiled as he toasted her, and then kissed her. "I love you, my darling." They kissed again. And they spent a quiet evening at home, watching TV again, and she talked about going home. She didn't want to intrude on him, and she did have her own apartment, after all, but he wouldn't hear of her leaving. He wanted to move some of her things in that week. He couldn't see the point of her staying in the dismal emptiness of her old town house, and she had to agree with him. It didn't have much appeal, not now, when she could be with him, which was all she wanted.

He drove her to work the next day, and told her he'd bring her home after the six o'clock news, and then take her back for the late show. And when Zelda saw her, smiling at her desk, she knew something had happened to her. But she didn't pry. She just guessed, and hurried down the hall, feeling happy for her. And when he stopped in at noon, Zelda knew exactly who it was, and precisely what must have happened.

"It worked!" Bill beamed.

"What did?" A bear had attacked a child at the zoo, and the child had nearly died, and Adrian had to make a decision about what part of the tape to run, but she was happy to see him anyway, as she looked up and saw him smiling broadly. "What worked?" she said a little more gently. It had been a busy morning, but everything seemed to be bathed in a haze of happiness and pleasure.

"Your idea. About Harry being the baby's father. It works out perfectly. And everyone on the show is pleased, especially the director. George Orben is a pleasure to work with, and everyone is delighted about his getting a bigger part. You're a genius!"

"Anytime, Mr. Thigpen. Anytime." She smiled. She was still hoping that one day his job offer might work out, and she could be working on his show instead of in the newsroom.

"Can you go out to lunch?" He looked hopeful, but she shook her head. There was too much going on, the bear at the zoo, a policeman had been brutally murdered an hour before, and the government had fallen in Venezuela.

"I don't think I'm going to get out of here till after the six o'clock news." He nodded, kissed her, disappeared, and was back half an hour later with a huge hamburger, a cup of soup, and a fruit salad.

"It's all good for you. Eat it."

"Yes, sir." And then she whispered, "I love you," under her breath, and saw out of the corner of her eye the look of disapproval on her secretary's face, and she realized what she had done. Her secretary didn't even know she and Steven had separated, and here she was kissing another man. There were several interested stares, and she knew that they would be even more so, once people started figuring out that she was pregnant.

"Who was that?" one of the editors asked her bluntly as Bill left.

"His name is Harry," she said mysteriously, "his wife died several months ago." She was paraphrasing his new plot for his soap, but of course no one knew it. ". . . She was Helen's best friend . . ." The editor raised an eyebrow, shook his head, and went back to work, as Adrian went back to work too. And when he turned to look back at her as he left, he saw that she was smiling.

CHAPTER

••22••

SEPTEMBER SPED BY WITH HARD WORK AND HAPPY NIGHTS, and blissful weekends. And toward the end of the month, people were beginning to suspect that she was pregnant. She was almost six months, and no matter how loose her clothes, it was easy to figure out that there was something beneath them. She had not asked for maternity leave yet, though, and she had decided to work till the very end, and take time off after it was born, which seemed simpler.

"If I take time off before, I'll die of boredom," she told Bill, and he didn't disagree. He thought that as long as the doctor said she was in good health, she should do what she wanted. And he had suggested to her again that she think about working on his show after the baby came and maybe hand in her notice in the newsroom in December.

They went out a fair amount, to quiet restaurants where they could relax like The Ivy and Chianti and the Bistro Garden, and then occasionally to the noisier, livelier ones like Morton's, and Chasen's, and, of course, Spago. And they talked to the boys at least twice a week, and they were fine too. And the ratings on Bill's show were better than ever. Everything was going smoothly, and Bill kept reminding her that the next time she went, he wanted to join her at the doctor. It was his baby now, too, no matter whose genes were involved, but they had made love often enough, and grown close enough that somehow, he felt he should have been the father, and Adrian didn't deny it.

She had heard nothing from Steven since June, or from his attorney since July, and she didn't worry about it. She assumed that the divorce was still in the works, but she didn't think about it very much. She was too busy at work, and too happy with Bill. And she hadn't slept in the town house since August, the night the boys left.

But the call from her attorney on October first still surprised her. He was calling to tell her that Steven wanted the condo put on the market. She had expected it, but she was startled anyway. It was nice knowing that she had a place to live, a place of her own, even if she didn't live there.

"They want to be sure you won't be there when it's shown," the lawyer said.

"That's fine," she said coolly.

"And they want you to make your key available to the realtors, and leave the apartment in good order."

"That's not difficult. Did they tell you he'd taken every stick of furniture with him? All I have is the bed and my clothes in the closets, one carpet, and a stool in the kitchen. I'll do my best to leave it neat." Somehow as dismal as it all was, she realized that it was also amusing.

"And you haven't refurnished?" Her attorney sounded surprised by what she had just told him. She had forgotten to tell him before. And Steven's attorney hadn't told him that, but he suspected that there was a lot more that Steven's attorney hadn't told him, like why he was rejecting his own baby, and ending his marriage to a woman who was both reasonable and decent.

"No, I haven't. The apartment is empty."

"It might not show well that way. They probably think you've refurnished."

"Steven should have thought of that before he cleaned it out. I'm not going to furnish it just so he can sell it out from under me."

"Do you have any interest in buying him out, Mrs. Townsend?"

"No, I don't. And even if I did, I couldn't afford it." The lawyer had told them what he wanted for it, and she thought it was too high. But if he got it, then she'd get half, so she wasn't going to argue. "How's the divorce coming?" she asked cautiously. It was still a delicate subject with her.

"Everything is in progress." He hesitated and then decided to ask, even if her husband didn't want to know. "How is your pregnancy going?"

"Fine." And then, "Did Steven's attorney ask about it?"

"No, he didn't," he said regretfully, and she only nodded. "Is there anything else?"

"No. Just the apartment. We'll proceed with the realtors, and advise you who'll be handling it. How soon could you start showing it?"

She thought about it for a minute and then shrugged. "Tomorrow, I guess." There was really nothing to do. Even her closets were fairly neat, especially now that half her belongings were across the complex in Bill's guest room closet.

"We'll be in touch." She thanked him and they hung up and she was still pensive when Bill picked her up to take her home after the six o'clock news. He did that a lot now. And people talked. They knew who he was, but they were curious about the implications, and she continued to make no comment whatsoever about being pregnant. And when one woman she didn't like had asked, she had looked her right in the eye and said, no, she wasn't.

"Something happen today?" He sensed her mood as they drove home. He had picked up fresh crab for dinner.

"Nothing much," she lied. She was still disturbed about the call from her lawyer.

"You seem quiet."

"You're too smart for your own good." She leaned over and kissed him. "My attorney called today."

"What's up?" For a moment he looked worried.

"Steven's putting the town house on the market."

"Do you mind?" He frowned as he glanced at her while he drove home. He never really enjoyed their conversations about Steven. But she didn't love hearing reminiscences about Leslie either.

"Sort of. It's nice to know I have a place of my own, even though I never use it."

"Why? What difference does it make?"

"What if you get tired of me, or we have a fight or . . . I don't know . . . what'll we do when the boys come back for Thanksgiving?" Even though she doubted that it would be sold by then.

"We tell them we love each other and you're having a baby, and we're living together, that's what we tell them. No big deal."

She smiled ruefully at him. "You've been writing soap operas for too long. That might sound normal to you, but it wouldn't to most people, and it won't to Adam and Tommy. And maybe if I lived there all the time, they'd feel crowded and resent me." She had been thinking about it all day and she was worried about it.

"So what are you telling me? You want to get your own place?" He looked markedly unhappy.

"No, that seems foolish. I'm just telling you that I'm not thrilled he's selling it. It's just nice to have it."

"How much does he want for it?" She told him and he whistled. "That's an awful lot, but at least you get half of that, I assume, if he gets it. Maybe it'll be nicer having money in the bank than an apartment you don't use and just sits there."

She sighed, nodding at the wisdom of what he'd just said. "You're probably right, and it's no big deal. It's an adjustment, that's all." And there had been a lot of them since June. And also a lot of very wonderful changes.

"Does he want to talk to you?" Bill asked calmly as they pulled into his parking space. They were driving the woody. But she shook her head. He didn't.

But she called Steven at his office the next morning. She recognized the secretary's voice, and politely asked to speak to her husband.

"I'm sorry, Mr. Townsend is not available. He's in a meeting."

"Could you please let him know I'm calling," she countered.

"I'm not sure I can disturb him."

"Please try," she urged, getting increasingly annoyed. He had obviously told his secretary that if his wife ever called, not to put her through, and Adrian didn't deserve that.

The secretary disappeared and came back on the line two minutes later. It hadn't been long enough to tell anyone anything, she was just faking. "I'm sorry, Mr. Townsend will be tied up all day, but I'd be happy to take a message." Tell him to drop dead, she was tempted to say into the phone, but she didn't. And there were other possibilities, too, but she resisted them all.

"Just tell him I called about the apartment," she started to say, and then decided to really leave him a whopper, "and the baby." The bomb dropped and there was silence. "Thank you very much."

"I'll tell him right away," the secretary said in haste, as though he didn't already know. But Adrian knew that Steven would hate getting the message. If his secretary knew, sooner or later, people would start talking.

But he didn't call. His attorney did, half an hour later. Steven had called him within seven minutes. And the attorney had tried to call her attorney but couldn't reach him. So he called Adrian himself so he could call Steven back immediately and assuage his client's panic.

"Is there a problem, Mrs. Townsend? I understand you called your . . . Mr. Townsend this morning."

"That's right. I wanted to speak to him." For a mad moment, she had wanted to ask him why he was doing this to her, why he was taking everything away that had been theirs, and had rejected their baby. Now that it was moving, that it was alive, that she felt it, and could see the bulge that it caused in her body, she was even less able to understand how he could push them both away. It still didn't make sense, and she wanted to talk to him about it. It had nothing to do with how much she loved Bill. She did. But Steven was still the baby's father.

"Would you mind telling me why you were calling him?" He tried to sound kind. Steven had been adamant in his instructions.

"Yes, I would. It was personal."

"I'm sorry." He paused and Adrian understood all over again.

"He's not going to speak to me, is he?"

He didn't want to answer her directly, but the lack of an answer told her the same thing just as clearly. "He feels that . . . it would just be too difficult for both of you, particularly given the circumstances." He was afraid she was going to get emotional and try and force the baby on him. He had no idea that she was living with a man who genuinely loved her, and wanted her baby. And he would never have been able to understand it.

"Is there a problem with the pregnancy? Something that relates to Mr. Townsend, in spite of his legal stance vis-à-vis the child?" She wanted to tell him to shut up, to knock off the legalese and deal with her like a human being. But the sad thing was that he was trying.

"No, never mind. Just tell him to forget it." Which was exactly what he wanted. He had told the attorney that he wanted to forget everything about her, but the lawyer would never have told her.

She hung up the phone, and she was even more depressed that afternoon, and Bill sensed it again, but figured it was still about the apartment, even though he thought it was silly. But he had no idea that she had tried to call Steven, just to talk to him, just to ask him why, it wasn't that she even wanted to change his mind anymore, she just wanted to know why he hadn't loved her, and had refused to accept their baby. There had to be a reason, something more than just a difficult childhood. But she didn't want to tell Bill. She knew that it would hurt his feelings. Instead, she just sat quietly in the living room, and suggested they call the boys after dinner. Talking to them always cheered her up. And the next day, her lawyer called her again and gave her the name of the real estate agent who would be showing the apartment.

That weekend, she and Bill went away, and on Monday she felt better. The apartment didn't seem so important anymore, and she realized that she didn't need a place of her own. She was perfectly happy living with Bill. And the apartment she had shared with Steven wasn't worth trying to hang on to.

They had gone to stay with friends of his in Palm Beach, an actor who used to be on the show in his youth, and had gone on to make several very successful pictures. He was an interesting man, with a lovely family and a wife Adrian really liked. It had been a perfect weekend, and they had teased Bill a lot about the baby. They assumed it was his, and they didn't find it at all unusual that they weren't married. But they had also been very warm to the idea, and Janet, the actor's wife, had been wonderfully supportive about the "marvels" of being pregnant. There were times when Adrian wondered if she would ever survive it, and other times when she actually forgot she was pregnant at all. It seemed to depend on the day and the mood and what else had happened. But the thing to keep in mind, Janet had reminded her, was that at the end of the road, the reward was not fat thighs, which went away, Janet promised, but the greatest wonder of all: a baby. They had both come back from the weekend feeling refreshed and excited about the baby. Bill pulled out some of the books he had bought her that they had never read, and read her all kinds of things that would have terrified her if she hadn't been in such a good mood. And in the end, they made love, which was much better.

And the next morning, at work, her attorney called her again and surprised her by announcing that there was an offer for the apartment, and Steven wanted to accept it. It was within ten thousand dollars of his asking price, and Adrian couldn't believe it.

"Already?"

"We were very surprised, too, and the buyer wants to close in thirty days, if that's all right with you. We realize that that may be too soon for you." But all of a sudden she didn't care. It would be November by then, and the boys would be coming home for Thanksgiving, and Bill insisted that he wanted her to continue to stay with him, and he had already suggested that they turn the guest room into a nursery sometime in the next few months, which had bowled her over. "How do you feel about the thirty-day closing?" the attorney asked her directly.

"It's fine." He was surprised to hear it.

"And the price?" She sat quietly for a minute, but only because in her head, she was saying good-bye to the apartment and to Steven.

"It's fine too."

"You accept it?"

"Yes." Christ. Push, push, push.

"I'll get the papers over to you this afternoon. You can sign them and I'll send them back to your husband's attorney."

"Fine."

"We'll send them right over." And when he did, it seemed odd to see Steven's signature looking up at her. She hadn't seen any part of him in so long that seeing his handwriting was like a jolt into the past. But there was nothing else, no note, no letter, nothing jotted on the forms. He had completely removed himself from her life and he wanted to keep it that way, no matter what. It was almost as though he was afraid of her, but she couldn't understand why. It seemed so unreasonable, but maybe it no longer mattered.

She showed the papers to Bill that night and he said they looked fine, but he made a couple of suggestions, about the escrow, and how to handle the deposit, and suggested she talk to her divorce lawyer about them. And he warned her to be careful that she got her fair share out of the proceeds from the apartment. And then he asked her something he'd been wondering for a while, but hadn't wanted to bring it up, because he didn't want to upset her.

"What about spousal support? Has he offered you anything? And support for the baby?"

"I haven't asked for anything," she said quietly. "I have my salary. And he's already told me that he won't support the baby. He's renouncing all his rights before it's born, I told you that." She looked upset talking about it. "I don't want anything from him." If he didn't want her, and the baby, then she didn't want his money. But Bill thought her sentiments were both noble and stupid.

"What if you get sick? If something happens to you?" he asked her gently.

"I have insurance," she said, shrugging. And then he turned to her with a look of quiet exasperation.

"Why are you letting this guy off so damn easy, Adrian? Are you still in love with him? He deserted you. He owes you something, and the child." And then he felt his heart sink as she shook her head and reached out to touch him.

"You know, I'm not in love with him. But I was married to him . . . he was my husband . . . he still is technically . . . and," she almost gulped on the word, after everything Bill had done for her, but it was still the truth, "he's the baby's father." She didn't want to hurt him, but it was true, and it meant something to her, and he knew it.

"That means a lot to you, doesn't it?"

She looked down at her hands and then looked up at him again as she nodded and spoke very softly. "Yes, it does. Not a lot. But something. It's his child, Bill. What if he comes to his senses one day? He has a right to something . . . some part of it . . . I don't want to slam all the doors on him, in case one day he wants that."

"I don't think he ever will." Bill spoke just as quietly. He didn't want to fight with her, and as he listened to her, he wondered if there was any point in his fighting Steven. Bill didn't want to get hurt. But he didn't want to lose her, or the baby, either. "I think you're dreaming if you think he'll come back. I think he's made his position clear."

"He might change his mind."

"Do you want him to, Adrian? Do you want him back?"

He looked her right in the eye and she shook her head, and

he believed her. And without another word, he took her in his arms. "I'll die if I ever lose you." She knew that, and she would have died if she lost him, too, and yet . . . there was still the specter of Steven. . . .

"I don't want to lose you either."

"You won't." And then he smiled. As he held her, he could feel the baby kicking.

"Thank you for being so good to me."

"Don't be silly." He kissed her and they sat together for a long time, but their conversation worried him afterward. He knew how strong her loyalties were, and even though she loved him, to her it was still important that Steven was really the baby's father. And Bill knew that there was nothing he could do to protect himself anymore. He just had to love her, and take his chances.

CHAPTER

··23··

THE APARTMENT SOLD QUICKLY AND SIMPLY, AND IN THE
first week of November, the deal closed, and she and Bill
packed up her things and moved them to his place across the
complex. It was all very simple, and much less emotional than
she had feared. There was nothing left to hold on to, or feel
sentimental about. Steven had taken it all with him five
months before, even the album with their wedding pictures.
She wondered what he had done with it, and figured he had
probably thrown it out. It was odd. It was so completely gone,
everything had disappeared as though nothing had ever happened. She tried to explain it to Bill as she put the rest of her
belongings in his guest room.

"It's almost as if we were never married. I feel as though I
never knew him." And yet at the same time, Bill knew that
her loyalties to Steven were tremendous.

"Maybe you didn't. There are people like that sometimes."

But he was happy to see that she didn't look depressed. She was getting a little tired these days, but she still felt pretty well. She was seven months pregnant, and they were both excited about seeing the boys over Thanksgiving. They were due to come out in two weeks. But the week before, she had to go to the doctor. And this time, Bill came. He had wanted to come for months, but she always seemed to go when he had a crisis on the show or a major network meeting. But this time, he had told his secretary that he would be gone for two hours no matter what came up, and he drove Adrian to see her doctor. Shortly after meeting Bill she had switched to a woman doctor who had been recommended by several friends, and Adrian really seemed to like her. And when Bill met her he could see why. Jane Bergman was intelligent and direct and treated the entire process as though it was normal and natural, and she reassured them both that she had every reason to believe that the birth would be normal and easy. She also seemed perfectly comfortable with the fact that they were living together and not married. One of the reasons why Adrian had changed was because her previous doctor had known about Steven and there would have been too many questions. This woman had no idea that the baby wasn't Bill's, but someone else's. And she let Bill listen to the baby's heart, and he beamed as he heard it.

"It sounds like a hamster," Bill said seriously, listening to the baby's heartbeat.

"That's a nice thing to say," Adrian laughed. But Bill was extremely moved by having heard it, and touched by her vulnerability as she lay there with her enormous belly. Dr. Bergman said the baby was a good size, and recommended they take a Lamaze class. They both knew what it was, but Adrian wasn't sure what it entailed, and it had been more than eight years since Bill had done one with Leslie.

"It might make a difference," she said easily. She was a

woman about Bill's age, and she seemed very competent to him, and he was glad he'd come. He liked her. And he said as much to Adrian as they drove back to the office.

"I wish I could have it at home," Adrian said longingly, looking out the window.

"Oh, Jesus," Bill groaned. "Don't even say that."

"Why?" She sounded plaintive, and almost childish, and she was making him extremely nervous. "It would be so much nicer."

"And so much more dangerous. Be nice, and listen to Dr. Bergman. We'll do the Lamaze class right after the boys come." That would give them a month to do it before the baby came. But he had noticed lately that Adrian was starting to get very nervous. For seven months she had managed to avoid it and pretend she wasn't pregnant, but suddenly it was coming close, and she had to face it. She asked Bill a lot of questions, about the boys when they were born, and she had started reading the books. But he suspected that she was afraid of the pain and possible complications. And to him, the baby was starting to look enormous.

"I love you," he reminded her as he left her in the hallway outside the newsroom.

"Hi, Harry!" one of the editors called out as he hurried past, and Bill stared at Adrian in confusion.

"Who's Harry?" She started to laugh, remembering the story she had told months before when they had pressed her.

"You are. I told them you were Harry . . . and you were a widower, your wife had been one of Helen's best friends . . ." She put on a serious face as she summarized his soap, and he started to roar with laughter.

"You're impossible. Go back to work, and stop worrying about the baby."

"Who's worried?" She pretended to be glib, but he knew she was worried in spite of what she said, and he didn't blame her. She had the added stress of going through a divorce while she was pregnant.

"See you later, sweetheart." He kissed her again and hurried back to work, after promising to pick her up after the evening show, and take her out to dinner.

They went to Le Chardonnay, and they had a wonderful meal and a delightful evening. He had just won another award for the show, and there had been a lot of press about it, and he was very pleased about it. And she was proud of him, too, and he insisted on giving her credit.

"You keep the ratings up with your crazy ideas." She fed him a lot of wild plots for the show, and he was still hoping she'd come to work for him after the baby. And they were laughing and talking about it, as a couple sat down at the next table. And Bill didn't know what had happened, but Adrian's face suddenly went pale as she stared at them. She was looking at the man as though she'd seen a ghost, and he looked horrified when he saw her. And then he turned away and continued to talk to the woman he was with. She was young and sleek, and attractive, and she looked very athletic. But she wasn't half as pretty as Adrian, although she did look a few years younger. But Bill wasn't looking at the other girl, he was looking at Adrian across the table. And then he turned and realized who the man was next to them. It was Steven.

She was still staring at him, and without a word to Bill, she leaned forward to speak to her husband.

"Steven . . ." She reached out toward his table, as though to catch his attention, but only the girl turned to look at her, wondering what she wanted. Steven turned away, turning his back on her, pretending to call the waiter. "Steven . . ." She said his name more clearly, and the girl looked as though she didn't know whether to smile or back away, the expression on Adrian's face was so odd, and so upset, and she looked so hugely pregnant.

And then, as though he knew he couldn't avoid her any longer, he spoke to the girl in a harsh voice as he stood up. "Let's go. The service in this place is dreadful." He was on his feet and halfway to the door before the girl could say another word, and she looked at Adrian in confusion and dismay as though to apologize, and all she could say was "I don't think he heard you."

"Yes, he did," Adrian said, her face pale as ice, her hands clammy. "He heard me perfectly." And there was absolutely nothing wrong with the service.

"I'm sorry." The girl nodded and dashed after him, and Adrian saw her talking to him, but he yanked her out the door and they were gone, as she sat there shaking. Bill was paying the check, and he also looked ashen. He didn't say a word, and they walked outside into the cool air, as Adrian caught her breath. She was feeling sick, after their wonderful dinner. And as they reached the street, they were just in time to see him drive away with the girl in his Porsche.

"Why did you speak to him?" Bill asked when they got into the woody. "Why did you bother?" He looked upset, and she turned to him with anger in her eyes. She was in no mood to argue with him, or with anyone. Steven had made himself abundantly clear, as though he hadn't already.

"I haven't seen him in five months, and I was married to him for two and a half years. Is it so odd that I would say something to him?"

"Given the way he's treated you, yes, it is, don't you think? Or were you going to thank him for all the nice things he's done for you lately?" The truth was, Bill was jealous, and he hated himself for making a fuss over it. But he had hated the look in her eyes, the anguish on her face, as she reached out to him. And he hated Steven for hurting her. He wanted him out of her life forever.

"Don't pick on me." She started to cry, and she looked

ghostly pale in the car as she rubbed her stomach. Even the baby was upset. It was kicking violently, and all she wanted to do was go home and lie down and forget him, but she knew she couldn't. "He didn't even look at me."

"Adrian," Bill said through clenched teeth, "the guy is a total shit. How long is it going to take you to accept that? A year? Five? Ten? You keep waiting for him to come back and throw roses at you and the baby. And I keep telling you, he's not going to. Did you get the message tonight? He wouldn't even speak to you, he got up and walked out. This is not a man who gives a damn about you or your baby." And Bill suspected that he never had, although he didn't say that.

"How can he do that? How can he not feel anything for his own child? He's repressing it, but sooner or later he'll have to face it."

"The only one who'll have to face anything is you. He's gone, baby. Forget him." She didn't answer, and they drove the rest of the way home in silence, but when they got home, they started arguing again, and Adrian went to bed in tears in the guest room, and the next morning she was subdued as they met over breakfast in the kitchen. He didn't say a word to her. He let her make her own breakfast for once, and then finally looked at her over the sports page.

"What exactly is it you're expecting from him? Why don't you clarify it for me, just so I understand once and for all what it is you want from him." And what he was up against from the competition.

"From Steven?" He nodded. "I don't know. I just expect him to deal with the fact that we're having a baby. He doesn't even know what he's rejecting. I can accept the fact that he's divorcing me, because he thinks I betrayed him. But I can't accept the fact that he's turning his back on his own child. One day he'll regret it."

"Of course he will. But that's the price he'll have to pay.

And maybe he'll never come to his senses. And how can you say you betrayed him? Did you fool him? Did you get pregnant on purpose?"

"Absolutely not." She looked insulted. And it was a question he had never asked her but always wondered. He wondered if that was why she felt so guilty. "I knew how strongly he felt about it and I was always careful."

"I thought so." He almost smiled, he loved her so much, and he hated their arguments, but at least there weren't many, and they were only on one subject. Steven. "But it doesn't hurt to ask. Go on. What do you want from him?" He really wanted to know, for his own sake, and for hers. They needed to face it.

"I just want him to acknowledge the baby. To admit that it's his, to deal with that fact. I think he's run away from it since the beginning. I want him to see it and say okay, I understand, it's mine but I really don't want it . . . or yes, it is, I was wrong, I love my baby. But I don't want him to run away from me forever, because I keep thinking he'll come back at some point, and be sorry, and want us back, and then he'll screw up my life, and the baby's, and yours and his own, and whatever I do, I'll always feel guilty. I need to feel free of him, completely, before I can really go on with my life, and in order to feel that, I need him to address the issue squarely or at least talk to me, and explain why he feels the way he does. He hasn't even had the decency to talk to me since he left the apartment." It was the first time she had stated it so clearly and it finally made sense. She couldn't really believe he was gone for good and she wanted direct confirmation from him that he understood what he was giving up and that he really meant it. It made sense, but Bill didn't think she was going to get it. Steven wasn't that kind of person, and he had already shown her that, for five months and the night before. He was going to run away, divorce her through attorneys, and give up the baby without ever seeing it. That was the way he was, and she just had to face it.

"I don't think you're going to get anything more out of him than you've gotten. He just can't deal with it directly."

"How do you know that?"

"Look at him last night. Is that a guy with guts who's going to confront you? He practically ran out the door, ten feet ahead of his girlfriend."

"Is that what she was?" She looked intrigued and he looked annoyed.

"How the hell do I know?"

"She looked very young," she said thoughtfully, and he groaned.

"So do you, because you are. So stop that, and what difference does it make any way? The point is that you have to let go of him, Adrian. That's the real issue."

"But what if he comes back later?" It was something that worried her a lot. She was sure he would come back into her life after she had the baby.

"You deal with it when it happens."

"But the baby has a right . . ."

"I know, I know." He slammed a fist on the kitchen table and she jumped. "The baby has a right to its natural father, right? I've heard it before. But what if his or her 'natural father' is an asshole? Then what? Wouldn't it be simpler to just let it go now?"

"What if Leslie had told you she wanted to leave you when she was drunk? Wouldn't you feel an obligation to see how she felt when she was sober?"

"Maybe. Why?"

"Because I think Steven has been drunk on fear since the days I told him I was pregnant. And as soon as he calms down, stops panicking, and sobers up, he's going to feel different."

"Maybe not. Maybe he really does hate kids. Maybe you should listen to him. Maybe he means it."

"I just want to know from him that he knows what he's doing."

"Maybe he doesn't. Are you going to hold your life up forever?" More to the point, was she going to hold theirs up? But he also knew it wasn't easy just forgetting a man with whom she had had a baby, and to whom she had been married for two and a half years before she got pregnant.

"You think I'm stupid to give a damn, don't you?"

"No." He sighed and sat back in his chair at the kitchen table. "I just think you're wasting your time. Just forget him."

"I feel like I'm stealing something from him," she explained, and caught his attention. "I'm taking his baby away from him, and giving it to you, because you want it. But what if he comes back and says, hey, that's mine, give it back to me . . . what then?" It was a good point, but Bill still didn't think he'd ever change his mind about her or the baby. He was a fool not to, but Bill sincerely believed that he wouldn't.

"You'll just have to wait and see. We're not going anywhere. We're not moving to Africa with the baby." No, but they were getting more and more involved with each other, and he knew it. He already felt as though the child were his, and in some ways, he knew that Adrian was trying to protect him from getting hurt and Steven from making a mistake that he would regret forever. "You can't be responsible for everyone. Let each of us make our own decisions, and if they're lousy decisions, that still isn't your problem." And then he beckoned to her, as he put aside his paper. "I love you . . . I want the baby . . . and if he comes back and changes his mind, we'll just have to face it. What's the worst that could happen anyway? He gets visiting rights? That's not so awful. We could live with that," and then, as he looked at her, he felt a whisper of terror. "Or would you go back to him yourself?" he asked her, and held his breath as he waited for the answer. She shook her head, but there was the slightest hint of hesitation.

"I don't think so."

He felt as though he was going to faint as she said it. "What do you mean, you don't *think* so?"

"I mean no. But it would depend on the circumstances . . . on a lot of things . . . Bill, I don't love him anymore, if that's what you're asking. I love you. But there's more than just us . . . there's the baby."

"Would you go back to a man you didn't love, for the sake of his child?"

"I doubt it." But she couldn't swear that she wouldn't.

He got up and left the table then, and it was a difficult few days until they both calmed down again. And finally, they made a truce, and spent the weekend in bed, talking and making love, and trying to explain their positions. She just wanted to be sure that Steven wasn't going to change his mind and want the baby. She thought he should at least see it when it was born. And Bill didn't like the idea, but he was willing to accept it. And after Steven's performance the night before, he considered it highly unlikely that he would come to see it.

"And after that, will you marry me?" he asked her seriously, and she beamed when he asked her.

"Yes, I will. If you still want me." But she didn't want him to tell the boys they were getting married until all the details were out of the way, the termination papers, the divorce, and they were sure about Steven. Bill still felt it was a courtesy her ex-husband didn't deserve, but he was willing to indulge her. And he was thrilled to think that eventually they would be getting married. "Do you think the boys will mind?" she asked worriedly. She was starting to worry about everything, but the doctor had explained that at this stage, anxiety was to be expected. She was worried about the delivery, the labor, the pain, the baby's health, all the normal things that women worried about, and Bill also knew that the divorce was a strain on her, and so had been selling the apartment. And she had held up beautifully, but now she was starting to worry about little things. And he suspected that her obsession about being fair to Steven was part of the same process.

She was still tenser than usual when Adam and Tommy came. She was terrified that they were going to be upset about the baby. And she decided to be honest with them. They looked undeniably surprised when they saw her stomach when she and Bill picked them up at the airport.

"Wow!" Tommy said, looking awestruck. "What *happened?*"

"Don't ask questions like that!" Adam scolded.

"I'm having a baby," Adrian explained unnecessarily, that much was obvious, even to Tommy.

"Is it Daddy's?" he asked, and Adam kicked him.

"No, it's not," she explained, once they were at home, drinking hot chocolate in the comfortable kitchen. "It's my husband's. But we're still getting divorced. In fact . . ." She was going to be totally up front with them, and Bill had already said that he would support her. ". . . that's why he left me. Because he didn't want a baby. So we're getting a divorce, and he's giving up all his rights to the baby." She said it very simply and the boys looked shocked, particularly Adam.

"That's awful!"

"No, it's not," Tommy said matter-of-factly. "If she weren't getting divorced, she wouldn't be with Daddy, and she wouldn't have been there to save me at Lake Tahoe last summer."

"That's true," Adrian laughed. They had a way of reducing it to practical basics.

"When's the baby coming?" Adam wanted to know.

"In January. In about seven weeks."

"That's pretty soon." Adam looked very sorry for her.

"Where are you going to live? In your apartment?" But this time their father interrupted.

"No, right here, with us . . . with me." He smiled. "We're going to put the baby in the guest room."

"Are you going to get married?" Tommy looked hopeful, and Adam didn't look as though he'd be averse to the situation either.

"Eventually," Bill supplied. "But not for a while. We need to sort things out first."

"Wow!" Tommy was visibly pleased, and Adam leaned over and hugged her. He was horrified by the story of her husband deserting her, and later he told his father that he thought he should marry her before she had the baby.

"I'll keep it in mind, Son." And then he answered him seriously. "I'd like to. But we have to wait for her divorce to be final."

"When will that be?"

"Pretty soon. We'll let you know what's happening." It seemed like a lot for them to absorb, but by the next morning, everyone was back to normal. The television was on, there was laundry everywhere, the boys were hopping all over the place, and Bill was making breakfast in the kitchen. It felt like one happy, normal family, and Tommy told her he hoped the baby was a boy, because girls were so dumb, but Adam only smiled and told her that whatever it was, they would love it. His gentleness made her cry, and she tidied the apartment up afterward when they went out for a while with their father. And when they came home, they brought her a huge bouquet of flowers.

She and Bill cooked Thanksgiving dinner for them, and it was a beautiful holiday for all of them. The only flaw in a perfect day was when Bill overheard her calling her mother.

"No, he's fine," she had just said, "he had to go to London on business." And then she saw Bill's face, and after she hung up, he cornered her in the kitchen. Their Thanksgiving dinner was over by then, and the boys were already asleep in their bedroom.

"What was that all about?" But he knew without her telling him. She was lying to her mother about Steven.

"There's no point in upsetting her. No one in my family has ever gotten divorced, and it's the holidays, for heaven's sake."

"He's been gone for six months, Adrian. You've had plenty of time to tell her." And then something else occurred to him. "Have you told her yet about the baby?" She shook her head, and he sat down in a chair and looked at her. "What kind of game are you playing? Why are you protecting him?"

"I'm not." Tears filled her eyes again. "I just don't want to get into it with her. I didn't tell her at first because I thought he'd come back, and now it's so awkward, and I don't need the pressure. They always give me a hard time. I'll tell her later." There were tears in her eyes and it was hard for her to make him understand how awkward things had always been with her family.

"When are you going to tell them? After our third child is born? Or at the baby's college graduation? Maybe you ought to give her a little hint sometime before that."

"What do you expect me to say? I've never been close to her. I don't want to talk to her about it."

"You could just tell her you're having a baby."

"Why?" But even she knew it was a stupid question.

"What are you waiting for?" He looked her dead in the eye, and for once fear touched her heart. He looked hurt as well as angry. "Are you waiting for him to come back, so you can clean it all up for them?" He had hit a nerve and he knew it.

"Maybe I was at first . . . and now it's all so damned complicated. How can I ever begin to explain it?"

"You're going to have to eventually . . ." unless Steven came home . . . but he wasn't going to get into that again with her. "Look, it's your life. They're your parents. I just don't understand what you're doing."

"Neither do I sometimes," she admitted to him. "I'm sorry, Bill. Everything got so screwed up when he left, and I didn't tell anyone. I was too embarrassed to at first, and then it was too late, and now it's ridiculous. Hell, half the people at work still think I'm cheating on my husband." She smiled at him, and he pulled her closer to him.

"You drive me crazy sometimes, but maybe that's why I love you."

"And that's why Harry loves Helen, who was best friends with . . ." She started to laugh and he swatted her behind with the kitchen towel as he put the last dish away.

"Stop that! It's beginning to sound like the begats in the Bible."

"I'm sorry, Bill . . . sometimes I make a real mess of things."

"We'll get it all sorted out sooner or later." He believed that they would, but he was beginning to hope that it would be sooner, rather than later.

CHAPTER

••24••

THE LONG THANKSGIVING WEEKEND WENT MUCH TOO quickly. And there was so much to talk about, now that the boys knew Adrian had moved in, and that she was having a baby. Adam was particularly fascinated with it, and wanted to touch her stomach to see if he could feel it move, and he was thrilled when it kicked repeatedly and he felt it. He turned wide eyes to her as Bill smiled at them.

"It's neat, isn't it?" It filled Bill with wonder too, each time he felt it.

And they were highly amused when they all went for a walk in the park, and before they went, try as she might, Adrian could not tie her own sneakers.

"I feel as though I'm leaning over a beach ball."

"So do I," he whispered as he knelt to help her with her shoes. They still made love whenever they had the time and the energy, but for the same reason she couldn't tie her shoes, it was rapidly becoming something of a challenge. "You know, this is something that could only happen to me," he laughed as he finished tying her laces, and sat down on the floor looking up at her. She was peering at him over her enormous stomach.

"What?"

"Falling in love with a woman who is eight months pregnant."

She chuckled, seeing the humor of it too. It was certainly a most unusual courtship. "Maybe you can use it as research for the show. Maybe Harry could desert Helen and she could fall for someone else," she suggested cheerfully, putting on one of his sweaters.

"No one would believe this," he grinned, and they went out to play ball in Penman Park with Adam and Tommy.

The next day, the boys flew home, and the house seemed too quiet again without them. But now there was a lot to do before the holidays. The newsroom was going wild, and the cast of his show always seemed to get more than a little worked up before Christmas. The pressures of their own lives and the imaginary traumas of the show seemed to combine to make them all come slightly unglued. And Adrian was trying to get the nursery ready too. Every night between the two shows, she would sit for hours, making skirts for the bassinet, or trying to figure out how to hang the curtains.

"Here, let me do that!" Bill was always chasing her off ladders or wrestling with assembling the crib himself. And then they would look at each other and laugh. It was all getting very exciting. And the boys were excited too. They hadn't seemed to resent the baby at all. They were too sorry for Adrian being abandoned by her husband, and too pleased at the idea of sharing the wonder of the baby. Now every time they called, the first thing they asked was whether or not she'd had it. But Bill promised they would call immediately, and the boys would be the first to know. They were hoping for a boy, but Bill secretly wanted a girl, not that it really mattered.

They attended their first Lamaze class after Thanksgiving. Adrian managed to sign up for one at the hospital that started right after the evening news show. And they appeared with a dozen other couples, all of whom, save one, were first-time parents. She felt a little strange being there, and she felt awkward about doing exercises and doing Lamaze with a roomful of strangers. But Bill and her doctor had insisted that it would help her.

"Help me do what?" she argued with him on the way over, eating a turkey sandwich that was left over from lunch. She would have to go right back to work after the class, for her late broadcast. "The baby's going to come out anyway, whether I huff and puff or not." All she knew was that Lamaze had something to do with breathing.

"It'll help you relax," he said calmly.

And then, almost jealously, she looked over at him as she ate the pickle. "Did you do this with Leslie?" It was beginning to irk her that he had done all this before, and he seemed to know a lot more about the mysteries of her pregnancy than she did.

But he was noticeably vague. He didn't like comparing his previous life to this one. This one was different from anything he'd ever shared with anyone, and it was unique. "Yeah . . . sort of . . ." was all he would say, but he continued to insist that the natural childbirth class was worth doing.

"I still think I'd rather have the baby at home." It was a refrain he'd heard before, and wouldn't even let her consider.

They parked in the hospital garage, walked into the hospital, and followed a number of extremely pregnant-looking women up to the third floor, where they all gathered with what the lecturer referred to as their "significant others." They were invited to make themselves comfortable on the floor, where they sat cross-legged on exercise mats, and introduced themselves, and their husbands. There were two teachers, a nurse, two girls who didn't work, a secretary, a postal employee, a swimming instructor who looked as though she was in fantastic shape, a hairdresser, a musician, and a woman who tuned pianos. And their assortment of mates was equally diverse. If anything, Adrian and Bill were the most sophisticated, and the most successful, but they just said they worked in TV, in the production end, and no one was impressed. The only thing that they all had in common was their pregnancies. Even their ages were widely different. Of the two women who didn't work, one was nineteen and still in college, and her husband was only twenty. And the postal employee was forty-two, her husband fifty-five, and this was their first baby. And somewhere in between was a range of people in their twenties and thirties, of various sizes and shapes and interests. Adrian was faintly intrigued with them, and she spent more time looking around than exercising until they were invited to stop for a "coffee break." The women drank sodas and water, while the men drank tea and coffee. And everyone looked more than a little nervous.

The instructor addressed all of them then and assured them that if they practiced enough, the breathing techniques would really help them. And to illustrate her point of how well it could work, she showed them a film of a natural delivery using Lamaze, from beginning to end. And as Adrian watched the woman on the screen writhe in pain, she gripped Bill's hand in horror. It was the woman's second child, the instructor said. The first had been a "medicated birth," she said with disdain. And this one was supposed to be a great improvement. They could hear every push and groan as she labored on the screen, and Adrian found the blow-by-blow descriptions of what was happening to her anything but comforting. She looked as though she were going to die, and finally, using the pant-blow technique, and then pushing until her face was dark red, there was a long, reedy wail, and a terrible series of grunts and screams, and a tiny red face appeared between her legs and she started to cry as she smiled, and everyone in the delivery room exclaimed as her baby was born. It was a girl, and the woman lay back victoriously as her husband beamed and helped cut the cord. And then, as the lights went on, the movie was over. Adrian looked horrified by what she'd seen and they didn't say another word until they left and were back in Bill's car on the way to the station.

"Well," he said quietly, "what did you think?" He could see that she was upset, but he had no idea to what extent, until she looked at him with wide eyes filled with terror.

"I want an abortion." He almost laughed, she looked so sweet, and he leaned over and kissed her, feeling sorry for her. He had thought the film was a little extreme. There would have been ways to make the entire process seem a little less awesome. And he wasn't sure that showing a film of an actual birth was such a great idea to a roomful of first-time mothers. "Primips," as the Lamaze teacher had called them.

"It won't be so bad. I promise." He loved her more than ever before. And he just wanted everything to turn out all right, and for her to have a healthy baby, and for it to be easy for her. He still remembered what a hard time Leslie had had, and how scared he had been himself when Adam was born. But Tommy had been a lot better. And he was hoping that he could use the little he knew and remembered, to help Adrian this time. The only thing he hated about it was the prospect of seeing her suffer.

"How do you know it won't be so bad?" she asked angrily. "Have you ever had a baby? Did you see that woman's face? I thought she was going to die while she was pushing."

"So did I. So it was a lousy film. Forget it."

"I'm not going back."

"That won't solve anything. Let's at least get the breathing down, so I can help you."

"I want a general anesthetic," she said matter-of-factly, but when she broached the subject to Jane, her doctor, the next time they went, she only smiled sympathetically.

"We only do that in very rare cases, in instances of a serious emergency when we don't have time to do a cesarean with an epidural. And there's no reason at all to think that you'll have any problem at all. Just go to the classes, Adrian, and you'll be surprised at how smoothly it goes for you when you're in labor."

"I don't want to have it," Adrian repeated to Bill as they left the doctor's office. She was matter-of-fact, and absolutely terrified.

"It's a little late for that, sweetheart," he said calmly. She was wearing a pink dress and ponytail as they walked back to his car. She was scared to death at having the baby now, ever since the first Lamaze class, and they had been to two now.

"That stupid breathing doesn't work. I can't even remember how to do it."

"Don't worry. We'll practice." And that night, he made her lie down and pretend she was having a contraction. He pretended to time the pain, and she tried the breathing technique, and halfway through it she stopped, and slipped a graceful hand into his trousers. "Stop that! Will you be serious!" He tried to get her hand out of his pants, but she was tickling him and he was laughing.

"Let's do something else," she announced with a wicked gleam in her eye as she attacked him.

"Adrian . . . be serious! Stop it!"

"I am serious!" But not about breathing.

"That's what got you into this in the first place."

"Maybe you've got a point." She tried to roll over on her stomach but she couldn't get far. The lump, as she referred to it at times, seemed to be getting bigger by the hour. And it was extremely peppy, she could feel kicks almost constantly, especially at night, and it only seemed to relax in the early morning. "Maybe I'll just stay pregnant. It's too much trouble to get this thing out." It was like building an ocean liner in the basement.

"I wouldn't mind seeing you skinny again," he said wistfully, "you had kind of a cute figure when I met you."

"Thanks," she said to him, rolling onto her back like a beached whale. Lying like that, she looked absolutely enormous. "You don't like my figure now?" She was half serious, and he knew he had to be careful. He lay next to her, on his stomach, and propped himself up on his elbows as he kissed her.

"I happen to think you're the most beautiful woman I know, pregnant or not."

"Thank you." She smiled and tears came to her eyes, and then she put her arms around his neck like a child, and the tears brimmed over. "I'm scared," she confessed, and she touched his heart as she said it.

"I know you are, baby, but it's going to be fine. I promise."

"But what if it isn't? What if something happens . . . to me . . . or the baby?" It sounded stupid, but she was afraid she was going to die. She kept thinking of the woman in the film, going through awful pain and screaming. No one had ever told her it was going to be like that. She just thought the baby came out, somehow, and that was it. No one had ever admitted that it could be that painful.

"Nothing's going to happen to you or the baby. I won't let it. I'll be there every second, holding your hand, and helping you. And it'll be over before you know it."

"Is it really that bad?" She looked into his eyes earnestly, and he didn't want to tell her how bad it had been for Leslie. It had almost driven him crazy to see it.

"Not necessarily. I think for some people it's fairly easy."

"Yeah. If they have hips like the Panama Canal," she said sadly, because she didn't.

"You'll be fine." He kissed her gently on the lips, and she slipped her hands into his shirt and touched his shoulders. And then she ran her hands down his back, and he felt a tremor of excitement. They were kissing, and she was touching him, and he gently let his hands wander over her body, and then he grinned in the midst of their passion. "I should be shot for molesting a woman in your condition." The absurdity of it struck him for a moment and then he forgot it.

"No, you shouldn't," she teased, and he marveled at how much she still turned him on. He rolled over on his back and laid her on top of him, as they took their clothes off. And half an hour later, they lay spent, and he looked at her guiltily. He was terrified he might cause her to go into labor, but the doctor hadn't told them not to.

"Are you okay?" he asked nervously, looking at her as though she might explode at any moment.

"Never better." She looked at him as though she were drunk, and then she giggled.

"I'm disgusting," he said, watching her. "I shouldn't do that."

"Yes, you should. I'd much rather make love to you than have the baby. And at least I can't get pregnant."

He frowned then as he looked at her. "I thought you told me you were a virgin."

"I am," she said happily. It seemed miraculous to her that their relationship was still so passionate, and she was more than eight months pregnant.

"Want to try the breathing again?" he volunteered as they lay in bed. He felt as though he had to do something to redeem himself for his unbridled passion.

"I thought we just did," she said benignly. And then she

glanced at the clock in dismay. It was ten o'clock, and she had to get up and go back to work. She was still planning to work full-time till the eleventh hour. Zelda had already volunteered to cover for her, anytime Adrian wanted her to, but so far Adrian hadn't called her. She was planning to start her maternity leave the same day she was due to have the baby. And Bill had already told her he thought she was pushing.

"Why don't you at least relax for a few weeks before that?"

"I'll have plenty of time to relax *after* I have the baby."

"That's what you think." He grinned. He remembered only too well the nights without sleep, the broken sleep from nursing a baby who wanted to eat every two or three hours. He tried to tell her that, but she still wanted to work till the end. She felt fine and insisted that she needed the distraction. But every time she went in to work, Zelda practically groaned when she saw her.

"How do you walk around with that?" she asked, pointing to Adrian's stomach. "Doesn't it hurt?"

"No." Adrian smiled. "You get used to it."

"I hope not," Zelda sympathized. It was something so foreign to her, and she had no desire to make it familiar. Babies were just not something she wanted. Nor was a husband. And she liked Bill a lot, but she admitted to Adrian early on that just being with them made her nervous. It was all much too married. But she was happy for Adrian. No one deserved a good man more than she did. And there was no doubt in Zelda's mind, he was a good one. Not like that son of a bitch Steven. She had run into him a few times. He went to the same gym she did, but he hadn't seemed to notice her. And she had seen him there several times with different girls, always pretty, always young, and she was willing to bet that none of them knew that he had walked out on his wife because she was having a baby.

She had asked Adrian once or twice if she ever heard from

him, but Adrian always shook her head, and it seemed to be a sensitive subject, so she stopped asking.

Bill drove Adrian to work that night, as he did every night now, and spent an hour at his own desk while she was working and then she would come to his office to pick him up, and sometimes they would sit and chat for a little while, in his comfortable office. They never seemed to run out of things to say, or ideas that they shared, or new plots for the show. They were a perfect match in many ways, and they had a good time, in bed and out, and they were both laughing as they headed for the elevator and she stopped with a funny look on her face.

"What's up?" He looked at her worriedly.

"I don't know. . . ." She leaned against him, surprised by what it had felt like. Her whole belly had gotten hard as a rock, and felt as though it were being squeezed in a vise. She knew what it was from the description in the Lamaze class. "I think I just had a contraction." She looked scared, and he put an arm around her. But she felt fine now. It had come and gone, but she looked up at him with an expression of panic.

"You've been working too hard. You've got to slow down, or the baby will come early."

"It can't do that. I'm not ready for it." The nursery was almost finished, but her head wasn't prepared for what she'd have to go through. "I want to enjoy Christmas before I have it."

"Then stop knocking yourself out," he scolded. "Tell them you can't do the late show anymore. They'll understand. Hell, you're eight months pregnant." And she wasn't even sure she was coming back. She was going to use her maternity leave to decide if she wanted to go to work for Bill. It still scared her a little to become that dependent on him.

They drove home and on the way, she had two more contractions. But when they got home, he gave her a small glass of white wine and insisted that she drink it, and miraculously the contractions stopped, and she looked delighted. She had been scared to death that she was about to have the baby. "That really worked."

"Of course." He looked pleased with himself as he kissed her. And then, for an instant, he looked guilty. "Maybe we shouldn't be making love anymore." He wondered if their earlier indulgence had done it.

"The doctor didn't say anything. And I think those are just those warm-up contractions to get things ready."

"The more you have now, the easier it'll be."

"Good. Then let's make love again." She polished off the wine, and grinned up at him, looking like an elf with an enormous stomach as she said it.

"I think you're perverted." And the awful thing was that he actually wanted to make love to her. He wanted to make love to her all the time. How could he have fantasies about a woman who was eight months pregnant? But he found that he loved her more each day, and somehow she seemed sweet to him the way she was. She was so vulnerable, and so cute and so cuddly. He leaned over and kissed her then, but he managed to ward her off when she tried to get sexy. "If you don't stop this, Adrian, you'll have triplets."

"Now there's a thought," but she sobered quickly when she contemplated the delivery. "I bet that must hurt."

"See, be grateful you're only having one." There was a long silence in the dark, and then she whispered to him again.

"What if it's twins and they don't know it?"

"Believe me, nowadays they'd know it." She was worried about everything, and she seemed to make a dozen trips into the nursery every night, checking things out, folding undershirts, looking at tiny little bonnets and booties and nightgowns. It touched him to see her like that, and more than once, it made him think of what a jerk Steven was for giving all that up. It meant so much to Bill, and absolutely nothing to Steven.

Bill had wallpapered the room for her, in a white paper with little pink and blue stars and a pretty pink-and-blue-rainbow border. He had put the four-poster bed away, in a storage locker he had in the basement, and they had bought nursery furniture together at the beginning of December. Everything was ready finally the week before Christmas. And they'd bought a Christmas tree, and decorated it with old-fashioned ornaments and cranberries and popcorn.

"I wish the boys could see this," he said proudly. It was a beautiful little tree, and the apartment looked pretty and festive. The boys had gone skiing in Vermont, and Adrian and Bill had talked to them several times before they left. But it wouldn't be the same for him, having Christmas without them. They were coming out in February, for their spring break, and that was going to work out perfectly. If the baby came on time, it would be three weeks old by then, and Adrian would be more or less recovered, except for the sleepless nights. She had decided to nurse the baby, and they were going to leave the baby in a basket next to their bed, so she wouldn't have to get up every time the baby was hungry.

She took a day off to finish her Christmas shopping, and for them it was going to be a double holiday. On the first of January, Bill was going to turn forty. She had bought him a beautiful gold watch at Cartier on Rodeo Drive. It had cost her a fortune but it was worth it. It was something he would wear for the rest of his life, and it was designed according to one that had been made for a sultan in the 1920s, and was appropriately called "The Pasha." And she knew he would love it. And for Christmas she had bought him a tiny portable telephone that folded into a case the size of a razor. It was the perfect gadget for him, since he liked to be accessible to the show all the time, and they were always panicking trying to reach him. She had bought him other things, too, a new sweater, some cologne, a book he'd been admiring about old movies, and a tiny, tiny television he could watch in his bathroom, or even while he drove the woody, if he had to go somewhere but wanted to keep an eye on the show. She'd had a wonderful time shopping for him, and they had bought new skis and boots for the boys, and shipped them east well before Christmas. It was going to be the first time Tommy had his own equipment, but they were both outstanding skiers. And she had sent them each a gift just from her, beautiful ski parkas, and an electronic game for each. They could play them in the car next summer when they all went on their big vacation. But this time they had already decided to go to Hawaii for a month and rent a condo there, they were all feeling a lot less enthused about another camping trip at Lake Tahoe.

It was three days before Christmas when Adrian was wrapping everything. She wanted to get it done before Bill came home. They were going to the annual Christmas party at his show, and she wanted to hide all his presents. She had put most of them in the baby's crib, with the comforter over them, and she was smiling to herself as she wrapped the tiny telephone. She knew he was going to love it, and he hadn't wanted to be extravagant and buy it for himself. It was nice being able to spoil him. And when she was finished, she went to get the mail, and she was startled when she saw the envelope from City Hall. She opened it without thinking, and gasped when she saw the papers.

On the twenty-first of December, her divorce had become final. She was no longer married to Steven, and although he could not remove it from her, he had stated a preference that she no longer use his surname. And the papers terminating his parental rights to their unborn child were included. Legally, the baby was no longer his. It was Adrian's, period. The baby had no legal father. And his name would not be on the birth certificate, as the lawyer had explained to her the previous summer. She sat staring at the papers for a long time, and tears slowly filled her eyes and spilled onto her cheeks. It was silly to get so upset at this late date, she told herself. It was no surprise. She had expected it. And yet it hurt anyway. It was the ultimate, final rejection. A marriage that had begun with hope and love had ended with total rejection. He had rejected everything about her, even her baby.

She quietly put the papers away in her drawer in Bill's desk. He had graciously shared everything he had, his heart, his space, his apartment, his life, his bed, and he was even willing to take on her baby. It was amazing how different the two men were, how opposite in every way, and yet she was still sad about Steven, and she still wished that he could have brought himself to care about the baby.

Bill came home while she was getting dressed, and as usual he sensed that something had happened. He thought she was scared about the baby again, and lately she had been on a rampage of anxiety, worrying if the baby would be normal. They had told her in the Lamaze class that all of these concerns were normal, that there was no need to feel it was a premonition of something truly awful.

"Are you having contractions again?" he asked, sensing she was upset about something.

"No, I'm okay." And then she decided not to beat around the bush. She never did with him. He knew her too well anyway. "My divorce papers came today. And the termination of parental rights. It's all official."

"I could say congratulations, but I won't." He looked at her carefully. "I know what that feels like. Even when you expect it, it's kind of a shock." He put gentle arms around her and kissed her and tears filled her eyes again. "I'm sorry, baby.

That's not nice for you at a time like this. But one day, it'll just be a memory and it will no longer matter."

"I hope so. I felt so lousy when I got them. I don't know . . . it was like flunking out of school, like really knowing you'd blown it."

"You didn't blow it. He did," he reminded her, but she sat down on the bed and sniffed.

"I still feel like I did something wrong . . . I mean . . . for him not to want the baby, I must have really handled it badly."

"From what you've told me, I don't think it could ever have been any different. If there was any humanity to the man, he'd have come around by now," and he didn't need to remind her that Steven hadn't. He hadn't even been willing to acknowledge her when they met in the restaurant in October. What kind of man would do that? A real son of a bitch, and a selfish one, was Bill's unspoken answer. "You just have to put it behind you." She nodded, and she knew he was right, but it was hard anyway. And she was quiet that night at his office Christmas party. Everyone was in high spirits and more than a little drunk, and suddenly she felt fat and uncomfortable and depressed and ugly. She had a lousy time, and Bill left early to take her home. He could see that she wasn't having fun, and the others wouldn't really miss him. They'd understand. And even if they didn't, Adrian was his first concern. She was having contractions again when they went to bed, and for once she didn't feel the least bit interested in making love to him.

"Now I know you're really depressed," he teased her. "It might even be terminal. Should I call the doctor?" He was playing at being concerned and he made her laugh, but she still looked sad as they lay in his bed. The baby's basket, covered in white lace, was already standing in the corner at the ready. Her due date was only two and a half weeks away, and she was still very nervous about it. So far, the Lamaze class hadn't reassured her, even though the information was abundant and useful. But the realities of childbirth still terrified her. But she wasn't even thinking about that tonight, she was just thinking about Steven and their divorce, and the fact that the baby had no father.

"I have an idea," he smiled. "It's a little unusual, but not totally inappropriate. Let's get married on Christmas. That gives us three days to get the blood test and the license. I think that's what it takes. That and about ten dollars. I might even be able to scrape up the money." He was looking at her tenderly, and although he was joking, he was serious about the proposal.

"That's not right," she said sadly.

"What, about the ten dollars?" He was still trying to keep it light. "Okay, if it's more, I'll scrape it up somehow."

"No, I'm serious, Bill. It's not right for you to marry me out of pity. You deserve more than that, and so do Adam and Tommy."

"Oh, for God's sake." He lay back in their bed and groaned. "Do me a favor, don't rescue me from myself. I'm a big boy and I know what I'm doing, and I happen to love you."

"I love you too," she said mournfully. "But it's not fair."

"To whom?"

"You, or Steven, or the baby."

"Would you mind explaining to me by what deviated, neurotic route you came to that conclusion?" Sometimes she exasperated him, especially lately. She worried about so many things, and she felt so obligated to be fair to everyone . . . him . . . and the baby . . . and even rotten Steven.

"I'm not going to let you marry me under duress, feeling that you owe me something, or have an obligation to help me out, or that the baby ought to have a father. When you get married, it should be because you want to, not because you have to, or think you owe it to someone."

"Has anyone ever told you that you're nuts? Sexy . . . beautiful . . . great legs . . . but definitely nuts. I am *not* asking you to marry me because I feel an obligation. I happen to be madly in love with you, and have been for six months, or hadn't you noticed? Remember me, I'm the guy you've been living with since last summer, the guy whose kid you saved, and whose kids, plural, think you walk on water."

She looked pleased by what he said, but she still shook her head. "It's still not right."

"Why not?"

"It's not fair to the baby."

He looked at her almost harshly then. He had heard this argument before and he didn't like it. "Or are you really saying it's not fair to Steven?"

She hesitated for a moment and then nodded. She felt an obligation to save him from himself too. "He doesn't know what he's giving up. He has to have a chance to understand that decision, to think it out clearly, after the baby's born, before I move on and shut him out forever."

"The law doesn't seem to agree with you. They approved those papers, Adrian. He no longer has any claim to that baby."

"Legally, you're right. But morally? Can you really say that?"

"Christ, I don't know what I can say anymore." He got out of bed and paced the room, glancing at her, and almost tripping over the little white basket. "I know one thing. I've stuck my neck way out for you . . . and my heart . . . and my guts . . . and whatever else you want. And I've done it because I love you, *and* the baby. I don't need to wait to see it, or check it out, to decide if it's cute or not, or take my emotional temperature the day it's born. It is and you are and I am, and *we* are exactly what I've always wanted. I'm telling you that I want to marry you, for better or worse, in sickness or in health, *forever.* That's all I want, just the two of you. And for the last seven years I've been too damn scared to offer that to anyone. I've been too scared even to let myself think it. Because, as I told you before, I never wanted to care that much again, or have a woman walk out on me and take my children. This baby isn't mine, it's his, as you keep pointing out to me, but I love it as though it were mine, and I don't want to lose it. I don't want to play games with you. I don't want to sit here waiting until he comes back, and takes back everything I've come to love. I don't think he will anyway, and I've told you that before too. But I'm also not going to sit here with my door open forever, waiting for him to come to his senses, or get bored with the bimbos in his life, and come back to you and the baby. As far as I'm concerned, Adrian, he can't have you. But if he does want you, and you want him, you'd both better make up your minds quick. I want to get on with our life, I want to marry you, I want to adopt that baby you've been carrying around in you for nine months while I feel it kicking. I'm not going to sit here with my heart and my guts wide-open forever. So if you want to talk about fair, let's talk about it. What's fair? How long is fair? Just how long am I expected to be 'fair' to Steven?"

"I don't know." She was impressed by everything he'd said. And she loved him more than ever. She wanted to go to him now, but she still felt she had to wait. But he was right too. It wasn't fair to expect him to wait forever.

"What sounds fair to you? A week? A month? A year? Do you want to give him a month after the baby's born, and just make sure via his attorneys that he still doesn't want any contact with the child? Does that sound reasonable?" He was trying to be fair, too, but she was driving him crazy.

"I'm not going to go back to him," she explained. There was no longer any doubt in her mind. But sometimes Bill wasn't as sure. He still worried about it when she talked about being fair to him. And women were odd sometimes about the men who had fathered their children, they gave them more understanding, more leeway. It wasn't that way with men, who could never be entirely sure who their children were. But women could. They knew. And he wondered if in some ways, she would feel bound to Steven forever through their baby. He hoped not. But she couldn't answer that yet either. "It's just the baby, Bill . . . it's just . . ."

"I know . . . I know . . . I understand . . . you just scare me sometimes." He sat down next to her on the bed and there were tears in his eyes now too. "I love you."

"I love you too," she said softly as he kissed her.

"Shall we give it a month then? A month after the baby's born. We contact the bastard after the baby comes, we give him a month to change his mind, and after that we forget him forever? Is that a deal?"

She nodded somberly. It sounded reasonable to her, and it was more than Steven deserved. He had signed the termination papers after all . . . termination . . . dissolution . . . it sounded almost like a murder, and in some ways it had been. In some ways what he had done to her had almost killed her. But on the other hand, Bill had saved her. And for that she would be eternally grateful. In truth, she owed Bill far more. And yet . . . Steven had been her husband. It was all so damn confusing. To whom did she owe the greatest loyalties? To whom did she owe the most? To Bill because he'd been there for her . . . and yet . . . she hated herself for feeling torn, but she did. In her heart, there was only one. But in her mind, there were always two. And that was the problem. But they had agreed on a month after the baby was born. And that seemed fair to her too. And after that, the door would be closed to Steven forever. For her, and the baby. He didn't even know it, but she was giving him a gift of time and choice that he hadn't even wanted.

"And then you'll marry me?" Bill pressed her, and she nodded with a shy smile. "Are you sure?" She nodded again, and then looked down demurely and spoke in a whisper.

"I have a confession to make first."

"Oh, shit. Now what?" He was at his wit's end. It had been a long night and he was tired.

"I lied to you." He was getting worried as she went on, barely able to look at him.

"About what?"

He could hardly hear the words as she confessed. "I'm not really a virgin."

There was a long silence, and he scowled at her with a look of immense relief as she suppressed a giggle. "Slut!" he growled at her, and then, in spite of himself and the remorse he knew he would feel afterward, he made love to her again, and when it was over, they slept peacefully in each other's arms until morning.

CHAPTER

··25··

ADRIAN HAD THE DAY OFF ON CHRISTMAS DAY, AND THEY
stayed in bed for a long time, dozing and snuggling and then
the phone rang at nine-fifteen. It was Adam and Tommy,
calling from Stowe, where they were skiing with their mother.
They were both excited and full of life, and after they hung
up, Adrian smiled and wished Bill a merry Christmas. They
both leapt out of bed, and went to their respective hiding
places and came back with their arms laden with brightly
wrapped presents. His were all wrapped by stores, and hers
were wrapped the way she cooked. But he loved everything
she gave him. He was crazy about the television and the
phone, and he put the sweater on under a red leather baseball
jacket she had bought him just two days before when she was
walking down Melrose.

And she loved her presents too. He had bought her a beautiful green suede dress from Giorgio, for after the baby, and a

Hermès bag, the black alligator "Kelly" one she had coveted every time they walked past there. And books, and a pair of funny pink shoes with watermelons on them, and three beautiful nightgowns and a robe for when she had the baby. And he had bought her all kinds of silly little trinkets, a gold key chain, and an antique pen, and a Mickey Mouse watch that she loved, and a book of poetry that said everything she felt for him. She was crying by the time she had finished opening all of it, and he looked immensely pleased by her reaction. And then he disappeared again, and returned with a small box wrapped in turquoise paper and white satin ribbon.

"Oh, no, not more!" She hid her face in the black leather gloves he had bought her at Gucci. They had little red bows on them and she loved them. "Bill, you can't!"

"You're right." He grinned. "I won't, and I didn't. But just for the hell of it, why don't you open this one?" But as she looked at it, she was afraid to. Instinct told her that this one was a biggie. "Go on . . . don't be so chicken. . . ." With trembling fingers, she opened it, and found first a cardboard box in the same blue as the paper with Tiffany written across it. And then, a heavy black suede box within it. And slowly, slowly, she opened it, and gasped. It was a diamond band, made of baguettes, and she sat staring at it in wonder. "Go on, silly." He took it from her gently. "Put it on . . . if it fits . . ." He knew that her hands were slightly swollen, and he had guessed at her ring size. But when he slipped it on for her, it fit perfectly.

"Oh, my God . . . oh, Bill . . ." She sat looking at him in disbelief, as tears rolled down her cheeks. "It's so beautiful, but . . ." She had already told him the other day that she wasn't ready yet to get married. And it was a very handsome wedding ring, the kind a few lucky women get after twenty years of marriage. But his show had just won yet another award, and she knew that although he was discreet about it, it was making a fortune, so he could afford it.

"I thought you should look respectable when you go to the hospital. So it's actually an engagement ring, but I thought it was prettier than a big rock, and this way," he said shyly as he looked at her, "it'll look kind of married. I'll get you a plain gold one if you want when we get married." It was beautiful, and she loved it. And she loved him even more. He was incredible. And as she looked at the ring on her left hand, she was dazzled. She had taken her gold wedding ring off finally, two months before, because it had gotten too small for her as her hands swelled, and in spite of her condition, it no longer seemed appropriate to wear it.

"My God, Bill, this is gorgeous!"

"Do you really like it?" He looked so pleased and she was so touched by everything he had done for her.

"Are you kidding? Like it! I love it!" She grinned and lay back in their bed again, displaying the ring with a broad smile, and noticing that it had a huge amount of sparkle. "I'm going to impress the hell out of the nurses when I have the baby."

"Funny." He squinted at her. "You don't look engaged." He patted her stomach then, and felt the baby kick him. "It must be a girl," he said happily.

"Why?" She was still looking at her ring. She couldn't believe it.

"She stamps her feet all the time," he said matter-of-factly.

"Maybe she wants a ring like her mother's." She smiled and leaned over to kiss him, doubly glad that she had bought the beautiful Cartier watch for him that she was going to give him on New Year's Day for his birthday. It had eaten a sizable piece of her profits from the sale of the condo, but she thought it was worth it. And she was saving the rest of the money for the baby. Bill had already told her that he wanted to pay her hospital bill, and she had insisted that she wouldn't let him.

"You're sure you don't want to reconsider and get married right away?" he asked hopefully, still trying to persuade her. If nothing else, it would mean putting his name on the baby's birth certificate, which seemed a lot nicer than the "father unknown" that was her only choice now, or just to leave it blank, as the attorney had suggested. But if she and Bill got married, they could always have it adjusted and add his name later.

But she looked sad as she looked at Bill, not wanting to hurt him. "I still think we should wait." They had agreed on February, as an outside date, if all went well, and Steven didn't pose a problem by altering everything, and changing his mind about the baby. It was a period of grace Bill still felt strongly he didn't deserve. But she still seemed to think he would come flying through the delivery room doors the moment she had the baby. And somehow, Bill felt sure she would come to her senses and be more realistic after she had the baby. Right now, she still seemed to need the fantasy that one day Steven would have regrets about the baby. Maybe it was her way of protecting herself from the sad reality that Steven didn't care about her or the baby.

They spent a quiet afternoon, and he cooked dinner for them that night, a turkey that he worked on all afternoon, as she relaxed on the couch, and took a nap, still wearing the beautiful ring he had given her that morning.

And Zelda commented on it when she went to work the next day. It was impossible to miss it, and the redhead's eyes flew wide-open when she saw it.

"Wow! Did you get married over the weekend?"

"Nope." Adrian smiled mysteriously. "Engaged," she said, and laughed to herself. She seemed awfully pregnant to be contemplating a mere engagement.

"That's quite a ring," Zelda said admiringly.

"He's quite a guy," Adrian added, and went back to see one of the editors in the newsroom.

She spent the rest of the week trying to tie up loose ends, and trying to explain all of her projects to Zelda. She was going to be leaving in two weeks and it seemed like an impossible task to get everything wrapped up before she left. And halfway through the week someone contacted her from Bill's show, and told her they were planning a surprise party for his fortieth birthday. They wanted her collaboration in getting him there, and she was happy and excited for him. His actual birthday was on New Year's Day, and they were going to have the party that afternoon, right on the set, with a band, and past and present members of the cast, and as many of his friends as they could contact. And Adrian thought it sounded great. She could hardly contain herself on New Year's Eve, keeping the secret.

They had dinner with friends on New Year's Eve, it was a small party that a writer he knew was giving at Chasen's, and afterward as they drove home, Adrian was very sleepy. Bill had had a fair amount to drink, but he wasn't drunk, and it was just after midnight when they got home, and he climbed into bed as soon as he was undressed, and was almost asleep when she got in beside him.

"Happy New Year," she whispered, and he smiled. "Happy birthday too!" She was thinking about the party the next day, but he was already asleep before she'd finished the words, and as she looked down at him, she leaned over and kissed him. He was so sweet, and so good to her, and she loved him so much. She lay there, awake for a while, tired, but no longer as sleepy as she had been an hour before, and then suddenly as she lay there, she felt a sharp kick, and then a tightening of everything from her chest to her thighs, so much so that she could hardly breathe, but it didn't really hurt her. It was another practice round, she figured. She was almost used to the warm-up contractions now. They happened mostly on busy days, or when she was very tired, and she didn't really mind them. She lay there, thinking peacefully for a little while, and she felt another tightening, and then another. And she decided to try one of his tricks, without bothering him. She went and helped herself to half a glass of wine, and took a sip. But this time it didn't stop them. By three o'clock, the contractions were coming regularly, but she still didn't believe they were for real, so she turned the light off and tried to go to sleep, but every time she had one it woke her up, so finally after turning from side to side, Bill stirred and asked her what was the matter.

"Nothing," she grumbled. "It's those stupid contractions."

He opened one eye in the dark and looked at her lying next to him. "Does it feel like the real thing?"

"No." They were making her uncomfortable, but she knew that was only because she was tired, and she was certain that she wasn't in labor. The baby wasn't due for another two weeks, and there was no reason for it to come early. She had seen the doctor only the day before, and she had seen nothing unexpected either, even though she had pointed out that technically, the baby was now full term, and could come anytime from now on, and until two weeks after her due date.

"How long have you had them?" Bill murmured as he turned away on his side again.

"I don't know . . . three or four hours." It was almost three-thirty.

"Take a hot bath." That was another of his magic recipes, but that one worked too. She had tried it several times when she had contractions, and it always stopped them. And the doctor had told them that when it was the real thing, nothing would stop it, not wine or hot baths, or standing on her head. When the baby wanted to come, it would. And she hated to get out of bed and take a bath now just to stop the contractions. "Go on," Bill nudged her, "try it, so you can get to sleep."

She padded into the bathroom shortly after that, and he smiled as he watched her waddle, and then dozed off as he listened to her run the tub, and it seemed like hours later when he heard her next to him again, but all of a sudden he felt her stiffen and make a strange noise. It woke him instantly and he looked at her, her face looked tense and her whole body went rigid when she clutched him.

"Baby, are you okay?" He looked worried as he watched her face and saw beads of perspiration on her forehead as soon as he switched on the light. The bath had definitely not stopped the contractions. And then he smiled as her body relaxed, and there was fear in her eyes. He took her hand in his and kissed her fingers. "I think our little friend wants to celebrate New Year's with us. What do you think, sweetheart? Shall I call the doctor?" But it was obvious to him that she was in labor.

"No . . ." She squeezed his hand again. "I'm okay . . . really . . . oh, no!" She shouted suddenly. "No, I'm not . . . oh, Bill!" She grabbed his hand and squeezed hard, forgetting everything they had taught her about breathing. But he reminded her and she panted her way through it. But it was abundantly clear to him that they didn't have time to waste. She was suddenly in a lot of pain, and it was time to go to the hospital. He helped her sit up, and she caught her breath, and went to her closet with a dazed look. She was tired and scared, and she was starting to tremble. And a minute later she came out of her closet again with a look of panic. He ran to her instantly, and helped her into a chair, but she couldn't speak now when she had a contraction. And as she sat there, gasping for air, she remembered the agony of the woman in the movie. But it seemed even worse than that. She couldn't catch her breath, and suddenly the pains were coming one on top of the other.

"Don't move . . . stay calm . . . keep breathing . . ." He was talking to himself as much as to her, as he ran and got a big loose dress out of her closet. He helped her off with her nightgown, slipped the dress over her head, and found an old pair of loafers.

"I can't go looking like this," she said between pains. He had pulled her worst dress out of the closet.

"Never mind, you look gorgeous." He pulled on jeans, a sweater over his head, and slipped into a pair of Docksiders that were under the bed, and kept an eye on her while he called the doctor. She promised to meet them at the hospital within half an hour, and he slowly helped Adrian out of the chair, but before they'd crossed the room she had a blinding contraction. He was beginning to wonder if he should call an ambulance, or if they'd waited too long, but he was determined that she not get her wish to have the baby at home, and he tried to encourage her to walk out with him as soon as the contraction was over. He had her hospital bag in his hand, and they almost made it to the front door before she had another one. They were making slow progress, and she started to cry almost the minute this one started. "It's all right, sweetheart . . . it's all right. We'll get you to the hospital in a few minutes and you'll feel better."

"No, I won't," she cried, clinging to him for dear life. "Oh, Bill . . . this is awful . . ."

"I know, baby, I know, but it'll be over soon, and we'll have a beautiful baby." She smiled up at him through her tears and tried to breathe through the pain, but it wasn't easy. He was right, though, it worked, to a point, but she was rapidly getting to the point when she couldn't do it.

It seemed to take hours to get back to where he had left the car, but he finally got her into the woody and threw her bag onto the backseat. And then he drove as fast as he could to the hospital, hoping that he'd be followed by the highway patrol.

For once, he wouldn't have minded being stopped. He was hoping for a police escort, in case she actually had the baby. But she didn't and no one came, and he drove into the emergency entrance and honked, praying that someone would come to help him. An attendant appeared a moment later, as Adrian gripped him, unable to breathe through the contraction. They helped her into a wheelchair, and she was whimpering as they rolled her in at full speed with Bill running along beside her.

"I can't . . . Bill . . . oh . . ." She was hardly able to speak anymore, and he saw that she was trembling violently, and threw his jacket over her as he tried to keep her distracted.

"Yes, you can . . . come on . . . you're doing fine . . . good . . . good . . . it's almost over." They were just words, but to her, they were all she had to cling to. He knew that once they were in a labor room, she would be attached to a monitor and they would be able to see exactly how ferocious the contractions were, and how long they were lasting, when they reached their peak, and when they were diminishing so he could tell her a contraction was almost over. But they had none of that now, and all she had was the pain and a sense of terror that it was going to get worse and she would totally lose control. She was starting to think that she was going to die, and she snapped at Bill when he tried to help her out of the wheelchair.

The doctor was already there, waiting for them, and she helped Adrian into bed, along with a cheerful young nurse, whom Adrian took an immediate dislike to. She was definitely not at her best, and she started to get hysterical when they took off her dress and tried to get the tight belt of the monitor on as another contraction ripped through her.

"Hang in, Adrian . . . this'll just take a minute," the doctor said, assisting the nurse with expert hands while Bill tried to keep Adrian breathing. She was having a rough time, and she suddenly looked at them, startled.

"It's coming out!" She was horrified as she looked frantically from Bill to the doctor. "It's coming . . . the baby is coming!"

"No, it isn't." The doctor tried to force her to calm down, and told her to pant, while Bill tried to remind her how, but she was screaming and she kept insisting that the baby was coming. "Don't push." The doctor was almost shouting at her now, and suddenly two more nurses appeared in the room, and the doctor frowned as she looked at the monitor and then spoke to Bill as she washed her hands at the sink in the room. "She's having enormous contractions . . . and long ones . . . she may be farther along than we think." She spoke quietly and Adrian was screaming.

"It's coming . . . it's coming . . ." She was crying incoherently and Bill wanted to cry too. He couldn't stand seeing her in pain, and it got worse as the doctor examined her. She felt as though there was a searing pain shoving its way right through her, and the doctor nodded with satisfaction.

"It's almost time to push, Adrian . . . just a few more contractions."

"No!" she screamed, and then struggled to sit up, fighting the monitor until she dislodged it from her swollen middle. "I won't! I can't do this!"

"Yes, you can," the doctor said again, as Bill tried unsuccessfully to soothe her. It made him feel sick to watch her in pain, and she was writhing in the bed as the doctor conferred with the nurses. It was much worse than the training film and Bill wanted to ask them why they didn't give her something for the pain, but the doctor interrupted him when he tried to ask her. "Would you like to have your baby right here, Adrian? You're going to have your baby very soon. I can see its head now. That's it . . . come on . . . you can start pushing." Adrian gave a hideous scream, and she looked at Bill as though begging him to save her. One of the nurses attached handles to the bed, and another fixed stirrups at the other end, and suddenly everything was draped in blue paper, and they had handed Bill a shower cap and a green gown, and the entire room was transformed, as he held Adrian's shoulders. "That's it . . . come on . . . push the baby out of there!" the doctor urged her on, and Adrian continued to insist that she couldn't. Her whole being seemed to be controlled by pain and Bill wanted to beg them to give her something for it. And she screamed every time she pushed as he held her and cried. But no one noticed his tears. Adrian was crying too. They both were, and then suddenly as she fell back again, and then sat up and pushed again, there was a long, reedy wail, and Bill looked up in amazement. He looked at Adrian and she was smiling through her tears and then she was screaming again as she pushed the baby out, and fell back against the pillows exhausted. "It's a boy!" the doctor said, and Adrian and Bill were both crying and laughing, and he looked at the tiny being who was looking at them with big startled eyes and a tiny nose just like his mother's. She was straining to see him, too, and then she gave an awful moan as the doctor delivered the placenta.

"He's so beautiful," Bill said in a hoarse voice, "and so are you." He leaned down and kissed her and she turned to him with a look that they would never share again, a look and a feeling that was born only of this moment, but that they would both remember forever.

"Is he okay?" she asked weakly.

"He's perfect," the doctor announced, doing a little sewing on Adrian. They had just given her a local, but she hadn't even noticed. And the pediatric resident had just arrived to check out the baby. But the baby looked fine. He weighed eight pounds and fourteen ounces, a healthy size, and Bill kept saying that the baby looked just like his mother, but she thought he looked like Bill, which didn't make any sense, but Bill didn't want to say that.

He helped take the baby to the nursery while they cleaned her up, and he was back again half an hour later. It was only five-fifteen. For a first baby, he had come remarkably quickly. They'd only been in the hospital since four-thirty. But to Adrian for those last few moments, it had seemed endless.

"I'm so sorry it was so hard for you," he whispered as he leaned over her, marveling at how different she looked than only moments before. Her hair was combed, her face and body washed, and she had even put on lipstick. She was a totally different person than the woman who had been hysterical and screaming in anguish.

"It wasn't that hard," she said quietly, and it was odd, as he looked at her, she seemed suddenly more grown-up now. It was as though in a moment, she had become more of a woman. And before that, she had been a girl. In some ways, she was right, she really had been a virgin. "It really wasn't that bad," she said happily. "I'd do it again. . . ." She smiled and he started to laugh. She was saying exactly what he had predicted. "Is he okay?"

"He's wonderful. They're making him all clean and pretty for you, and then they're going to bring him back." And a few minutes later, a nurse came back with the baby, all clean and smelling sweet, wrapped tightly in swaddling clothes and a blanket. He opened his eyes when the nurse handed him to her, and Bill and Adrian looked down at him in wonder. He was perfect in every way, and a miracle beyond anything Adrian had ever dreamed of. It reminded Bill of Adam and Tommy in some ways, but this had been different too. Different, and very special. He felt much closer to her suddenly, even closer than he had before, as though they shared one soul, one mind, one heart . . . and one baby. As though the three of them shared a single heartbeat. And the baby opened his eyes and stared at them, as though trying to remember if he knew them.

Adrian started to cry again, but they were tears of joy. Everything about this little person had been worth it. He was worth all the pain, the confusion, the anxiety she'd been through. He was even worth the loss of her marriage to Steven, and she was now suddenly doubly glad that she hadn't let Steven force her to abort him. It was a hideous thought, as Bill helped her unwrap him a little and put him to her breast. He took to it at once, as Bill felt tears fill his eyes as he watched them. It was all so simple, so easy, so much what life had been intended for. Two people who loved each other and the children who entered their lives like tiny blessings.

"What'll we call him?" she whispered to Bill.

"I keep thinking Thigpen would be nice. It's a hell of a name, though."

"I happen to like it," she said tenderly. She would never forget what he had done for her, how he had been there from the beginning to the end, and she knew she couldn't have gotten through it without him. The medical team seemed much less important. "I'm having the next one at home," she announced then, and Bill groaned.

"Please . . . could I just catch my breath? It isn't even six o'clock in the morning." But he was happy to hear her talk about "the next one." And as she smiled at him, she realized it was New Year's Day, and it was his birthday.

"Happy birthday." She leaned forward and kissed him as the baby watched them. He made little snuffling noises now and then, but he seemed perfectly at ease between them.

"That's quite a gift!" It had been a beautiful way to turn forty, a reminder of how precious life was, how simple and rare. The gift of a baby from the woman he loved. It was perfect. "What do you think about Teddy, by the way?"

She thought about it for a minute and then countered. "How about Sam?"

He nodded, looking down at him. He was a beautiful child, and the name seemed to suit him. "I love it. Sam Thigpen." And then he looked at her, not wanting to ask any questions. Was it to be Sam Thigpen, or Sam Townsend, or her maiden name, Sam Thompson? But it was much too soon to ask her.

Bill stayed with her until eight a.m., and then he went home to shower and clean up and have breakfast. He promised to be back no later than noon, and told her to get some sleep too. And when he left, tiptoeing softly out of the room, he turned back once, and watched them, the baby sleeping in the mother's arms, the two of them so peaceful and so loved, and for the first time in a long time, he was completely fulfilled and at peace, and totally happy.

CHAPTER

··26··

ADRIAN WOKE UP AGAIN ABOUT AN HOUR AFTER BILL HAD left. The baby was still asleep, but the nurses came in to check how she was doing. She was doing fine and she was still having small contractions. But everything appeared to be okay, and she lay quietly for a long time, thinking, after they left her. There were two calls she had to make, and this seemed as good a time to make them as any. She felt almost electrically charged, as she lay looking at her sleeping baby. It was the most exciting day of her life, the happiest moment, and in some ways, she wanted to share it.

She called Connecticut first, and the call was difficult, but the good news made it a little better.

"Why didn't you tell me?" her mother asked, shocked by the news that she had a new grandchild when she had never even known Adrian was pregnant. "Isn't he normal?" It was the only reason she could think of for Adrian having not told her. But it was typical of the kind of relationship Adrian had had in recent years with her parents. Ever since she'd married Steven. And her parents made no bones about the fact that they didn't like him. They had been right, perhaps, but it had permanently marked their relationship with their daughter.

"I'm sorry, Mom. Things were kind of a mess out here. Steven left in June. And . . . I just thought he'd come back and I didn't want to tell you about the baby till he did . . . I guess that was pretty dumb."

"I guess so." There was a long silence. "Is he paying you alimony?" It struck her odd that that was all they thought of.

"No, I didn't want any."

"Is he going to fight you for custody of the baby?"

"No." She decided to spare them the details of that, and she also decided not to tell them about Bill, or her mother might think that she was having an affair and that was why Steven had left her. There was plenty of time to give her the details later. Adrian had just wanted to tell her about the baby.

"How long will you be in the hospital?" Her mother was so painfully matter-of-fact, it was difficult to feel close to her, even now that Adrian had just become a mother.

"Maybe till tomorrow." She wasn't sure. "Or a couple of days. I don't really know yet."

"I'll call you when you get home. Do you still have the same number?" It told its own tale that she even had to ask, but as seldom as it was, it was usually Adrian who called her.

"Yes." She'd had her phone installed at Bill's when she gave up her condo. It had been easier to do that at the time than make explanations. "I'll call you, Mom."

"Okay, and . . . congratulations . . ." Her mother still sounded as though she didn't know what to make of it, and her father had been out. It had saddened her to call them somehow, but at least she had done her duty.

And the next call was even harder. Her attorney had gotten

Steven's number inadvertently, but he had suggested to Adrian that she try not to use it. She got her address book out of her bag, and holding the baby in her left arm, she dialed the number. And as she did, she looked down at Sam. He was so beautiful and so sweet and so peaceful. He was everything she had wanted him to be, and more. He was four hours old, and already she felt as though she had always known him.

"Hello!" It was a familiar voice on the phone, but she hadn't heard it in months, and suddenly she felt awkward when she heard him.

"Hello . . . Steven . . . I . . . it's Adrian. I'm sorry to call you." There was a long silence while he said nothing at all. He couldn't imagine why she'd called him or how she had gotten his unlisted number.

"Why are you calling me?" He acted as though she had no right even to speak to him, and she felt her hand shake as she listened.

"I thought you had a right to know . . . the baby was born this morning. It's a little boy, and he weighed eight pounds fourteen ounces." She suddenly felt even more stupid for calling while there was an even longer silence. "I'm sorry. I guess I shouldn't have called . . . I just thought . . ."

And then, finally, a voice. "Is he normal?" It was the same thing her mother had asked, and somehow the question seemed offensive.

"Yes, he's fine," she said quietly. "He's really beautiful."

And then, hesitantly, "Are you all right? Was it awful?" He sounded almost like the man she had once known as he asked her.

"It was fine." There was no point explaining to him what it was like. It had been much harder than she thought it would be, but even now it didn't seem so bad, now that she had Sam in her arms and it was over.

"It was worth it." And then, hesitantly, "I wanted to call

. . . I just thought . . . I know you signed those papers, but I wanted to give you a chance to see him, if you want to." It was kinder than most women would have been, but Adrian had always been like that. "I don't expect you to, of course . . . I just thought I'd let you know, in case . . ." Her voice drifted off and his cut into hers.

"I'd like that." She looked stunned as she heard him. She had always planned to offer this opportunity to him, but she never really expected him to take it. "Where are you?"

"At Cedars-Sinai."

"I'll come over sometime this morning." And then, in an odd, wistful voice, "Does he have a name?"

She nodded, as tears rolled down her cheeks. She hadn't expected this, and now it had upset her. She hadn't seen him since June, when he'd left her. And now, after all this time, he wanted to see his baby. "His name is Sam." She spoke almost in a whisper.

"Give him a kiss from me. I'll see you later." She was even more shocked by what he'd just said. He sounded so different suddenly, so mellow, and now she was afraid of what would happen when he came to see her. She lay thinking of it all morning as she held the baby close to her, and he never stirred as he slept on. And it was almost lunchtime when she heard the door open and saw Steven standing there, looking at her in gray slacks, a blue shirt, and a blazer. His hair was longer than it had been before, he had a tan, and he was more handsome than ever.

"Hello, Adrian, can I come in?" He stood looking at her, hesitating in the doorway, and she nodded as she tried not to cry when she saw him. But her efforts were useless. The tears slid slowly down her cheeks as he walked toward her. Suddenly she remembered how much she had once loved him, what high hopes she had had, how confident she had been that

their marriage was forever, and how heartbroken and desolate she had been when he left her.

He only saw her at first, as he advanced toward her slowly,
carrying a large bunch of yellow roses, and then as he stood
next to her, he saw the baby suddenly, wrapped in his little
blue blanket, his tiny pink face like her own precious rosebud.

"Oh my God . . ." He stared down at him. "Is that him?"

She nodded, smiling through her tears at the silly question.
"Isn't he beautiful?"

This time Steven nodded, and there were tears in his eyes as
he looked first at the child that was his, and then the woman
who had borne him. "What a fool I was . . ." They were the
exact words she had fantasized, but never really expected.

She nodded, crying openly, she couldn't disagree with him.
But no one could have dissuaded him at the time, his own
attorney had tried and gotten nowhere. "I think you were just
very frightened."

"I know I was. I just couldn't imagine myself having children, and making the kind of sacrifices one has to make. I still
can't imagine it," he said honestly. But he was overwhelmed
by the sight of his baby. *His* child. *His* creation.

"He's beautiful, isn't he?" he said quietly, staring down at
him, as she watched, and then finally, Steven looked up at her,
but his eyes were matter-of-fact, not tender. "It must have
been hard for you these past months." She nodded, not wanting to tell him about Bill. That was none of his business.
"Where are you living?" It was odd that he should ask her
now, after all this time, and she answered cryptically. All this
time he had never cared where or how she was. And now he
did, or did he?

"At the same address, across the complex." He assumed that
she must have bought something smaller with the money she
had derived from their town house.

"That's nice." And then he stared down at his son, and

gently touched the tiny fingers. "He's so small . . ." And he was so perfect.

"He weighed almost nine pounds," she defended Sam, but Steven could only look at him in wonder. He saw no one he knew there, except maybe Adrian, but he looked like a person unto himself and Steven didn't really mind that. And then Adrian looked at him hesitantly, her hands still shaking from the shock of seeing him again. "Would you like to hold him?"

Steven looked terrified suddenly, and then he startled himself and her by nodding and holding his arms out. And Adrian gently handed the baby to him. The baby was his son, after all, and this was why she had called him. To see if he cared, to give him one last chance to reach out to the child he had rejected. She settled the baby in his arms and felt a sob catch in her throat as she watched him looking down at the sleeping infant in silent wonder. He sat in a chair next to the bed, afraid to move, looking terrified, his arms still, as though he was afraid the baby might leap up and bite him. But he sat there, staring at him, and as she watched him the door opened, and Bill walked in, carrying a huge bouquet of flowers, two dozen helium-filled balloons, and a huge blue bear that he set down awkwardly in the doorway. He started to walk into the room, as Steven bent over her and handed the baby back to her, and all Bill could see from where he stood was the cozy scene of the reunited threesome. Adrian looked up at Bill with startled eyes, and Steven stood near her, as though he had never left her, and for the first time, the baby began to cry, as though he sensed that something terrible had just happened.

"Oh . . . I'm sorry . . . I see this isn't a good time," Bill said to the room at large, afraid to look at Adrian's eyes, for fear of what he might see there.

"That's all right," Adrian said awkwardly, "this is Steven Townsend, my . . ." And then she almost choked on the words, she had been about to say "my husband." And she saw

Bill's face go pale and she wanted to beg him to stop it, to stop being hysterical and come in, and Steven would be leaving in a moment, but she found that she could say nothing, as Steven stared inhospitably at him, and Bill started to back out of the room without waiting for an explanation.

"I'll come back later."

"No . . . Bill . . ." But he was already gone, hurrying down the hall, feeling a rock in his throat, the same rock that had lodged there when Leslie had told him she wasn't moving to California. It was all happening to him again, the loss, the pain, the grief, the loneliness . . . but this time he wasn't going to let it.

And in her hospital room, Adrian was looking distressed as Steven watched her. "Who was that anyway?" Steven asked irritably. He had been visibly annoyed by the interruption.

"A friend," she said softly. She saw that Steven looked angry suddenly, but they both knew that he had no right to, and now he was looking down at her with a serious expression. He had been doing a lot of thinking since her phone call, and since seeing the baby.

"I owe you an apology," he said somberly, as Adrian agonized silently over what Bill must be feeling. She hadn't expected Steven to come so soon, and when he had offered to, she was glad to get it over with, so she and Bill could get on with the business of living. She had promised herself she'd call him, but she had never expected this, or Bill to walk in on them. Suddenly everything was upside down, and she wasn't sure what to do with the crying baby. She rang for the nurse, who volunteered to take him to the nursery for a while, as Adrian turned to Steven with a look of anguish. "I'm sorry if I hurt you, Adrian." And as he said it, she found herself remembering the night he had ignored her at Le Chardonnay when she was six months pregnant. "These last six months must have been very hard on you," he said, barely describing what she'd been through. And without Bill to take care of her, she didn't know how she would have survived it. "But they've been hard on me too." Adrian couldn't believe what she was hearing. She wasn't the one who had divorced him. And as she listened to him now she realized that she was still angry at him for what he'd done. Angry and hurt and she wasn't sure she would ever forgive him. "You challenged me in a way that rocked me to my very core, in a way, it was a complete betrayal." He went on as Adrian stared at him. He was as selfish as ever. "But . . . for the sake of my son . . . our child . . . I think in time, I might be willing to forgive you."

She stared at him with open eyes, unable to believe what she was hearing. He was willing to forgive *her*. "That's very kind of you," she said quietly, "and I appreciate it very much." She almost choked on the words. "But Steven, you're not the only person who was hurt. And I'm sorry if you felt betrayed. But you abandoned me when I was pregnant. You completely shut me out. You took all our furniture, kicked me out of our home, divorced me, and gave up your rights to our baby. You wouldn't even speak to me when I called you." It was quite a list, but he seemed unimpressed as he continued.

"Be that as it may." He ignored everything she had just said. "I think for the child's sake, we should go back together."

"Are you serious?" She stared at him almost in horror. This was not what she had planned, no matter how fair she wanted to be to him. And he was even more insensitive than he had been, and like everything else in his life, the baby was an ego trip for him, and now that he had seen it, that it was okay, and a son, he was suddenly willing to consider taking it on, after deserting them so completely. And this was the opportunity she had wanted to give him. But what she had expected, if anything, on his part, was genuine feeling for the baby. Not even anything for her, or if he did feel something, she would have expected some kind of tenderness and kindness. Some remorse, or regret, some vestige of decency and caring. But that was Bill she was thinking of, she suddenly realized. This man had none of that inside him.

"I don't think you understand," she went on. "Steven, you gave everything up because you didn't give a damn about either of us. You deserted us. And the only reason why I called was on the off chance that you'd regret it. I wanted you to have a chance to see the baby. But you don't care about anyone. You have no feelings whatsoever about what you've done. The only one you care about is yourself, and you have the nerve to imagine yourself 'betrayed.' I'm not even convinced you care about the baby or ever could care. You're so wrapped up in yourself that you don't give a damn about me, or him. And I think you're impressed that you have a 'son,' but that's it. Who is he to you? What does he mean? What are *you* prepared to give *him*?" It was an important question, and Steven looked more than ever annoyed to be questioned.

"Shelter, food, an education, toys . . ." He couldn't think of anything else and she shook her head. He hadn't made the grade. He never would. And now she knew that. It was what she had had to see, and now she was glad that she'd called him.

"You forgot something very important."

Steven thought about it, but nothing came to mind as he looked from her to the child and back again. And he looked handsome, but he also looked empty.

"You forgot love. That means more than shelter, food, education, or anything. It means more than computers, tennis rackets, furniture, stereos, apartments, jobs. Love. It was the one thing I think you forgot entirely in our marriage. If you had loved me, you wouldn't have walked out on me and the baby."

"I loved you . . . but *you* didn't love me. You broke a solemn promise to me never to have children." And he meant it.

"I couldn't help it." She had no regrets. "And I'm not sorry now."

"You should be," he said sorrowfully, "for the grief you caused me."

"The grief I caused *you*?" Adrian stared at him amazed, as he got up and walked around the room, glancing at the huge bear Bill had left just inside the doorway.

"The truth is, you betrayed me," he said again, "and if I'm willing to forgive you now, for the child's sake, you ought to be very grateful." She couldn't believe her ears as she stared at him.

"Well, I'm not." She looked at him and said bluntly. And then she asked him the most fearful question. "Steven, do you love the baby? I mean really *love* him? Do you want him more than anything . . . want to spend your life making his life better?"

He looked at her mutely for a long time. "I'm sure that I could learn to in time." But she saw as she looked at him that something inside him had died long since and she had never known it.

"And if you feel threatened by us again, then what? You walk out? Or you sell the apartment? Or you just file for termination?" He had been cruel to her, and indirectly to his own child, and they both knew it, no matter what he said now about "betrayal."

"I can't make you promises for the future. I can just say I'll try. But I think you owe it to me to come back and give it a try." She *owed* it to him. How endearing. How tender.

"On what basis? Are you asking me to marry you again?" She wanted to clarify everything once and for all now. This was the confrontation she had longed for.

"No, I . . . I think we should try it. I think you should come back and try it for six months, for a year, while I see if . . ."

"If you like being a parent, is that it? And if you don't?"

"Then there's no harm done. The papers are already in place, we shake hands and wish each other well." It sounded like a business agreement.

"And Sam?" He was already real to her, a special, precious person.

"In that case, he's yours."

"How nice. And how do I explain it to him later on? You tried it out and didn't like him? No, you don't get to rent fatherhood, Steven, to try it on. You either do it or you don't, like marriage, like love, like real life. This is not one of your tennis games, where you get to sample different partners and pick the ones who play the worst, so you can massage your ego." He looked furious at what she had just said, but it was all true, and he knew it.

"Then just exactly why did you call me? Wasn't that what you wanted from me? Or are you trying to find the best offer?" The new diamond ring on her finger hadn't gone unnoticed, nor had Bill with his many offerings abandoned in the doorway.

"I don't need your best offer anymore. But I wanted to be sure I gave you a last shot at your son, before you gave him away forever. I thought you deserved that. I thought there was always the off chance that you would regret it bitterly one day, and that you might fall in love with him when he was born. But you didn't. All you want is to try him out like a car on a rental plan, and you want me back to maintain him, because you're 'willing' to forgive me for *my* 'betrayal,' as you call it. But the betrayal is not mine, but yours, and the baby is mine now." He looked nonplussed, and not overly distressed at what she had just said. She wondered if he might even be relieved. But whatever he was, he hadn't changed. She knew that for sure now.

"You can tell him I offered to take you back and you refused, since you're so concerned with what you're going to tell him later."

"On a trial basis, Steven. That's nothing." Suddenly, she realized that she was shouting, but she didn't care. It felt good to finally be shouting at him. "I want to love him unconditionally, through thick and thin, handsome or ugly, good moods or bad, in sickness and health, with every ounce of love I have to give him. That's what I want to give our baby." There were tears in her eyes, and as she said the words, she realized that it was exactly what she wanted to give Bill, everything she had to give, forever.

"There is no such thing as unconditional love, except among fools," he said cynically.

"That's what I am then." It was what she had offered him once upon a time, and what he had walked out on.

"Good luck then." He stood looking at her for a long moment, and any feeling they had once had seemed to have dissipated between them. And then, a little more gently, "I'm sorry things didn't work out, Adrian." But he didn't really seem sorry to be giving up his baby. For a brief moment, he had been intrigued with him, fascinated, but the moment was already over. The moment the nurse had taken the baby from the room, Steven seemed to forget him.

"I'm sorry too." She looked up at him, wondering who he really had been all the time she thought she knew him. "I'm sorry for you," she said quietly.

"Don't be." She felt free finally, looking at him, and she was doubly glad she had called him. He was honest with her, there was nothing for him to lose now. "I wasn't ready for this, Adrian. I suppose I never would be." They were the most honest words he had ever said to her, no matter how intriguing the beauty of their newborn baby. But he just wasn't Bill, and she realized clearly now that she no longer loved Steven. She hadn't in months, not since Bill . . . or maybe ever since the baby, but she hadn't known it.

"I know." She nodded slowly at him, and then laid her head back against the pillows, it had been a long morning. "Thank you for coming." He touched her hand with his own, and then turned and walked out of the room without saying a word, and this time she knew that he was gone for good, and she was sorry, but she knew that she would never miss him. She lay in bed, thinking about Bill then, and desperately worried about what he'd thought when he saw her with Steven. All she wanted was for him to come back again, and she would be able to explain it.

But as she thought of Bill, Steven walked down the hall with a long, solemn stride, and he stopped for a moment at the nursery, and saw their baby. A blue bundle in an acrylic bassinet, propped up so the nurses could see him better, and the little blue card on the basket read "Thompson, baby boy, 8 lbs. 14 oz. 5:15 a.m." He bore her maiden name as Steven had requested through the courts. And as he looked at him, Steven waited to feel something he never had before, but he just didn't. He was beautiful, and he was so unbelievably small and vulnerable. He made you want to reach out and touch him. And he would never forget what it had been like to hold him, but he had been relieved when Adrian took him back, as he was now, knowing that the baby was Adrian's, not his. It was nice to know that he was someone else's. Steven had thought about trying it for a while, maybe just to get her back, but in the end, it was a relief now knowing that he didn't have to. And even he had realized that their relationship was over. She wanted too many things that he didn't. She wanted too much from him.

"Your boy?" An old man with a cigar and a bald head asked

with a broad smile, as Steven looked at him curiously and shook his head. No. Not his boy. Someone else's. And then he left, with his smooth stride, feeling at peace again. For Steven, the agony was over.

CHAPTER

••27••

ADRIAN WAITED ALL DAY FOR BILL TO COME BACK, BUT HE never came, and she called the apartment endlessly, but he never answered. By four o'clock she was desperate to find him. She was in agony over what he must have thought, and she wanted to explain, and tell him the outcome of Steven's visit. But she just couldn't find him. She was worried about his surprise party, too, remembering that everyone was counting on her to get him to his office where the entire cast and crew were going to surprise him. She called the office directly finally, figuring that the others had to be there by then, and finally at six o'clock, someone answered the phone and she could hear all the noise in the background. She tried to shout loud enough so they could hear her above the din, and finally, the assistant director realized who was calling.

"Adrian? Oh, congratulations on the baby!" Bill had told everyone about Sam, but those who knew him well thought he was strangely quiet. And they just figured he was tired after a long night with Adrian in labor. As it turned out, he had happened on the party completely by accident. After he left Adrian, he'd gone home, and then, needing to clear his mind, he had gone to the office. And he had arrived only slightly later than he should. It was as though, with or without her, he had been destined to get there.

"Is Bill there?" Finally, she had found him.

"He just left. He said there were some things he had to do. But it's a hell of a party." The A.D. sounded more than a little drunk, and they were having such a good time, they hardly missed their guest of honor. He had slipped away, touched by what they'd done, but anxious to be alone. It had already been quite a birthday.

Adrian tried to call him at home again, but he had the machine on. She couldn't believe that he had just slipped through her fingers like that, or that he wasn't going to give her a chance to explain what had happened. He had always known that she wanted to contact Steven after the baby was born, but he hadn't expected to see him sitting next to Adrian, in her hospital room, holding the baby, and he had immediately made a brutally painful assumption. And as Adrian continued to lie in her hospital bed, waiting for him, she began to fear the worst when he never came back to see her. He must have been so angry at her that he didn't want to see her again, and there was nothing more she could do to find him. She couldn't leave her room, or the hospital, and she felt trapped and helpless.

She held the baby for most of the afternoon, and put him in his little bassinet next to her for the entire evening. When her dinner tray came, she sent it away, and she put the big blue bear in a chair, and sat looking sadly at his roses. And all she wanted was to see him and tell him how much she loved him.

"Would you like a sleeping pill?" the nurse asked at eight

o'clock, but she only shook her head, and the nurse made a note on the chart about possible postpartum depression. They had noted the fact that she had eaten nothing for dinner or lunch, and she even seemed unexcited about nursing her baby. She was quiet and uncommunicative, and as soon as the nurse left the room, she dialed the apartment again, and the answering machine was still on, and she left an anguished message for him to call her.

She picked up the baby again, and held him close to her for a long time, looking at the tiny nose, the sleeping eyes, the perfect mouth, the tiny, gently curled fingers. He was so sweet and so tiny and so perfect, and she was so engrossed in watching him that she didn't hear the door whoosh open at nine o'clock, and he stood there for a long minute, watching her, willing himself not to feel anything for her or the baby, as she turned her head suddenly and saw him. Her breath caught, and without thinking, she reached out a hand, and then started to get out of bed, which wasn't entirely easy.

"Stay there," he said gently, "don't get up. I just came to say good-bye." He sounded cool and calm, and he walked closer to the bed, but he kept his distance. He looked remarkably dressed up, and somehow she sensed that it wasn't from the party. The party had been a surprise, and he had been wearing a sweatshirt and jeans for that, but now he looked as though he was dressed for something important. He was wearing an English tweed suit, a cream-colored shirt, and Hermès tie, and serious-looking brown shoes, and there was a winter coat over his arm, and suddenly she knew that he was going.

"Where are you going?" she asked worriedly, sensing instantly that everything had changed between them. All in a few hours, since that morning. Only twelve hours before they had been like one heart, one soul, and now he had torn himself away from her and he was leaving. But she knew why. She only wondered if she could heal the hurt she had caused him.

"I thought I'd go to New York to see the boys for a few days."
He glanced at his watch. "I have to leave in a few minutes, to
catch the red-eye." She felt her heart sink as she looked at
him, and all she could feel was panic, and a desperate fear that
she would lose him. It almost took her breath away as she
watched him look uncomfortably around the room and then
back at her, but he seemed anxious to avoid looking at the
baby.

"Do the boys know you're coming?"

"No," he said somberly. "I thought I'd surprise them."

"How long will you be gone?" She didn't know what to say
to him, except to tell him that she was sorry, that she'd been a
fool, that she shouldn't have cared what Steven thought, that
he was a jerk, and she was, too, and that she loved Bill more
than life itself, and Sam was going to grow up to be their baby
. . . if he stayed, if only Bill would stay . . . if only he would
forgive her.

"I don't know how long I'll be," he answered, holding his
coat in his arms and looking at her longingly. "A week . . .
two . . . I thought maybe I'd take them on a little vacation
after they get back from Vermont, if Leslie will let me. . . ."
He was always at the mercy of someone else to get to the
people he loved . . . Leslie, Adrian . . . Steven . . . but he
couldn't let himself think of that now. It would just be good to
see the boys again, and get out of California. He'd had enough.
He needed a break. And his birthday present to himself was to
get out of town and let someone else take care of his problems.
They had plenty of scripts to work with while he was gone,
and if they couldn't figure it out, they could invent it.

"I hired a nurse for you, by the way. She'll come in by the
day, or stay overnight if you need her, when you leave the
hospital. I didn't meet her myself, but the agency said she's
terrific." He thought of everything, and Adrian's eyes welled
up with tears as he said it.

"You didn't have to do that. I can take care of myself."

"I thought you might need help with the baby. Unless . . ." He hadn't even thought of that, and then he looked at her curiously, feeling even more foolish. ". . . Are you going back to my place, or Steven's?" She realized then what he thought, and her heart ached for him. And it was all her fault, which made her feel even worse for the pain she had caused him.

"I'm not going to Steven. Now or ever. I'm not going anywhere with him." She said it so absolutely that he looked at her very strangely.

"I got the impression this morning that . . . I thought . . . I knew you were going to call him," he explained. "I just didn't know you were going to do it quite so soon. I should have been prepared for that," he said quietly, "but I wasn't. It took me by surprise when I walked in on the three of you . . . and I was so excited about Sam and everything, and . . ." He looked so sad as he looked at her that the tears rolled down her cheeks as she looked at him and then down at the baby.

"I just wanted to get it over with . . . I know it was wrong of me, but I wanted him to see the baby . . . and release him, spiritually, or give him his blessing, or something. I don't know what I thought, I don't know what crazy delusions I've had all this time about owing Steven something because of the baby. Maybe I felt guilty about taking something so wonderful from him and walking off with it, and maybe even sharing it with you. But the truth is, he doesn't even realize what having a baby is. He doesn't know what love is. And to him the baby is nothing more than a hardship. He's a jerk and a fool, and I was an even bigger one to even marry him in the first place." She looked miserably at Bill and started to sob, as she held the baby, and suddenly the baby started to wail, too, and Bill put his coat down and rushed forward to help her.

"Here, let me do it . . ." He was calm and smooth and his hands were sure as she watched him. "Is he hungry?"

"I don't know. I nursed him a little while ago, but I don't think he's figured it out yet."

"Maybe he's wet." He checked expertly, and then deftly wrapped him up tightly again in the blanket while she silently marveled at how good he was at everything he touched, from screenplays to soufflés to babies. "He just wanted to be wrapped up tight again, I think. You kind of let him get un-wound. They like to be all bundled up, like a cocoon. Here, I'll show you." He gave her a quick demonstration and handed the baby back to her with sure hands, while she blew her nose and thanked him.

"I don't know what I was thinking of when I called Steven. But as soon as he was here, I knew it was a mistake, and then you walked in, and before I could say anything, you were gone again." She started crying all over again, and a nurse walked in and shook her head again, thinking that Adrian was definitely manifesting the early signs of postpartum depression. Either that or her husband was giving her a hard time, but there was something going on here. "And I tried to call you all day," Adrian went on, "and I couldn't find you anywhere!" she said accusingly. "And today was your birthday!"

"I know it was." He smiled. She looked so pathetic and so upset, and so childlike with a blue bow in her hair. She looked like a teenager, holding someone else's baby. "But it was so damn awkward when I walked into the room and he was here. I didn't expect him. And it just all looked so cozy."

"Well, it was very moving at first," she explained, wishing Bill would sit down, but she didn't want to suggest it for fear that he'd remember he had to catch the red-eye. "He looked at the baby as though he'd never seen one. But he's such a goddamn horse's ass, and so pompous. I don't think he's ever loved anyone or anything in his life, except maybe his tennis racket or his Porsche. He was 'willing to *forgive me* for be-

traying *him,* and take me and the baby back on a trial basis.'
Can you imagine?" She was still angry when she said it.

"And if he'd taken you back unconditionally? If he'd told
you that he loved you?"

"I realized that it was too late, that it was all gone if it was
ever there at all. And he and I never had what we have. We
had something very superficial and very young. I never knew
the meaning of the word *love* until I met you." She said it very
softly, and he set his coat down next to the blue bear and went
to the bed, where she still sat holding the baby.

"I couldn't stand the idea of losing you, Adrian . . . I just
couldn't. I've been through that before, and I know what it's
like." He looked down at the sleeping infant then. "And I
don't want to lose you either. I want both of you, and Tommy
and Adam whenever we can . . . forever. I have no right to
stand in your way. You were married to Steven, and you have a
right to go back to him if you want to. But if you've made up
your mind, if you're sure now, I need to know it. . . ." He
looked at her with eyes full of pain. He had come of age on his
fortieth birthday.

"I've never loved anyone more." She reached out to him
and he took her in his arms as tears rolled down her cheeks.
She felt as though she had been crying all day, but so had he.
He had had a rotten birthday. "I couldn't live without you."
She still trembled, thinking that, through her own stupidity,
she had almost lost him.

Bill smiled for a long moment, and didn't say anything as he
helped her set the baby down, and then he looked at her
again. "I love you. I just want you to know how much I love
you." And then he glanced at his watch and smiled, as he sat
on the edge of the bed next to her. "It looks like I just missed
the red-eye." But he'd been surprising the boys anyway, so
they wouldn't be disappointed. "Mind if I spend the night?"

He grinned at her and she laughed and blew her nose again. It had been an emotional day, and night before that.

"I'm not sure what the nurses would say." But neither of them seemed to care, as they snuggled in her bed, Adrian in her pink nightgown he'd given her for Christmas and Bill in his London tweeds, and then the nurse came in to check on her, saw them kissing, and quietly closed the door again. Mrs. Thompson was feeling much better.

"They're going to think we're misbehaving," Adrian whispered to him as the door whooshed closed behind the nurse.

"Good," he whispered with a grin.

"I have a birthday present for you." Adrian remembered the watch suddenly, as they continued to kiss and talk in whispers.

"Already?" Bill laughed. "Isn't it too soon?"

"You're disgusting." But he kissed her long and hard, and all was right with the world again as he held her.

"I have a surprise for you," he said thoughtfully, as they lay back side by side, against her pillows.

"What is it?" They were still speaking softly, for fear of waking the baby, and because suddenly their life seemed so simple and so peaceful.

"We're getting married in the next few days."

"It's about time." She pretended to scowl at him, flashing the ring he had given her for Christmas.

"I want my name on Sam's birth certificate," Bill said almost sternly.

"How about Samuel William Thigpen," she supplied with a shy smile, and he leaned over and kissed her.

"It'll do . . ." He smiled. "It'll do," pulling her close to him again, and feeling her heart next to his, with a single heartbeat.